D0946882

THE HANDHELD CALCULATOR

THE HANDHELD CALCULATOR

Use and Applications

Herman R. Hyatt
Bernard Feldman

Los Angeles Pierce College

John Wiley & Sons

New York • Chichester • Brisbane • Toronto

Library of Congress Cataloging in Publication Data:

Hyatt, Herman R
The handheld calculator.

Includes index.
1. Calculating-machines. I. Feldman, Bernard,
joint author. II. Title.

QA75.H93 681'.14 78-12332
ISBN 0-471-02276-4

Printed in the United States of America

10 9 8 7 6 5 4 3 2

Preface

This book can be used for two types of courses—one involving the use of scientific calculators, the other involving the use of nonscientific calculators. The only prerequisites are successful completion of an elementary (first-year) algebra course and access to an electronic handheld calculator. Either "algebraic entry" or "reverse Polish notation" calculators are appropriate.

The need for such courses was suggested by several observations. First, many calculator users are unaware of some of the capabilities of their calculators. Second, certain mathematical background concepts (for example, rounding off and significant digits) are often needed when calculator results are used. Third, the fact that even relatively inexpensive calculators offer a wider range of capabilities than a slide rule indicates a diminished need (if any) for traditional slide rule courses.

This book is divided into three main parts (A, B, and C) that describe calculator techniques together with an informal presentation of related mathematical concepts when needed. The three parts of the book are subdivided into sections, each of which begins with a list of objectives for that section and ends with a set of exercises. In the text of each section, newly introduced concepts or techniques are immediately followed by examples. Except for Section A-11, the exercises in the exercise sets are keyed to the numbered examples in the text.

PART A

This part, designed for both scientific and nonscientific calculators, covers calculator instructions for the operations of addition, subtraction, multiplication, division, and raising numbers to powers, as well as combinations of these operations. Part A also considers such concepts as rounding off numbers, significant digits, computations with exact and approximate numbers, and algebraic order of operations.

PART B

This part is for scientific calculators only. The concept of "function" is introduced informally, and operations relating to polynomial, trigonometric, exponential, and logarithmic functions are considered. Instructions for writing calculator sequences are given throughout Part B. Sections on graphing, elementary numerical equation-solving methods, and numerical trigonometry are provided so that students can use calculators on problems of significant mathematical interest.

PART C

This part is designed mainly for nonscientific calculators. Practice in the use of the ideas and skills developed in Part A is provided by way of sections that consider working with formulas, applications of percent, use of the Pythagorean theorem, and the elementary statistical concepts of average (mean) and standard deviation.

EXERCISE SETS

In each exercise set the odd-numbered exercises are matched with the even-numbered exercises—Exercises 1 and 2 are similar, Exercises 3 and 4 are similar, and so forth. Answers to odd-numbered exercises are given in the answer section of the book; answers to even-numbered exercises are given in the Instructor's Manual.

PRETESTING FOR PART A

Many students may already be familiar with some of the mathematical concepts introduced in Part A. Hence, the Instructor's Manual for this book includes a set of short pretests designed to determine whether a student could be excused from studying particular sections of Part A.

SUGGESTED COURSES

This book can be used with an individualized instruction approach, with the traditional classroom-lecture approach, or with a combination of the two approaches. Listed below are some possible groupings of sections to be covered in various time periods. AB courses are for scientific calculators only; the AC course is for nonscientific calculators. (An "independent study-mastery approach" course is described in the Instructor's Manual.)

COURSE AB-1 (12 hours)

Part A (3-4 hours): Include A-7, A-8, A-10, and A-11

Part B: B-1, B-2 as far as Example 1, B-6, B-8, B-12, B-13 (omit Exercises 13-18), and B-14 (omit Exercises 41-44)

COURSE AB-2 (16 hours)

Same as AB-1 but includes graphing and some numerical trigonometry.

Part A (3-4 hours): Include A-7, A-8, A-10, and A-11

Part B: B-1, B-2, B-3, B-6, B-7, B-8, B-9, B-11, B-12, B-13, and B-14

COURSE AB-3 (more than 16 hours)

Same as AB-2 but includes more numerical trigonometry and numerical methods for solving equations.

Part A (3-4 hours): Include A-7, A-8, A-10, and A-11

Part B: All

COURSE AC

Part A: All

Part C: As many sections as time allows, not necessarily in sequence

Contents

PART C NONSCIENTIFIC CALCULATORS: APPLICATIONS

THE HANDHELD CALCULATOR

PART A
BASIC CONCEPTS

A-0 Some Preliminary Concepts

This book is designed to be used with either a nonscientific or a scientific type hand-held calculator. Some typical calculators are shown in Figure A-0.1 on page 2.

There are three main parts to a calculator: a *display* in which lighted symbols appear, a *keyboard* with an array of keys, and one or more *registers* (which are internal and cannot be seen) in which numbers are stored during computations. Some calculators have symbols printed directly on the keys; others have symbols printed on the case near the keys; still others have both. We will refer to a key by its symbol, regardless of where the symbol is actually printed.

Any calculator to be used with this book must be able to show eight (or more) digits in the display and must have at least:

1. *Number entry keys* (the ten digits and the decimal point)

2. *Operation keys* for the four basic operations

3. An *equals key* [=] or an *enter key* [ENT]

In addition, scientific-type calculators must have at least the following keys available:

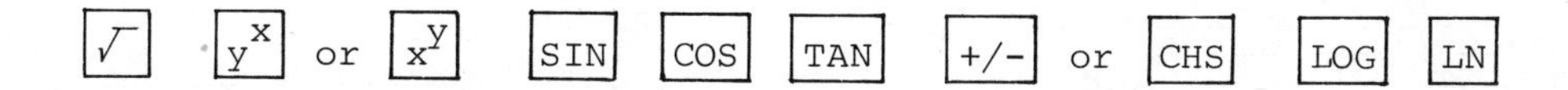

Calculators vary with regard to the capabilities designed into them. Consequently, your calculator may sometimes display a result that differs slightly from a result in the text. For example, the computations in this book were done on a calculator that can display up to eight digits *to the right* of the decimal point, while your calculator may be able to display at most seven digits. Such slight differences will not cause any difficulties in your work.

CLEARING ENTRIES

If you mistakenly enter a number in the display during a computation, a "clear entry" procedure can be used to "erase" the incorrect number from the display; entries in the register are left unchanged. Your calculator should have a key such as

[CE] [CE/C] [C/CA] or [CHX]

that operates as a *clear entry* key. If you cannot find such a key, see the instruction booklet provided with your calculator.

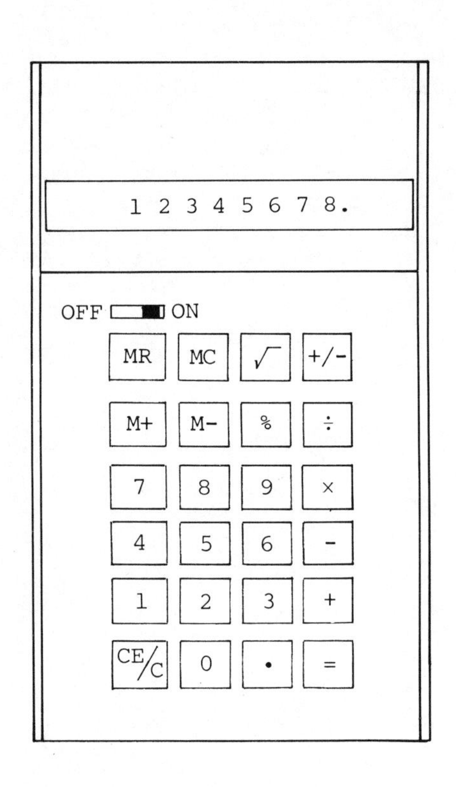
1 2 3 4 5 6 7 8.
OFF ON
MR MC √ +/-
M+ M- % ÷
7 8 9 ×
4 5 6 -
1 2 3 +
CE/C 0 • =

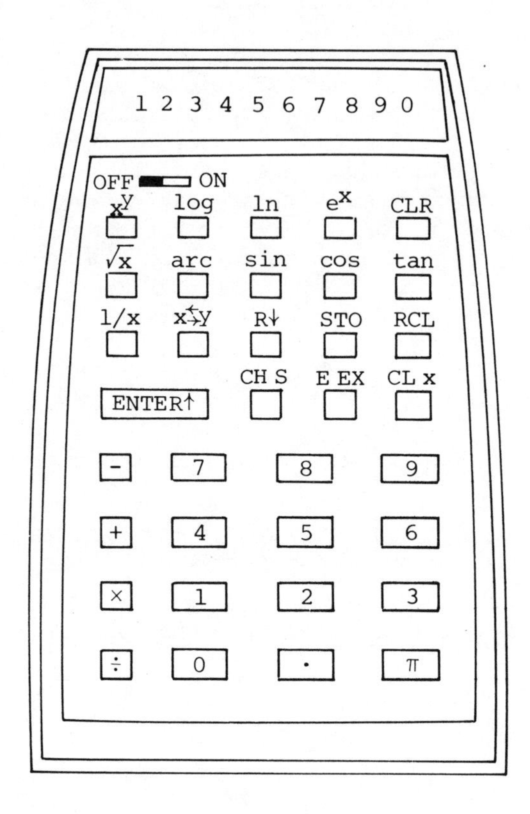
1 2 3 4 5 6 7 8 9 0
OFF ON
x^y log ln e^x CLR
$\sqrt{x}$ arc sin cos tan
1/x x⇆y R↓ STO RCL
ENTER↑ CH S E EX CL x
- 7 8 9
+ 4 5 6
× 1 2 3
÷ 0 • π

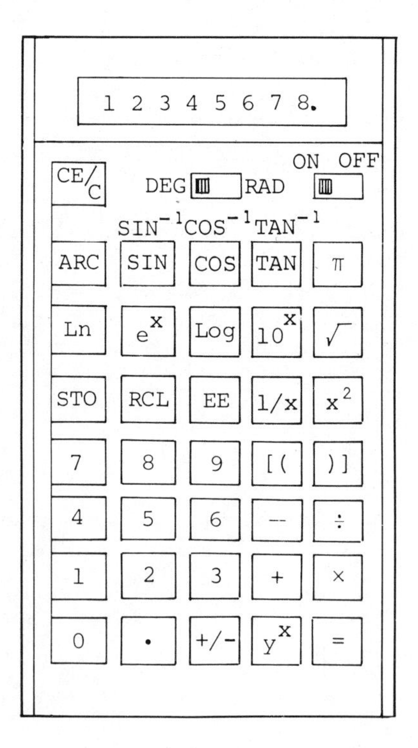
1 2 3 4 5 6 7 8.
CE/C
DEG RAD
ON OFF
SIN^{-1} COS^{-1} TAN^{-1}
ARC SIN COS TAN π
Ln e^x Log 10^x √
STO RCL EE 1/x x^2
7 8 9 [( )]
4 5 6 -- ÷
1 2 3 + ×
0 • +/- y^x =

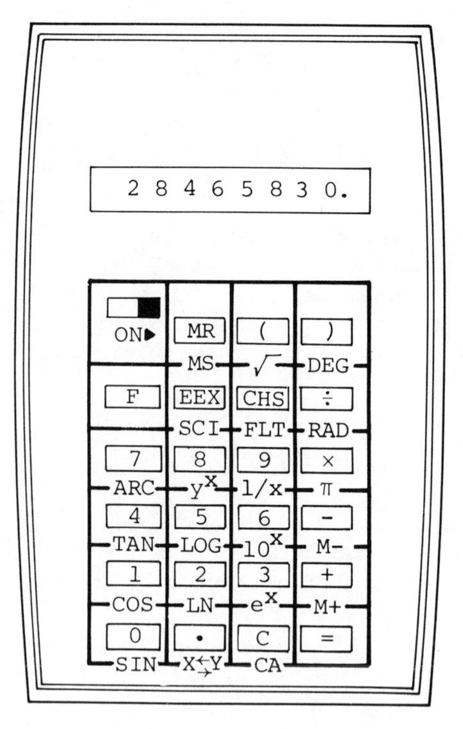
2 8 4 6 5 8 3 0.
ON▶ MR ( )
MS √ DEG
F EEX CHS ÷
SCI FLT RAD
7 8 9 ×
ARC y^x 1/x π
4 5 6 -
TAN LOG 10^x M-
1 2 3 +
COS LN e^x M+
0 • C =
SIN X⇆Y CA

FIGURE A-0.1

CALCULATOR SEQUENCES

Throughout this book we will show suggested sequences of keys to press. In such sequences, operations keys will be indicated by the appropriate symbol enclosed in a box; numerical entries will be shown without a box. For example, a calculator sequence for the computation

$$35 + 1.9 - 4.11$$

will appear as

35 [+] 1.9 [-] 4.11 [=] or 35 [ENT] 1.9 [+] 4.11 [-]

Such sequences are read, and followed, from left to right.

A list of symbols used in this book, together with the number of the page on which the symbol is introduced, appears before the index.

TWO MAJOR TYPES OF CALCULATORS

In mathematics, operations on numbers may be *binary*, meaning operations performed on *two* numbers, or *unary*, meaning operations performed on *one* number. *Addition, subtraction, multiplication,* and *division* are examples of binary operations; finding a *square root* of a number or the *reciprocal* of a number are examples of unary operations. All of the operations considered in this book are either binary or unary.

When using a calculator, the two most important things you need to know are: how to enter numbers into the calculator and how to tell the calculator which operation to perform. Different calculators do these things in different ways. Look at the keyboard of your calculator. If it has an [=] key, methods for entering numbers and performing operations are based on "algebraic notation"; we shall refer to such calculators as "[=] calculators." If the keyboard has an [ENT] key, methods for entering numbers and performing operations are based on "reverse Polish notation"; we shall refer to such calculators as "[ENT] calculators." In some sections of this book both types of calculators are discussed. When this is done, it is understood that you will read only the material designated as being appropriate for your type of calculator.

[=] CALCULATORS

[=] calculators are designed so that entering a computation into the calculator follows elementary algebraic notation. For binary operations, the operation key is pressed *between* entry of the two numbers. For example, the computation

$$4 + 5$$

is entered in the calculator just as you read it, by the sequence

[4] [+] [5] [=] → [9]

Note that pressing the [=] key instructs the calculator to complete the addition and display the result, 9. However, *it is not always correct to enter a computation just as you read it.* In this book we will consider those mathematical concepts necessary to know in order to correctly perform computations on your calculator.

For unary operations, the number is entered first. When the appropriate operation key is pressed, the operation is completed and the result is displayed. For example, we can compute the reciprocal of 4 by the sequence

4 [1/x] → .25

[ENT] CALCULATORS

For binary operations, [ENT] calculators require that two numbers be entered *before* the operation key is pressed. To separate the two numbers being entered, the [ENT] key is pressed *after* the first number is entered; the appropriate operation key is pressed *after* the second number is entered. For example, the computation

$$4 + 5$$

can be entered and computed by the sequence

4 [ENT] 5 [+] → 9

Note that pressing the operation key ([+] in this example) instructs the calculator to complete the operation and display the result.

The [ENT] key is not needed for unary operations. For example, to compute the reciprocal of 4, we can use the sequence

4 [1/x] → .25

SETS OF NUMBERS

We shall sometimes refer by name to certain sets of numbers. As you may recall, the *natural numbers* are

$$1, 2, 3, 4, 5, \ldots$$

The *whole numbers* are

$$0, 1, 2, 3, 4, 5, \ldots$$

The *integers* are

$$\ldots, -3, -2, -1, 0, 1, 2, 3, \ldots$$

A-1 Addition, Subtraction, Multiplication, and Division

OBJECTIVES

After completing this section, you should be able to

1. Perform additions, subtractions, and combined additions and subtractions on your calculator.
2. Check additions and subtractions.
3. Perform multiplications, divisions, and combined multiplications and divisions on your calculator.
4. Check multiplications and divisions.

The operation of ADDITION is used to find the *sum* (or *total*) of two or more numbers. The numbers to be added are called *terms* (or *addends*).

EXAMPLE 1

67.5 + 49.27 + 210.3 + 84 = 411.07, as computed by

[=] calculators:

67.5 [+] 49.27 [+] 210.3 [+] 84 [=] → 411.07

[ENT] calculators:

67.5 [ENT] 49.27 [+] 210.3 [+] 84 [+] → 411.07

Note that each of the expressions 8 + 4 and 4 + 8 names the same number, 12—that is, 8 + 4 = 4 + 8. Such statements illustrate a useful property of addition called the *commutative property*:

Changing the order in which numbers are added does not change the sum.

The commutative property of addition can be used to check the result of an addition—add the same terms but in *reverse* order. If the same sum is obtained, the result is assumed to be correct. For example, the sum in Example 1 can be checked as follows:

84 + 210.3 + 49.27 + 67.5 = 411.07

The operation of SUBTRACTION is used to find the *difference* of two numbers. Numbers to be subtracted may also be referred to as terms.

EXAMPLE 2

526 - 398.7 = 127.3, as computed by

[=] calculators:

526 [-] 398.7 [=] → 127.3

[ENT] calculators:

526 [ENT] 398.7 [-] → 127.3

A subtraction can be checked by an addition. For example, the result of Example 2 can be checked as follows:

Computation: 526 - 398.7 = 127.3

Check: 398.7 + 127.3 = 526

Subtraction is *not* commutative, as you can verify by noting that

398.7 - 526 = -127.3

and comparing the number -127.3 with the result (127.3) of Example 2.

Combined additions and subtractions can be done in the order in which the numbers and symbols are read, left to right.

EXAMPLE 3

25.32 - 6.94 - 12.003 + 18.5 = 24.877, as computed by

[=] calculators:

25.32 [-] 6.94 [-] 12.003 [+] 18.5 [=] → 24.877

[ENT] calculators:

25.32 [ENT] 6.94 [-] 12.003 [-] 18.5 [+] → 24.877*

The operation of MULTIPLICATION is used to find the *product* of two or more numbers. The numbers to be multiplied are called *factors*.

---

* [ENT] calculators can be instructed to display a preselected number of decimal places. See your instruction booklet.

EXAMPLE 4

9.4 × 47 × 13.52 = 5973.136, as computed by

[=] calculators:

9.4 [×] 47 [×] 13.52 [=] → 5973.136

[ENT] calculators:

9.4 [ENT] 47 [×] 13.52 [×] → 5973.136

The fact that 8 × 4 equals 4 × 8 illustrates a property of multiplication called the *commutative property*:

Changing the order in which numbers are multiplied does not change the product.

The commutative property of multiplication can be used to check the result of a multiplication—multiply the same factors, but in reverse order. If the same product is obtained, the result is assumed to be correct. For example, the product in Example 4 can be checked as

13.52 × 47 × 9.4 = 5973.136

The operation of DIVISION is used to find the *quotient* of two numbers. An expression such as $n \div d$ is called the *quotient* of n divided by d; n is the *dividend* and d is the *divisor*. Quotients may also be expressed in *fraction form* as $\frac{n}{d}$ (or n/d), in which case n is also called the *numerator* and d is called the *denominator*.

EXAMPLE 5

834.2 ÷ 1.94 = 430, as computed by

[=] calculators:

834.2 [÷] 1.94 [=] → 430

[ENT] calculators:

834.2 [ENT] 1.94 [÷] → 430

The result of a division can be checked by a multiplication; the product of the divisor and the quotient should equal the dividend. Thus, the division of Example 5 can be checked as follows.

Computation: $834.2 \div 1.94 = 430$

Check: $1.94 \times 430 = 834.2$

Division is *not* commutative, as you can verify by noting that

$$1.94 \div 834.2 = .00232558^{*}$$

and comparing the answer .00232558 with the result (430) of Example 5.

Combined multiplications and divisions can be done in the order in which the numbers and symbols are read, left to right.

EXAMPLE 6

$17.25 \times 7.2 \div 18 = 6.9$, as computed by

[=] calculators:

17.25 [×] 7.2 [÷] 18 [=] → 6.9

[ENT] calculators:

17.25 [ENT] 7.2 [×] 18 [÷] → 6.9

Given a quotient in fraction form, $\frac{n}{d}$, it is often useful to rewrite the quotient in *on-line* form, $n \div d$, for purposes of calculating.

EXAMPLE 7

$\frac{2.4 \times 1.05}{.84}$; the on-line form of the quotient is $2.4 \times 1.05 \div .84$. The calculations can be done by

[=] calculators:

2.4 [×] 1.05 [÷] .84 [=] → 3

[ENT] calculators:

2.4 [ENT] 1.05 [×] .84 [÷] → 3

---

* If the display on your calculator shows 2.3255 -03, read "-03" as instructions to *move the decimal point three places to the left*. For a discussion of this notation, see Section A-8.

EXERCISE SET A-1

Find each sum. Check each result by adding the numbers in reverse order. See Example 1.

1. 32.4 + 68.3 + 49.7
2. 748.96 + 872.54 + 127.96
3. 48.95 + 34.47 + 28.77 + 36.25
4. 645.9 + 247.62 + 345.96 + 174.82
5. 374.664 + 802.962 + 189.402 + 246.054 + 423.909
6. 981.503 + 476 + 346.057 + 745 + 348.334

Find each difference. Check each result by an addition. See Example 2.

7. 728 - 476.7
8. 976 - 372.9
9. 476.99 - 246.37
10. 802.35 - 477.68
11. 472,864 - 109,228
12. 190,496 - 87,472

Compute. See Example 3.

13. 47.6 + 68.7 - 24.9
14. 86.9 + 47.6 - 38.4
15. 486.95 - 78.24 - 102.76
16. 742 - 60.94 - 247.29
17. 342.9 - 68.4 + 74.1 - 104.4
18. 765.44 - 172.63 - 472.36 + 177.46
19. 872.33 - 241.75 - 163.18 + 346.91 - 104.65
20. 247.95 - 87.64 - 74.93 + 362.39 - 99.42

21. A company operates four restaurants, A, B, C, and D. The following table lists profits and losses (losses are indicated by numbers in parentheses) for each restaurant over a three-month period. Find the total profit (or loss):

    a. For each restaurant for the three-month period.
    b. For all four restaurants for each month.
    c. For all four restaurants for the three-month period.

	A	B	C	D	Totals
Jan.	$3124.56	$ 246.15	$1819.75	$ 874.15	$_______
Feb.	$2748.19	($ 212.27)	$ 976.88	($ 103.95)	$_______
Mar.	$2917.94	$ 311.95	$2045.12	($1674.27)	$_______
Totals	$_______	$_______	$_______	$_______	$_______

22. Follow the instructions of Exercise 21 for the following table of profits and losses.

	E	F	G	H	Totals
Oct.	$ 473.12	$ 412.19	$2642.07	$ 168.42	$_______
Nov.	$ 98.75	($ 845.96)	$2715.21	($ 42.77)	$_______
Dec.	$ 645.88	$1417.37	$3001.72	($ 185.19)	$_______
Totals	$_______	$_______	$_______	$_______	$_______

For each checking account statement, find the closing balance. (Hint: Start with the opening balance. Add deposits and subtract checks.)

23. Opening balance: $436.18

Date	Deposits	Checks
12/3		24.96
12/8		56.15
12/10	234.15	
12/15	51.09	217.25
12/21		101.96
12/31		33.75

Closing balance: $_______

24. Opening balance: $1065.53

Date	Deposits	Checks
2/5		645.24
2/7	415.25	215.99
2/19		68.77
2/20	415.25	110.00
2/28		86.33

Closing balance: $_______

25. Opening balance: $279.77

Date	Deposits	Checks
5/2		128.45
		31.18
5/10	95.70	
5/15		215.20
		20.12
5/21	118.15	166.08
5/27		31.50
5/31	80.90	16.72

Closing balance: $_______

26. Opening balance: $815.70

Date	Deposits	Checks
10/4		421.95
10/9	362.83	112.19
10/15		354.20
		116.19
10/17	195.00	224.78
10/25	345.72	95.19
10/30		66.00
		332.50

Closing balance: $_______

Find each product. Check your answers by multiplying in reverse order. See Example 4.

27. 375×61
28. 946×21
29. $.007 \times 57.6134$
30. $.876 \times .678$
31. $53.85 \times .047 \times 9.5$
32. $8.7 \times .87 \times .087$

Find each quotient. Check your answer by a multiplication. See Example 5.

33. $\dfrac{4154}{67}$
34. $\dfrac{1722}{82}$
35. $\dfrac{18,546}{6.6}$
36. $\dfrac{26,134}{7.3}$
37. $752.076 \div 96.42$
38. $424.821 \div 8.265$
39. $139.3184 \div 8.7074$
40. $801.528 \div 5.7252$

Compute. See Example 6.

41. $1.21 \times 12.76 \div .11$
42. $13.2 \div 1.1 \times 5.3$
43. $.144 \div .08 \times 7.9$
44. $6.4 \times 51.7 \div .016$

Rewrite each quotient in on-line form and compute. See Example 7.

45. $\dfrac{.0135 \times 4.67}{.27}$
46. $\dfrac{15.5 \times 47.9}{3.1}$

47. $\dfrac{175 \times 586}{700}$

48. $\dfrac{647 \times 819}{117}$

Find the cost of the given quantity.

49. 18 gallons of paint at \$9.50 per gallon.

50. 25 gallons of paint at \$8.75 per gallon.

51. 5.5 yards of cloth at \$2.50 per yard.

52. 13 yards of cloth at \$3.25 per yard.

In Problems 53-56, find the cost per ounce of each of the following items selling at the given price.

53. 12 ounces of frozen peas at 54¢.

54. 16 ounces of punch at 52¢.

55. 12.5 ounces of syrup at \$1.05.

56. 1.25 ounces of make-up at \$2.25.

57. How far can a car be expected to go if its gasoline tank holds 17.5 gallons of gasoline and its average gasoline mileage is 15.5 miles per gallon?

58. On a trip of 1763 miles, a car used 86 gallons of gasoline. What was its mileage in miles per gallon?

A-2 Rounding Off

OBJECTIVE

After completing this section, you should be able to round off a number to a specified number of places.

Figure A-2.1 shows the names of place values for the decimal number system: *whole number places* (to the left of the decimal point) are named to ten millions; *decimal places* (to the right of the decimal point) are named to ten thousandths. Familiarity with these place values is sufficient for most applications.

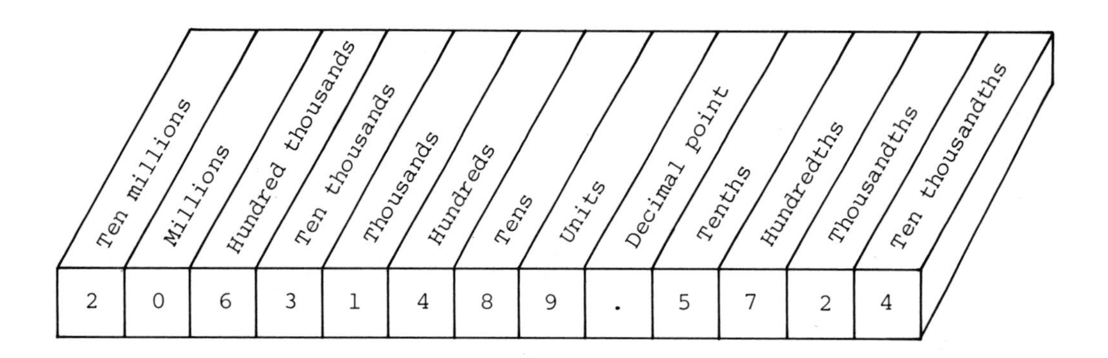

FIGURE A-2.1

EXAMPLE 1

Write the number 3729.1608 and underline the digit in the (a) tens place, (b) tenths place, (c) thousandths place, (d) thousands place, (e) units place, and (f) ten-thousandths place.

Solutions

a. $37\underline{2}9.1608$ b. $3729.\underline{1}608$ c. $3729.16\underline{0}8$

d. $\underline{3}729.1608$ e. $372\underline{9}.1608$ f. $3729.160\underline{8}$

A few calculators are designed to show exactly two decimal places in the result of *every* computation. Such calculators are said to be operating with *fixed decimal point*. On the other hand, when a calculator shows as many decimal places as may result from a computation, the calculator is said to be operating under *floating decimal point*. The results of such computations frequently include more digits than may be needed, or may be correct, for a given problem. Hence, we need the concept of *rounding off*.

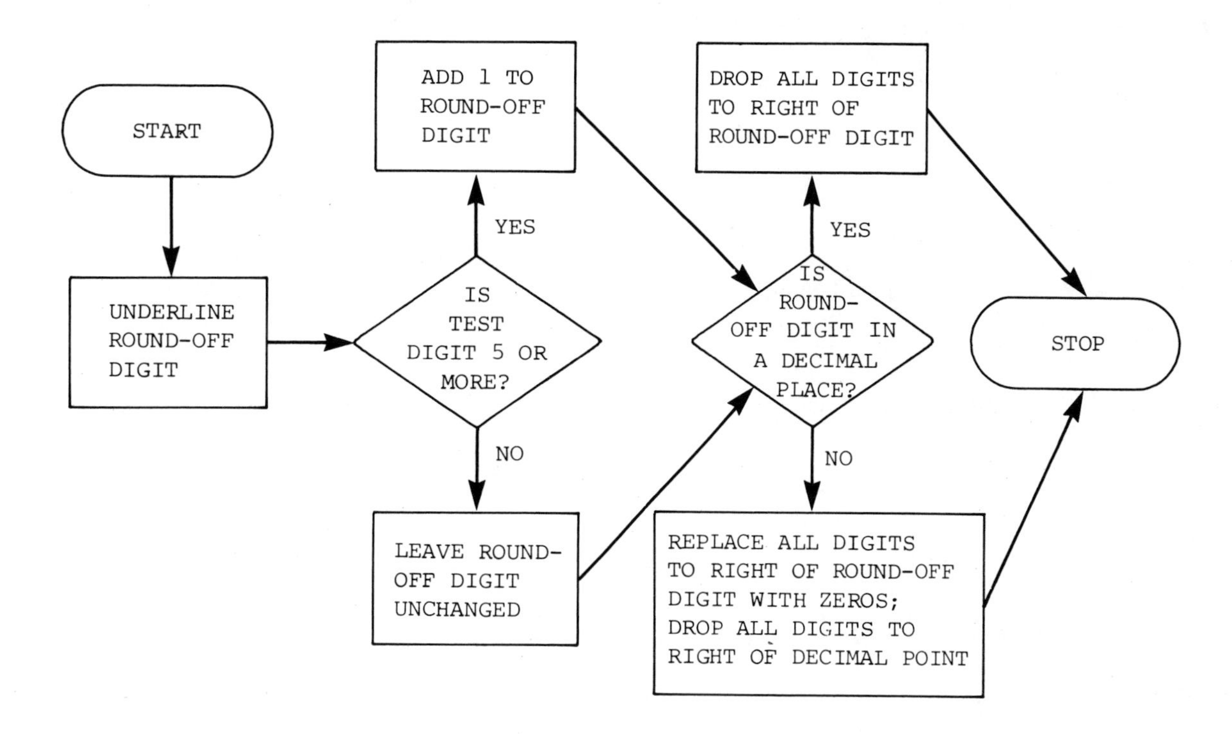

FIGURE A-2.2 Round-Off Procedure

The *flow chart* above indicates the rounding-off process most commonly used. In this procedure, the *round-off digit* is the last digit to be kept; the *test digit* is the digit immediately to the right of the round-off digit. For example, to round off 649.03574 to the nearest hundredth, underline the round-off digit, 3, in the hundredths place and proceed as follows:

649.03574 (test digit: 5; round-off digit: 3)

The test digit is 5; hence, 1 is added to the round-off digit.

649.0~~3~~574 (3 replaced by 4)

The round-off digit is in a decimal place, so all digits to its right are dropped.

649.0~~3574~~ (3 replaced by 4) → 649.04

EXAMPLE 2

In each case the round-off digit is underlined.

a. Round off to the nearest ten:

$$6\underline{4}9.03574 \rightarrow 6\overset{5}{\underline{\not{4}}}\overset{0}{\not{9}}.\not{0}\not{3}\not{5}\not{7}\not{4} \rightarrow 650$$

b. Round off to the nearest tenth:

$$649.\underline{0}3574 \rightarrow 649.\underline{0}\not{3}\not{5}\not{7}\not{4} \rightarrow 649.0$$

c. Round off to the nearest thousandth:

$$649.03\underline{5}74 \rightarrow 649.03\overset{6}{\underline{\not{5}}}\not{7}\not{4} \rightarrow 649.036$$

d. Round off to the nearest hundred:

$$\underline{6}49.03574 \rightarrow \underline{6}\overset{0}{\not{4}}\overset{0}{\not{9}}.\not{0}\not{3}\not{5}\not{7}\not{4} \rightarrow 600$$

e. Round off to the nearest unit:

$$64\underline{9}.03574 \rightarrow 64\underline{9}.\not{0}\not{3}\not{5}\not{7}\not{4} \rightarrow 649$$

In Example 2e, observe that the result is a whole number. Thus, instructions such as "round off to the nearest unit" may also be given as "round off to the nearest whole number."

Round-off instructions sometimes specify a particular number of places.

EXAMPLE 3

a. Round off to two decimal places:

$$28.3\underline{9}72 \rightarrow 28.\overset{4}{\not{3}}\overset{0}{\underline{\not{9}}}\not{7}\not{2} \rightarrow 28.40$$

b. Round off to three decimal places:

$$28.39\underline{7}2 \rightarrow 28.39\underline{7}\not{2} \rightarrow 28.397$$

In many engineering and scientific applications, the round-off rule described above is followed, except in the case in which the test digit is 5. In such cases we use the following ODD-FIVE RULE.

If a test digit, 5, is the last nonzero digit of a number:

1. Add 1 to the round-off digit if it is odd (1, 3, 5, 7, 9).

2. Retain the original round-off digit if it is even (0, 2, 4, 6, 8).

For example, to round off 96.035 to the nearest hundredth by the odd-five rule, first note that the test digit is 5 and it is the *last* nonzero digit. Next, because the round-off digit 3 is *odd*, add 1 to obtain 4 and drop the digit 5:

$$96.0\underline{3}5 \rightarrow 96.0\overset{4}{\underline{\not{3}}}\not{5} \rightarrow 96.04$$

To round off 96.025 to the nearest hundredth, where the round-off digit 2 is even, retain the 2 and drop the 5. Thus:

$$96.0\underline{2}5 \rightarrow 96.0\underline{2}\not{5} \rightarrow 96.02$$

EXAMPLE 4

Use the odd-five rule to round off the given number:

a. To the nearest thousandth.

(odd digit; add 1 to digit)

$$3.07\underline{1}50 \rightarrow 3.07\underline{1}\not{5}\not{0} \rightarrow 3.072$$

b. To the nearest hundred.

(even digit; retain digit)

$$69,\underline{4}50 \rightarrow 69,\underline{4}\not{5}\not{0} \rightarrow 69,400$$

In the exercises of this book, the odd-five rule is to be used only when specified.

TRUNCATION

The result of a computation may involve more digits than can be displayed by the calculator being used. In such cases the rightmost digits of the number are dropped, and we say that the number has been "truncated." Some calculators truncate numbers and round off the result, others truncate without rounding off. For example, the result of the division

$$20 \div 3$$

will be displayed as 6.6666666 on calculators that do *not* round off and as 6.6666667 on calculators that do round off. Consequently, *you may sometimes obtain answers on your calculator that differ slightly from the answers to the examples and exercises in this book.* You may want to use the division shown above to determine whether or not your calculator rounds off truncated answers.

EXERCISE SET A-2

Write each number and underline the digit in the (a) tens place, (b) tenths place, (c) thousandths place, (d) thousands place, (e) hundredths place, (f) ten-thousandths place, and (g) units place. See Example 1.

1. 6374.1592
2. 1234.5678
3. 20,468.13509
4. 75,123.02645
5. 1,034,592.00563
6. 2,135,004.505102

Round off each number to the nearest: (a) tenth, (b) hundredth, (c) thousandth, (d) whole number (unit), and (e) hundred. See Example 2.

7. 647.7742	8. 105.6344	9. 786.6825
10. 515.6079	11. 2486.8833	12. 1225.5703
13. 6874.0119	14. 7640.2959	15. 6015.63543
16. 4439.4256	17. 1584.9595	18. 19,905.09095

Round off each number to (a) one decimal place, (b) two decimal places, and (c) three decimal places. See Example 3.

19. 5.6755	20. 7.9855	21. 19.4607	22. 18.5908
23. 108.0675	24. 74.0785	25. 94.0507	26. 80.1806

Use the odd-five rule, when appropriate, to round off each number to the nearest (a) tenth and (b) thousandth. See Example 4.

27. 555.5555	28. 753.3545	29. 451.4545	30. 1456.1515

Round off each amount of money to (a) the nearest cent (hundredth) and (b) the nearest dollar (unit). Do not use the odd-five rule.

31. \$78.578	32. \$568.645	33. \$140.495	34. \$.575
35. \$.495	36. \$645.581	37. \$7.504	38. \$12.462

A-3 Exact and Approximate Numbers, Significant Digits

OBJECTIVES

After completing this section, you should

1. Be familiar with the meaning of *exact* and *approximate* numbers.
2. Know how to determine which digits of an approximate number are significant.
3. Be able to round off a given number to a specified number of significant digits.

Any number obtained by a counting process is an *exact* number. For example, if we say, "60 students are enrolled in a class," the number 60 is exact. Exact numbers may also arise by definition. In the statement, "One hour equals 60 minutes," the number 60 is exact. On the other hand, a number that is obtained by a process of measurement is an *approximate number*. Thus, if the distance between two cities, measured by driving from one city to the other, is given as 60 miles, this distance is an approximation to the actual distance, and the number 60 is an approximate number. The actual distance may be a little more or a little less than 60 miles.

EXAMPLE 1

In the statement:

a. "There are 12 employees in this office," the number 12 is *exact*; 12 is obtained by counting.

b. "There are 12 eggs in a dozen," the number 12 is *exact*; 12 is defined to be the number associated with "dozen."

c. "There are 12 gallons of gasoline in the tank," the number 12 is *approximate*; 12 is a measure of the amount of gasoline.

SIGNIFICANT DIGITS

When working with approximate numbers, the phrase *significant digits* is used to refer to those digits in a number that have meaning relative to the measurement process by which they were obtained. The following five rules can be used to decide which digits of an approximate number are significant.

1. *Nonzero digits* (1, 2, 3, 4, 5, 6, 7, 8, 9) *are always significant.*
2. *Zeros that are preceded and followed by significant digits are always significant.*
3. *Final zeros on the right of a decimal point are significant.*
4. *Final zeros on a whole number are assumed not to be significant unless further information is available.*
5. *When a number has no digits on the left of the decimal point, zeros between the decimal point and the first nonzero digit are not significant.*

In the examples illustrating each rule, the significant digits are underlined.

EXAMPLE 2

a. 14.24 has four significant digits (Rule 1).

b. .0036 has two significant digits (Rules 1 and 5).

EXAMPLE 3

a. 14.0024 has six significant digits (Rule 2).

b. 7001 has four significant digits (Rule 2).

EXAMPLE 4

a. 8.9000 has five significant digits (Rule 3).

b. .03600 has four significant digits (Rules 1 and 5).

EXAMPLE 5

a. In the statement, "Hawaii is 2400 miles west of Los Angeles," (without further information on how the measurement was made) assume that 2400 has only two significant digits (Rule 4).

b. If the distance between two cities is given as 2400 miles *to the nearest mile*, then the number 2400 has four significant digits (Rule 4).

Numbers can be rounded off to a specified number of significant digits by using the same procedure that is used to round off a number to a specified place value.

EXAMPLE 6

a. Round off to two significant digits:

37.804 → 37.~~804~~ → 38

b. Round off to four significant digits:

37.804 → 37.80~~4~~ → 37.80

EXAMPLE 7

Use the odd-five round-off rule.

a. Round off to three significant digits:

12.95 → 12.9~~5~~ → 13.0

b. Round off to two significant digits:

12.500 → 12.~~500~~ → 12

EXERCISE SET A-3

Specify whether the number in each statement is exact or approximate. See Example 1.

1. The wire is 100 cm long.
2. The board is 10 in. long.
3. There are 100 pennies in the drawer.
4. There are 200 postage stamps in this sheet.
5. One mile is 5280 ft long.
6. The thermometer reads 40° C.
7. This performance will last 30 min.
8. There are 60 minutes in 1 hr.
9. The barometer reads 25.8.
10. There are 100 lb of sand in the bag.

Specify how many significant digits are in each number. See Examples 2, 3, and 4.

11. 53.62	12. 133.44	13. .003	14. .00112
15. 15.02	16. 8.0092	17. 30,025	18. 155,013
19. 9.070	20. 82.400	21. 205.10	22. 18.0
23. 31.50	24. 1134.7	25. 62.01	26. 8305
27. 4.04	28. .0090	29. 3.0090	30. 302.001

Specify how many significant digits are in the number in each of the following statements. See Example 5.

31. The mountain is 2000 ft high.
32. The mountain is 2000 ft high, to the nearest foot.
33. To the nearest kilometer, city hall is 40 km from the city boundary.
34. City hall is 40 km from the city boundary.
35. The truck carried 600 lb of sand.
36. To the nearest pound, the truck carried 600 lb of sand.

Round off each number to (a) two significant digits, (b) three significant digits, and (c) four significant digits. See Example 6.

37. 62.352	38. 121.346	39. 18.507	40. 567.09
41. 8.3400	42. 12.600	43. .014767	44. .00687653
45. 50,037	46. 608,089	47. 134.85	48. 68.350

Use the odd-five rule to round off each number to (a) two significant digits and (b) three significant digits. See Example 7.

49. 1.255

50. 655.0

51. 32.45

52. .2450

53. 9.155

54. 315.0

A-4 Computations with Approximate Numbers

OBJECTIVES

After completing this section, you should

1. Be able to determine which of two or more approximate numbers is the least precise or least accurate.
2. Know the *addition-subtraction* rule and the *multiplication-division* rule for rounding off answers to computations with approximate numbers.

PRECISION

If the capacity of a tank is given as 235 gallons, it is assumed that the capacity was measured to the nearest whole gallon. If the capacity is given as 23.5 gallons, it is assumed that the capacity was measured to the nearest tenth of a gallon. We say that the number 23.5 "has greater precision" than 235. More generally, the *precision* of an approximate number is determined by the *least place value* in which a significant digit appears. (We do not use "precision" with reference to exact numbers.) Thus, when comparing approximate numbers for precision, the number with a *significant digit farthest to the right* is the number with the *greatest precision*. In Examples 1 and 2 below, the place value of the significant digit farthest to the right is named, in parentheses, after each number.

EXAMPLE 1

a. The number 16.700 (thousandths) is more precise than 16.70 (hundredths).

b. The number 4780 (tens) is less precise than 478 (units).

c. The numbers 95.3 (tenths) and 295.3 (tenths) have the same precision.

Most often we are concerned with which of two or more numbers is the *least* precise.

EXAMPLE 2

Which of the numbers 50.000, 27.8, and 42.39 has the least precision?

Solution

Consider the rightmost significant digit in each number: 50.000 (thousandths), 27.8 (tenths), 42.39 (hundredths). Because significant digits appear farther to the right in the numbers 50.000 and 42.39 than in 27.8, the number with the *least* precision is 27.8.

ACCURACY

The *accuracy* of an approximate number can be determined by counting how many significant digits appear in the number. *The greater the number of significant digits, the greater the accuracy.* (We do not use "accuracy" with reference to exact numbers.)

EXAMPLE 3

The number of significant digits in each number is specified in parentheses after the number.

a. The number 37.5 (three) has greater accuracy than .42 (two).

b. The number .042 (two) has the same accuracy as 88 (two).

c. The number .80 (two) has less accuracy than the number .0800 (three).

Most often we are concerned with which of two or more numbers is the *least* accurate.

EXAMPLE 4

Which of the numbers .09, 340, and 1.01 has the least accuracy?

Solution

Count the significant digits in each number: .09 (one), 340 (two), 1.01 (three). The number .09 with only one significant digit has the *least* accuracy.

PRECISION AND ACCURACY IN COMPUTATIONS

Computations that involve one or more approximate numbers lead to results that are also approximate numbers. Furthermore, the number of places to be retained in such results depends on the precision and accuracy of the numbers entered into the computations. Because most calculators compute with entered numbers as though they are exact numbers, it is important to have rules for controlling the results of such computations. Two rules used for computing with approximate numbers follow.

1. Additions-Subtractions: *Round off the result to as many places as the approximate number with the least precision.*
2. Multiplications-Divisions: *Round off the result to as many significant digits as the approximate number with the least accuracy.*

Note that both of these rules refer only to approximate numbers. If a computation involves both approximate and exact numbers, we consider only the approximate numbers when applying the rules, because exact numbers do not affect either the accuracy or the precision of the result.

EXAMPLE 5

Unless specified otherwise, assume all numbers are approximate.

a. Under floating decimal point operation,

$$25.608 - 21 + 37.4 + 6.13 = 48.138$$

The number with the least precision is 21 (units). Hence, by Rule 1, round off 48.138 to the nearest whole number to obtain 48 as the answer.

b. Under floating decimal point operation,

$$16.04 + 5.83 - 14 + 9.0 = 16.87$$

If 14 is given as an exact number, then the number with the least precision is 9.0 (tenths). Hence, by Rule 1, round off 16.87 to the nearest tenth to obtain 16.9 as the answer.

EXAMPLE 6

Unless specified otherwise, assume all numbers are approximate.

a. Under floating decimal point operation,

$$43.7 \times .014 \times 8.605 = 5.264539$$

The number with the least accuracy is .014 (two significant digits). Hence, by Rule 2, round off 5.264539 to two significant digits to obtain 5.3 as the answer.

b. Under floating decimal point operation,

$$843.052 \div 4 = 210.763$$

If 4 is given as an exact number, then the number with least accuracy is 843.052, which has six significant digits. By Rule 2, six significant digits are retained in the answer. The quotient is 210.763.

EXERCISE SET A-4

Assume all numbers are approximate.

Determine which number has the least precision. See Example 2.

1. 24.7; 24.70
2. 1205; 346.4
3. 1001.2; 10,001; 10,001.42
4. 1.60; 4.8; 3.445
5. .005; .0024; .00024
6. 300.5; 486.55; 4002

Determine which number has the least accuracy. See Example 4.

7. .07; 1.4
8. 560; 3.05
9. .150; 1.9; 14.66
10. 215; 2.150; 2.1
11. 404; 2012; 41.14
12. 19.9; 2.0; 20.2

Perform each calculation and round off answers according to the rule for adding and subtracting approximate numbers. See Example 5a.

13. 1.526 + 18.1427 + 4.068
14. 39.5704 + 9.60004 + 8.573
15. 249 + 249.6 + 249.86
16. 5108 + 376 + 99.14 + 75.28

17. 46.057 - 32.1351
18. 219.0036 - 174.383
19. 617 - 485.1308
20. 2828 - 1976.0312
21. 955.97 - 416.419 + 90.1 - 334.3133
22. 9.4961 - 6.205 + 7.22 - 5.7

Perform each calculation and round off answers according to the rule for multiplying and dividing approximate numbers. See Example 6a.

23. 2058 × 7.01
24. 706.0 × .49
25. 34.82 × 16.1 × .149
26. 96.01 × 3.81 × .513
27. 18 ÷ 6.003
28. 275 ÷ 24.125
29. .08062 ÷ .04
30. .4315 ÷ .625
31. 74,001 ÷ 2.13044 × 5.123
32. 9843 ÷ 3.08166 × .0688
33. 48.00 ÷ .1200 × 2.000
34. 3.95 ÷ 2.24 × 55

Perform each calculation and round off answers according to the rule for adding and subtracting, or multiplying and dividing, approximate numbers assuming (a) all numbers are approximate and (b) that the underlined number is exact. See Examples 5b and 6b.

35. 26.2 + $\underline{135}$ - 48.26
36. 473.47 + 340.5 - $\underline{58}$
37. $\underline{98.6}$ - 48.72 + 151.663
38. $\underline{302.5}$ - 68.74 - 108.649
39. 9.697 + 14.335 - $\underline{6.8}$ + 23.450
40. 136.842 - $\underline{75.90}$ + 22.630 - 12.1864
41. $\underline{360}$ × 8.09 ÷ 12.6
42. 12.96 × $\underline{72}$ ÷ 8.25
43. $\underline{2.5}$ × 6.81 ÷ .00545
44. 15.47 ÷ 3.9 × $\underline{12.1}$
45. 64 ÷ $\underline{86.9}$ × 9.095
46. 75.10 × $\underline{96.8}$ ÷ 19.07

A-5 Factoring

OBJECTIVES

After completing this section, you should

1. Know the meaning of *exact divisor, factor, prime number, composite number,* and *completely factored form.*
2. Be able to completely factor a number.
3. Be able to show that a given number is (or is not) a prime number.

When a number such as 75 is written as the product 3×25, we say that 3×25 is a *factored form* of 75. The process of changing a number to factored form is called *factoring*.

If one whole number is divided by a second whole number so that the quotient is a whole number, then the second whole number is an *exact divisor* of the first. Thus, because

$$75 \div 3 = 25$$

and 25 is a whole number, 3 is an exact divisor of 75.

An exact divisor of a whole number is also called a *factor* of the number. For example, 25 and 3 are two of the factors of 75.

EXAMPLE 1

a. 15 is a factor of 75 because $75 \div 15 = 5$, and 5 is a whole number.

b. 4 is not a factor of 75 because $75 \div 4 = 18.75$, and 18.75 is not a whole number.

COMPLETELY FACTORED FORM

A whole number greater than 1 that has no exact divisor except for itself and 1 is called a *prime number*. The first sixteen prime numbers are

$$2, 3, 5, 7, 11, 13, 17, 19, 23, 29, 31, 37, 41, 43, 47, 53$$

Whole numbers greater than 1 that are not prime numbers are called *composite numbers*. For example, 75 is a composite number because it has exact divisors other than itself (as shown above, 3 is an exact divisor of 75). When a composite number is written as a product of prime numbers, it is said to be *completely factored,* and the resulting product is called the *completely factored form* of the number. For example, $3 \times 5 \times 5$ is the completely factored form of 75. Because the order in which numbers are multiplied does not change the product, the order in which the prime factors of a number are listed does not matter. Thus, $5 \times 3 \times 5$ is also the completely factored form of 75.

Some numbers can be completely factored by inspection. For example,

$$15 = 3 \times 5, \quad 21 = 3 \times 7, \quad 25 = 5 \times 5$$

The following rules can be used to decide whether or not a given number can be exactly divided by 2 or 3 or 5 and can be helpful when writing the completely factored form of some numbers.

1. A whole number is divisible by 2 if the last digit to the right is an even digit (0, 2, 4, 6, 8).
2. A whole number is divisible by 3 if the sum of its digits is divisible by 3.
3. A whole number is divisible by 5 if the last digit to the right is either 0 or 5.

EXAMPLE 2

a. 54 is divisible by 2 because the last digit to the right is an even digit, 4.

b. 12,345 is divisible by 3 because 1 + 2 + 3 + 4 + 5 = 15, and 15 is divisible by 3.

c. 12,345 is divisible by 5 because the last digit to the right is 5.

If a number, N, cannot be readily factored by inspection or by using the divisibility rules for 2, 3, and 5, we can divide N by each prime factor in turn* (more than once, if necessary) to see if it is an exact divisor. The process ends when N is completely factored, or when we find that we have divided by the *greatest prime test divisor* of N. We can determine the greatest prime test divisor of a number in either of two ways.

1. On calculators with a square root key [√]:†

   Find the square root of N. The greatest prime number that is less than or equal to the square root of N is the greatest prime test divisor.

2. On calculators without a square root key:

   Guess a possible greatest prime test divisor and test it by multiplying it by itself. The greatest prime divisor, which, when multiplied by itself, results in a product less than or equal to N, is the greatest prime test divisor of N.

EXAMPLE 3

Find the greatest prime test divisor of 619.

Solution

With the square root key: $\sqrt{619}$ = 24.879711; as computed by

619 [√] → 24.879711 or by 619 [ENT] [√] → 24.879711

The greatest prime number less than 24.879711 is 23; hence, 23 is the greatest prime test divisor of 619.

Without the square root key: By guess, start with 19 (an arbitrary choice) and consider the products

$$19 \times 19 = 361, \quad 23 \times 23 = 529, \quad 29 \times 29 = 841$$

Because 529 is less than 619 and 841 is greater than 619, it follows that 23 is the greatest prime test divisor of 619.

---

*Refer to the list of the first sixteen prime factors on page 25.

†See Appendix A for a review of square root.

EXAMPLE 4

Completely factor 286.

Solution

First note that 286 is divisible by 2 because the last digit, 6, is an even digit. Thus,

$$286 \div 2 = 143 \quad \text{or} \quad 286 = 2 \times 143$$

Next, note that 143 is not divisible by 2, 3, or 5. Divide 143 by the next prime numbers of the list:

$$143 \div 7 = 20.428571$$

$$143 \div 11 = 13 \quad \text{or} \quad 143 = 11 \times 13$$

Thus,

$$286 = 2 \times 143 = 2 \times 11 \times 13$$

Because 2, 11, and 13 are prime numbers, the completely factored form of 286 is $2 \times 11 \times 13$.

The next example shows a convenient arrangement for completely factoring a number when several steps are involved.

EXAMPLE 5

$$\begin{aligned} 2925 &= 3 \times 975 \\ &= 3 \times 3 \times 325 \\ &= 3 \times 3 \times 5 \times 65 \\ &= 3 \times 3 \times 5 \times 5 \times 13 \end{aligned}$$

If none of the prime divisors, up to and including the greatest possible prime divisor, is an exact divisor of a number N, then N is a prime number.

EXAMPLE 6

Show that 619 is a prime number.

Solution

From Example 3, the greatest prime test divisor of 619 is 23. Note that 619 is not divisible by 2, 3, or 5. Divide 619 in turn by 7, 11, 13, 17, 19, and 23:

$$619 \div 7 = 88.428571 \qquad 619 \div 17 = 36.411764$$

$$619 \div 11 = 56.272727 \qquad 619 \div 19 = 32.578947$$

$$619 \div 13 = 47.615384 \qquad 619 \div 23 = 26.913043$$

Because 619 is not divisible by any of the prime numbers up to and including 23, it follows that 619 is a prime number.

EXAMPLE 7

Completely factor 12,999.

Solution

$$12{,}999 = 3 \times 4333$$

$$= 3 \times 7 \times 619$$

From Example 6, the number 619 is prime. Hence,

$$12{,}999 = 3 \times 7 \times 619$$

EXERCISE SET A-5

State which (if any) of the first two numbers is a factor of the third number. See Example 1.

1. 13, 9; 65
2. 14, 12; 196
3. 17, 14; 273
4. 23, 31; 1289
5. 33, 41; 615
6. 76, 89; 4104
7. 27, 29; 1479
8. 103, 69; 5459

State whether the given number is divisible by 2, 3, 5, or none of these. See Example 2.

9. 4696
10. 71,005
11. 69,445
12. 67,490
13. 749,180
14. 1899
15. 5481
16. 8303
17. 1763
18. 980,127
19. 64,359
20. 795

For Exercises 21-52, you may want to refer to the list of prime numbers on page 25.

Find the greatest prime test divisor of each number. See Example 3.

21. 754
22. 1075
23. 999
24. 3472
25. 2195
26. 2980
27. 853
28. 1010

Factor completely, if possible. See Examples 4, 5, and 6.

29. 364
30. 432
31. 650
32. 476

33. 4329
34. 1431
35. 109
36. 127
37. 1785
38. 1295
39. 3000
40. 2000
41. 419
42. 797
43. 429
44. 1001
45. 2185
46. 6355
47. 1827
48. 5225
49. 4655
50. 6975
51. 20,727
52. 14,157

Factor completely. See Example 7.

53. 3395
54. 3115
55. 2865
56. 10,311
57. 120,825
58. 68,025

A-6 Decimal Equivalents

OBJECTIVES

After completing this section, you should be able to

1. Compute the decimal equivalent of a fraction and determine whether the decimal equivalent is terminating or nonterminating.
2. Compute the reciprocal of any nonzero number.

Because a fraction represents a quotient, any fraction can be written in decimal form.

EXAMPLE 1

a. $\frac{4}{5} = 4 \div 5 = .8$

b. $\frac{5}{6} = 5 \div 6 = .83333333$

In Example 1a, note that no digits appear to the right of the digit 8. When the decimal form of a quotient has a last digit, as in .8, it is called a *terminating decimal*. In Example 1b we cannot tell from the display whether .83333333 is a terminating decimal, because eight-digit calculators can display at most eight digits. In fact,

$$5 \div 6 = .83333333...$$

where the symbol "..." indicates that there is no last digit. Such a decimal is called a *nonterminating decimal*. If the numerator and the denominator of a fraction do not have any common factors, and if the completely factored form of the denominator includes any prime factor other than 2 or 5, the decimal form is nonterminating. If 2 and 5 are the only prime factors, the decimal form is terminating.

EXAMPLE 2

a. $\frac{1}{8} = \frac{1}{2 \cdot 2 \cdot 2}$ Because no factors other than 2 appear in the denominator, the decimal form of $\frac{1}{8}$ terminates (1/8 = .125).

b. $\frac{7}{20} = \frac{7}{2 \cdot 2 \cdot 5}$ Because no factors other than 2 or 5 appear in the denominator, the decimal form of $\frac{7}{20}$ terminates (7/20 = .35).

c. $\frac{5}{6} = \frac{5}{2 \cdot 3}$ Because the denominator includes a factor (3) other than 2 or 5, the decimal form of $\frac{5}{6}$ does not terminate (5/6 = .83333333).

If the numerator and denominator of a fraction have common factors, the fraction must be reduced to lowest terms before deciding whether the decimal form is terminating or nonterminating. An efficient way to reduce a fraction to lowest terms is to factor the numerator and denominator completely and "cancel" any common factors.

EXAMPLE 3

a. $\frac{21}{60} = \frac{\not{3} \cdot 7}{2 \cdot 2 \cdot \not{3} \cdot 5} = \frac{7}{20}$ $\quad \frac{7}{20}$ has a terminating decimal form (see Example 2b).

b. $\frac{25}{30} = \frac{5 \cdot \not{5}}{2 \cdot 3 \cdot \not{5}} = \frac{5}{6}$ $\quad \frac{5}{6}$ has a nonterminating decimal form (see Example 2c).

DECIMAL EQUIVALENTS ON A CALCULATOR

The decimal form of a fraction, terminating or nonterminating, is called the *decimal equivalent* of the fraction. When we use a calculator to compute the decimal equivalent, the digits that appear in the display may be the entire decimal equivalent, or only the first seven or eight digits of the decimal equivalent. In either case we shall refer to the number in the display as the decimal equivalent of the fraction. We shall also consider rounded-off forms of decimal equivalents.

EXAMPLE 4

a. $\frac{9}{16} = .5625$ (under floating decimal point)

$= .6$ (to the nearest tenth)

$= .563$ (to the nearest thousandth)

b. $\frac{7}{12} = .58333333$ (under floating decimal point)

$= .6$ (to one decimal place)

$= .58$ (to two decimal places)

The decimal equivalent of a mixed number *greater than 1* can be obtained by replacing the fraction part by its decimal equivalent; the decimal equivalent of a mixed number *less than 1* can be obtained by replacing the fraction part by the *digits* of its decimal equivalent.

EXAMPLE 5

Because $\frac{3}{4} = .75$:

a. $9\frac{3}{4} = 9.75$

b. $.09\frac{3}{4} = .0975$

EXAMPLE 6

Because $\frac{2}{3} = .66666667$:

a. $8\frac{2}{3} = 8.66666667$

b. $.08\frac{2}{3} = .0866666667$

RECIPROCALS OF NUMBERS

The *reciprocal* of a nonzero number, n, is $\frac{1}{n}$; the reciprocal of the fraction, $\frac{n}{d}$, is $\frac{d}{n}$, where $d \neq 0$. Many calculators have a *reciprocal key* [1/x] for computing the decimal equivalent of the reciprocal of a number. (If your calculator has no such key, use the [÷] key and compute a quotient.) The [1/x] key operates only on the number in the display.

EXAMPLE 7

a. The reciprocal of 4 is $\frac{1}{4} = .25$; as computed by

1 [÷] 4 [=] → .25 or 4 [1/x] → .25

b. The reciprocal of .25 is $\frac{1}{.25} = 4$; as computed by

1 [÷] .25 [=] → 4 or .25 [1/x] → 4

The [÷] key is more convenient than the [1/x] key for computing the decimal equivalent of the reciprocal of a fraction.

EXAMPLE 8

The reciprocal of $\frac{3}{5}$ is $\frac{5}{3} = 1.6666667$; as computed by

5 [÷] 3 [=] → 1.6666667 or 5 [ENT] 3 [÷] → 1.6666667

The reciprocal of a mixed number can be obtained by first changing the mixed number to an improper fraction and then computing the decimal equivalent of the reciprocal of the resulting fraction.

EXAMPLE 9

The mixed number $3\frac{5}{7}$ equals $\frac{26}{7}$, where the numerator (26) can be computed mentally or by the sequence

7 [×] 3 [+] 5 [=] → 26 or 7 [ENT] 3 [×] 5 [+] → 26

The reciprocal of $\frac{26}{7}$ is $\frac{7}{26}$. The decimal equivalent of $\frac{7}{26}$ is .26923077.

EXERCISE SET A-6

Determine whether the decimal equivalent of each fraction is terminating or nonterminating. See Examples 2 and 3.

1. $\frac{3}{8}$ 2. $\frac{5}{16}$ 3. $\frac{17}{50}$ 4. $\frac{21}{25}$
5. $\frac{7}{12}$ 6. $\frac{17}{30}$ 7. $\frac{45}{80}$ 8. $\frac{29}{160}$
9. $\frac{21}{24}$ 10. $\frac{33}{48}$ 11. $\frac{26}{75}$ 12. $\frac{19}{70}$

Write the decimal equivalent of each fraction or mixed number (a) under floating decimal point, (b) to the nearest tenth, (c) to the nearest hundredth, and (d) to the nearest thousandth. See Examples 4 and 5.

13. $\frac{11}{12}$ 14. $\frac{7}{15}$ 15. $\frac{9}{16}$ 16. $\frac{11}{18}$
17. $\frac{25}{256}$ 18. $\frac{39}{128}$ 19. $\frac{119}{365}$ 20. $\frac{61}{360}$
21. $5\frac{5}{7}$ 22. $2\frac{3}{16}$ 23. $14\frac{43}{64}$ 24. $9\frac{25}{128}$
25. $.08\frac{3}{8}$ 26. $.3\frac{5}{16}$ 27. $.4\frac{1}{12}$ 28. $.05\frac{7}{18}$

For each number, (a) write its reciprocal as a fraction. Then, write the reciprocal of each number (b) under floating decimal point, (c) to two decimal places, and (d) to three decimal places. See Examples 7, 8, and 9.

29. 16 30. 32 31. 15 32. 18
33. .09 34. .07 35. .75 36. .45
37. $\frac{32}{5}$ 38. $\frac{16}{25}$ 39. $\frac{9}{11}$ 40. $\frac{7}{12}$
41. $5\frac{5}{7}$ 42. $2\frac{3}{16}$ 43. $8\frac{57}{360}$ 44. $12\frac{100}{365}$

A-7 Powers of Numbers

OBJECTIVES

After completing this section, you should be able to

1. Raise a number to a positive or a negative integer power.
2. Write products and quotients of powers of 10 as a single power of 10.

The product of two or more identical factors, such as

$$b \cdot b \cdot b \cdot b \cdot b$$

can be more concisely represented by the symbol b^5. This form of a product is called *exponential notation* and is often referred to as "raising a number to a power." In the exponential notation b^n, the number b is called the *base*, and n is called the *exponent*. The number b^n can be defined by the following three statements.

1. For $n = 1,2,3,\ldots$:

$$b^n = \overbrace{b \cdot b \cdot b \cdot \ldots \cdot b}^{n \text{ factors}}$$

2. For $n = 0$ and $b \neq 0$:

$$b^0 = 1$$

3. For n any integer $(\ldots,-2,-1,0,1,2,\ldots)$ and $b \neq 0$:

$$b^{-n} = \frac{1}{b^n}; \qquad \frac{1}{b^{-n}} = b^n$$

EXAMPLE 1

a. $9^1 = 9$

b. $9^4 = 9 \cdot 9 \cdot 9 \cdot 9$

c. $9^0 = 1$

EXAMPLE 2

a. $10^{-3} = \dfrac{1}{10^3}$

b. $\dfrac{1}{10^{-3}} = 10^3$

Most calculators have special capabilities for raising numbers to powers. Because these capabilities depend upon the type of calculator, you must know which type of calculator you have.

1. If your calculator has keys such as [SIN] and [LOG], you have a *scientific calculator*. For you, the material starting with the heading CONSTANT MULTIPLIER OR DIVISOR is optional (you may find it useful). Proceed from the heading POWERS ON SCIENTIFIC CALCULATORS (page 37) to the end of the section.
2. If your calculator does *not* have keys such as [SIN] and [LOG], you have a *non-scientific calculator*. Study the material starting with the heading CONSTANT MULTIPLIER OR DIVISOR (below), and omit the material headed POWERS ON SCIENTIFIC CALCULATORS. Then proceed to the heading POWERS OF 10 on page 38.

CONSTANT MULTIPLIER OR DIVISOR

Computing a series of products such as

$$7 \times 20, \qquad 7 \times 34.2, \qquad 7 \times 259$$

in which one of the factors in each product is the same, is called *multiplication by a constant* (we shall label it K-MULT). The factor that remains the same (in this case, 7) is the *constant factor*. Many calculators are capable of performing such multiplications with a minimum number of steps (some calculators require that a "constant" switch be turned to the ON, or K, position before proceeding with the computations).

In some calculators, the *first* factor entered into the calculator becomes the constant factor, in others, the *second* factor entered becomes the constant factor. In either type it is not necessary to re-enter the constant factor for each product. To determine whether K-MULT is available on your calculator, press the sequence

4 [×] [=]

If the result is 16, your calculator has K-MULT; if not, it does not, and you may omit Examples 3 and 4.

EXAMPLE 3

a. If the first factor entered is the constant factor, then

$7 \times 20 = 140, \qquad 7 \times 34.2 \doteq 239.4, \qquad 7 \times 259 = 1813$

computed by the sequence

7 [×] 20 [=] → 140, 34.2 [=] → 239.4, 259 [=] → 1813

b. If the second factor entered is the constant factor, then

$20 \times 7 = 140, \qquad 34.2 \times 7 = 239.4, \qquad 259 \times 7 = 1813$

computed by the sequence

20 [×] 7 [=] → 140, 34.2 [=] → 239.4, 259 [=] → 1813

Computing a series of quotients in which the divisor is the same in each quotient is called *division by a constant* (we shall label it K-DIV). The calculator procedure for such divisions is similar to that for K-MULT except that *the second number entered is always the constant divisor.*

EXAMPLE 4

$112 \div 1.4 = 80$, $56.84 \div 1.4 = 40.6$, $8.638 \div 1.4 = 6.17$

computed by the sequence

112 [÷] 1.4 [=] → 80, 56.84 [=] → 40.6, 8.638 [=] → 6.17

RAISING TO POSITIVE POWERS

Raising a number to a positive power can be done with or without K-MULT. To use K-MULT to raise a number b to a positive power n, it is only necessary to enter the base b in the calculator once, press the [×] key, and then press the [=] key *one time less than the number n.* Example 5 shows how to raise a number to a power with or without K-MULT.

EXAMPLE 5

$2.3^4 = 27.9841$

a. As computed with K-MULT:

2.3 [×] [=] [=] [=] → 27.9841

b. As computed without K-MULT:

2.3 [×] 2.3 [×] 2.3 [×] 2.3 [=] → 27.9841

Negative bases can be raised to integer powers as in the next example.

EXAMPLE 6

Compute: a. $(-2.4)^3$ b. $(-2.4)^4$

Solutions

a. First compute $(2.4)^3 = 13.824$. Then, note that a negative number raised to an *odd* power is negative. Hence,

$$(-2.4)^3 = -13.824$$

b. First compute $(2.4)^4 = 33.1776$. Then, note that a negative number raised to an *even* power is positive. Hence,

$$(-2.4)^4 = 33.1776$$

RAISING TO NEGATIVE POWERS

From Statement 3 at the beginning of this section, note that

$$6^{-3} = \frac{1}{6^3} = 1 \div 6^3$$

which indicates that raising a number to a negative power involves division. The division can be done with or without K-DIV. To use K-DIV for raising a number b to a negative power, enter b in the calculator once, press the [÷] key, and then press the [=] key *one more time than the number n.*

EXAMPLE 7

$6^{-3} = .0046296$

a. As computed with K-DIV:

6 [÷] [=] [=] [=] [=] → .00462962

b. Without K-DIV, there are choices. You can compute 6^3 and then compute its reciprocal. A better method is

1 [÷] 6 [÷] 6 [÷] 6 [=] → .00462962

POWERS ON SCIENTIFIC CALCULATORS

Scientific calculators have a *power key* [y^x] (or [x^y]), which is used to raise a positive number to a power. The power key operates on two numbers, the base and the exponent. On [=] calculators, the base is entered *before* and the exponent is entered *after* the [y^x] key is pressed. On [ENT] calculators, both the base and the exponent are entered *before* the [y^x] key is pressed. Sequences that involve the power key depend upon whether your calculator does or does not have an [F] key.* The next example shows both types of sequences.

EXAMPLE 8

$1.2^6 = 2.985984$, as computed by

[=] calculators:

1.2 [y^x] 6 [=] → 2.985984 or 1.2 [F] [y^x] 6 [=] → 2.985984

---

*On [ENT] calculators, the [F] key may simply be a solid-colored key with no label. (See your instruction booklet.)

ENT calculators:

1.2 ENT 6 y^x → 2.985984 or 1.2 ENT 6 F y^x → 2.985984

In the remainder of this book we will show only the y^x symbol in a sequence, with the understanding that you will use the F key if your calculator requires it.

To raise a number to a negative power, we use the *sign change key* +/- (or CHS).

EXAMPLE 9

$1.2^{-6} = .334898$, as computed by

= calculators:

1.2 y^x 6 +/- = → .334898

ENT calculators:

1.2 ENT 6 +/- y^x → .334898

Most calculators will not accept a negative number as a base to be raised to a power. However, negative bases can be raised to integer powers as in the next example.

EXAMPLE 10

Compute: a. $(-2.4)^3$ b. $(-2.4)^4$

Solutions

a. First compute $(2.4)^3 = 13.824$. Then note that a negative number raised to an *odd* power is negative. Hence,

$$(-2.4)^3 = -13.824$$

b. First compute $(2.4)^4 = 33.1776$. Then, note that a negative number raised to an *even* power is positive. Hence,

$$(-2.4)^4 = 33.1776$$

POWERS OF 10

Powers in the form 10^n, where n is any integer, are referred to as *powers of* 10. Products of two (or more) powers of 10 can be expressed as a single power of 10 by the following rule.

If m and n are integers, then

$$10^m \times 10^n = 10^{m+n}$$

EXAMPLE 11

a. $10^2 \times 10^3 = 10^{2+3} = 10^5$

b.* $10^2 \times 10^3 \times 10^{-4} = 10^{2+3+(-4)} = 10^1$, or 10

c. $10^5 \times 10^{-4} \times 10^{-1} = 10^{5+(-4)+(-1)} = 10^0$, or 1

Quotients involving powers of 10 can be expressed as products. For example, applying Statement 3, we have

$$\frac{10^4}{10^{-3}} = 10^4 \times \frac{1}{10^{-3}} = 10^4 \times 10^3$$

and

$$\frac{10^4}{10^3} = 10^4 \times \frac{1}{10^3} = 10^4 \times 10^{-3}$$

Note that in each case a power of 10 in the denominator is rewritten with the sign of the exponent changed and is included as a factor (not in a denominator). This technique can be used for combined products and quotients of powers of 10.

EXAMPLE 12

Write each expression as a single power of 10.

a. $\dfrac{10^2 \times 10^{-3}}{10^4 \times 10^{-2}}$ b. $\dfrac{10^5 \times 10^{-2} \times 10^2}{10^1 \times 10^3 \times 10^{-4}}$

Solutions

a. $\dfrac{10^2 \times 10^{-3}}{10^4 \times 10^{-2}} = 10^2 \times 10^{-3} \times 10^{-4} \times 10^2 = 10^{-3}$

b. $\dfrac{10^5 \times 10^{-2} \times 10^2}{10^1 \times 10^3 \times 10^{-4}} = 10^5 \times 10^{-2} \times 10^2 \times 10^{-1} \times 10^{-3} \times 10^4 = 10^5$

EXERCISE SET A-7

Express each product in the form b^n. See Example 1.

1. $2 \times 2 \times 2$
2. $5 \times 5 \times 5 \times 5$
3. $4 \times 4 \times 4 \times 4$
4. 3×3
5. 10
6. $10 \times 10 \times 10$
7. $6 \times 6 \times 6 \times 6 \times 6 \times 6$
8. $12 \times 12 \times 12 \times 12$

---

*Addition of positive and negative integers is considered in Appendix C.

Each expression below is in the form b^n. Rewrite each expression as a product of equal factors, or as 1 or as b. See Example 1.

9. 3^6 10. 7^3 11. 10^4 12. 8^0

13. 5^1 14. 12^1 15. 7^0 16. 4^5

Each expression below is in the form b^{-n}. Rewrite each expression as an equivalent expression with a positive exponent. See Example 2.

17. 10^{-1} 18. 10^{-2} 19. 7^{-3} 20. 9^{-4}

21. 4^{-2} 22. 5^{-1} 23. 3^{-5} 24. 6^{-5}

25. $\frac{1}{10^{-2}}$ 26. $\frac{1}{10^{-4}}$ 27. $\frac{1}{2^{-3}}$ 28. $\frac{1}{4^{-2}}$

Calculate each series of products or quotients using K-MULT or K-DIV. See Examples 3 and 4. (Exercises 29-36 are *optional* for scientific calculators.)

29. 12×3.4; 12×15.2; 12×25.6

30. 5.2×6.8; 5.2×2.9; 5.2×7.4

31. 1.4×4.6; 4.1×4.6; 9.3×4.6

32. 9.4×5.1; 6.8×5.1; 12.2×5.1

33. $58 \div 2.5$; $68 \div 2.5$; $75 \div 2.5$

34. $76 \div 1.25$; $89 \div 1.25$; $107 \div 1.25$

35. $11.4 \div 40$; $12.6 \div 40$; $19.8 \div 40$

36. $4.5 \div 7.5$; $9.6 \div 7.5$; $12.3 \div 7.5$

Calculate each power. See Examples 5 and 6 or 8 and 10.

37. 6^4 38. 4^5 39. 3^6 40. 2^8

41. 2^{12} 42. 2.5^4 43. $(-6.1)^3$ 44. $(-5.8)^4$

45. $.74^5$ 46. $.83^3$ 47. $(-.41)^4$ 48. $(-.75)^5$

Calculate each power. See Example 7 or 9.

49. 7^{-1} 50. 8^{-1} 51. 4.2^{-2} 52. 5.5^{-2}

53. 1.4^{-3} 54. $.86^{-3}$ 55. 3.05^{-4} 56. 3.5^{-4}

Express as a single positive or negative power of 10 or as 1. See Examples 11 and 12.

57. $10^2 \times 10^3$ 58. $10^4 \times 10^5$ 59. $10^{-3} \times 10^2$

60. $10^{-5} \times 10^4$ 61. $10^{-2} \times 10^{-3} \times 10^1$ 62. $10^{-4} \times 10^{-5} \times 10^8$

63. $10^1 \times 10^2 \times 10^{-3}$ 64. $10^{-1} \times 10^2 \times 10^{-3}$ 65. $\frac{10^{-1} \times 10^{-2} \times 10^{-3}}{10^2 \times 10^1}$

66. $\frac{10^2 \times 10^{-4}}{10^{-5} \times 10^1}$ 67. $\frac{10^{-3} \times 10^4}{10^{-6} \times 10^2}$ 68. $\frac{10^2 \times 10^1 \times 10^{-5}}{10^3 \times 10^{-4}}$

(Optional) Because $b^{-n} = 1/b^n$, the reciprocal key [1/x] can be used together with the [y^x] key to provide an alternate method for raising a number to a negative power.

EXAMPLE

$6^{-3} = .00463$ to three significant digits, as computed by

6 [y^x] 3 [=] [1/x] or 6 [ENT] 3 [y^x] [1/x]

Use the [1/x] key to compute the powers in Exercises 49-56.

A-8 Scientific Notation

OBJECTIVES

After completing this section, you should be able to

1. Multiply a number by a power of 10 without using a calculator.
2. Change a number from decimal form to scientific notation.
3. Do multiplication or division with numbers in scientific notation.
4. Enter a number in scientific notation into an [EE] calculator (if you have such a calculator).

Note that each of the following products has 6.29 as one factor and a power of 10 as the other.

$$6.29 \times 10^2 = 6.29 \times 100 = 629$$

and

$$6.29 \times 10^{-2} = 6.29 \times .01 = .0629$$

Comparing the factor 6.29 with the final form of each product, we see that only the position of the decimal point has changed; the significant digits remain the same. Note in particular that when multiplying by 10^2, the decimal point in the answer appears *two places to the right* of its original position. When multiplying by 10^{-2}, the decimal point appears *two places to the left* of its original position. Results such as these suggest the following "mental arithmetic" rule.

To multiply a number by 10^n, retain the original digits in the number. From its original position, move the decimal point as follows:

1. n places to the right if n is positive,

2. n places to the left if n is negative.

Add or drop zeros as needed.

EXAMPLE 1

a. $65.4 \times 10^3 = 65400. = 65,400$

b. $65.4 \times 10^{-3} = .0654 = .0654$

c. $.654 \times 10^2 = 065.4 = 65.4$

d. $.654 \times 10^{-2} = .00654 = .00654$

NUMBERS IN SCIENTIFIC NOTATION

It is possible to write a given number in different factored forms in which one of the factors is a power of 10. For example,

$$4305 = 430.5 \times 10^1 \qquad .4305 = 430.5 \times 10^{-3}$$

$$= 43.05 \times 10^2 \qquad = 43.05 \times 10^{-2}$$

$$= 4.305 \times 10^3 \qquad = 4.305 \times 10^{-1}$$

Observe that each of the numbers in the last lines of the examples above involves a factor (4.305) between 1 and 10, and another factor that is a power of 10. Any number written in the form

$$b \times 10^n$$

where b is a number between 1 and 10 and n is any integer, is said to be in *scientific notation*. Numbers not in scientific notation will be referred to as in *decimal form*. The following examples illustrate the process of writing numbers in scientific notation.

EXAMPLE 2

a. $9870.4 \rightarrow 9.8704 \times 10^n$, for some integer n.

In order for 9.8704×10^n to be equal to 9870.4, n must be +3 (according to the rule for multiplying by 10^n). Hence,

$$9870.4 = 9.8704 \times 10^3$$

b. $.0098704 \rightarrow 9.8704 \times 10^n$, for some integer n.

In order for 9.8704×10^n to be equal to .0098704, n must be equal to -3 (according to the rule for multiplying by 10^n). Hence,

$$.0098704 = 9.8704 \times 10^{-3}$$

To change a number from scientific notation to decimal form, apply the rule for multiplying by 10^n.

EXAMPLE 3

a. $5.00732 \times 10^6 = 5007320. = 5,007,320$

b. $5.00732 \times 10^{-6} = .00000500732 = .00000500732$

FINAL ZEROS AS SIGNIFICANT DIGITS

In Section A-3 we stated that final zeros on a whole number, such as 25,400, are assumed not to be significant digits. Scientific notation can be used, as in the following examples, to indicate when such final zeros *are* to be considered significant.

EXAMPLE 4

If 25,400 is written in the form

a. 2.5400×10^3, the factor 2.5400 indicates that both zeros are significant.

b. 2.540×10^3, the factor 2.540 indicates that only one of the zeros of 25,400 is significant.

c. 2.54×10^3, the factor 2.54 indicates that the zeros of 25,400 are not significant.

At this point we must once again consider two different types of calculators. Many calculators have the capability of computing directly with numbers in scientific notation. Such calculators usually have a key marked with a symbol such as

[EE], [EEX], or [EXP]

If your calculator has this capability, proceed directly from here to the heading SCIENTIFIC NOTATION CALCULATORS on page 45. If your calculator does not have this capability, continue from here and stop when you reach the heading SCIENTIFIC NOTATION CALCULATORS.

COMPUTATIONS WITH NUMBERS IN SCIENTIFIC NOTATION

For most computations involving multiplication and division, we can choose to compute directly using the decimal form or to compute after changing to scientific notation. However, in some cases, certain computing difficulties may be encountered because of calculators' limitations. The use of scientific notation frequently enables us to avoid such difficulties.

Numbers such as 3,456,000,000 and .000000007 cannot be entered into an 8-digit calculator. If such numbers are first changed to scientific notation, we can do computations with the resulting forms.

EXAMPLE 5

$$\begin{aligned} 3{,}456{,}000{,}000 \times .000000007 &= 3.456 \times 10^9 \times 7 \times 10^{-9} \\ &= (3.456 \times 7) \times (10^9 \times 10^{-9}) \\ &= 24.192 \times 10^0 = 24.192 \end{aligned}$$

On an 8-digit calculator, the result of the computation

$$1{,}100{,}000 \times 990{,}000 = 1{,}089{,}000{,}000{,}000$$

is displayed as 10890000, a truncated number. (On many calculators the keyboard "locks" so that other numbers cannot immediately be entered.) When the result of a computation is a number greater than 99,999,999 or less than -99,999,999, we say that an *overflow* has occurred (see Figure A-8.1).

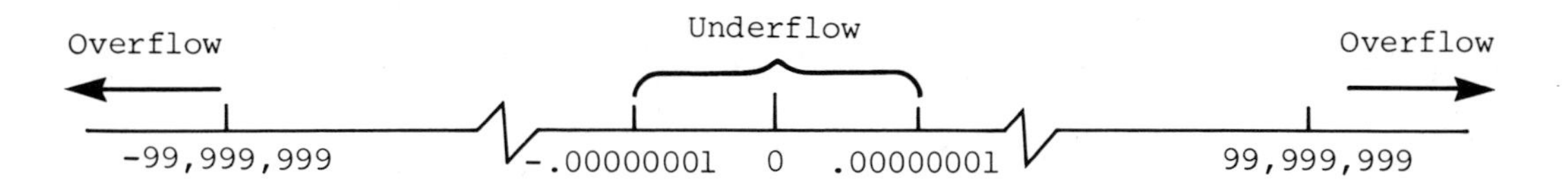

FIGURE A-8.1

On an 8-digit calculator, the result of the computation

$$.000002 \times .00008 = .00000000016$$

is displayed as 0 (zero); a number has been truncated. When the result of a computation is a number with numerical value less than .00000001 (.0000001 on some calculators), we say that an *underflow* has occurred (see Figure A-8.1).

In most cases the difficulties caused by an overflow or an underflow can be taken care of by changing numbers to scientific notation before computing.

EXAMPLE 6

a. $1{,}100{,}000 \times 990{,}000 = 1.1 \times 10^6 \times 9.9 \times 10^5$

$= (1.1 \times 9.9) \times (10^6 \times 10^5)$

$= 10.89 \times 10^{11}$

$= 1{,}089{,}000{,}000{,}000$

b. $.000002 \times .00008 = 2 \times 10^{-6} \times 8 \times 10^{-5}$

$= (2 \times 8) \times (10^{-6} \times 10^{-5})$

$= 16 \times 10^{-11}$

$= .00000000016$

SCIENTIFIC NOTATION CALCULATORS

Symbols such as [EE], [EEX], or [EXP] are used to name the *enter exponent key*. In this book we use only the [EE] symbol, with the understanding that you will use the appropriate key on your calculator. We shall refer to such calculators as [EE] calculators.

ENTERING NUMBERS IN SCIENTIFIC NOTATION

A number in scientific notation, $b \times 10^n$, is entered into an [EE] calculator as follows. First, enter the number b (in calculator instruction manuals, the factor b is usually referred to as the *mantissa*). Next, press the [EE] key and enter the exponent (the number n). If the exponent is negative, press the sign change key *after* entering the exponent.

EXAMPLE 7

Enter each number into the calculator in scientific notation.

a. 1.2345×10^4 b. 1.2345×10^{-4}

Solutions

In each case enter the mantissa 1.2345 first.

a. 1.2345 [EE] 4 Display: [1.2345 04]

b. 1.2345 [EE] 4 [+/-] Display: [1.2345 -04]

In Example 7, note that the last two digits in the display are used to show the exponent only.

COMPUTATIONS WITH NUMBERS IN SCIENTIFIC NOTATION

For most computations involving multiplication and division, we can choose to compute directly from decimal form or to compute after changing to scientific notation. However, numbers such as 3,456,000,000 and .000000007 cannot be entered directly into an 8-digit calculator. If such numbers are first changed to scientific notation, we can do computations with the resulting forms.

EXAMPLE 8

a. $3,456,000,000 \times .0289 = 3.456 \times 10^9 \times 2.89 \times 10^{-2}$

$= 9.9878 \times 10^7 = 99,878,400$

b. $.000000007 \times 86,400,000 = 7 \times 10^{-9} \times 8.64 \times 10^7$

$= 6.048 \times 10^{-1} = .6048$

In an 8-digit calculator, the greatest number (call it G) that can be displayed in decimal form is 99,999,999; the least number (call it L) is .00000001 (or .0000001 on some calculators). If the result of a computation is greater than G, or less than L, the [EE] calculator will automatically display the result in scientific notation.

EXAMPLE 9

a. $110,000 \times 990 = 1.089 \times 10^8 = 108,900,000$

b. $\frac{2,103,000}{.005} = 4.206 \times 10^8 = 420,600,000$

c. $.0002 \times .0008 = 1.6 \times 10^{-7} = .00000016$

Examples 8 and 9 illustrate how the use of scientific notation can extend the range of an 8-digit calculator. However, not more than five digits can be displayed for the mantissa of a number in scientific notation. Hence, if greater accuracy is required, a 10-digit or 12-digit calculator can be used.

EXERCISE SET A-8

Find each product without using a calculator. See Example 1.

1. 7.23×10^2
2. 4.76×10^2
3. 98.5×10^{-2}
4. 65.3×10^{-2}
5. $.225 \times 10^4$
6. $.123 \times 10^4$
7. $.0354 \times 10^3$
8. $.0108 \times 10^3$
9. 354×10^{-4}
10. 872×10^{-4}
11. 75.6×10^{-3}
12. 86.7×10^{-3}

Write each number in scientific notation. See Example 2.

13. 3476.8
14. 5242.5
15. 64.4
16. 89.2
17. 123.4
18. 248.6
19. .00561
20. .00742
21. .456
22. .789
23. .0006
24. .0007
25. 598
26. 4754
27. .0025
28. .0059

Write each number in decimal form. See Example 3.

29. 5.93×10^2
30. 4.75×10^2
31. 7.23×10^{-2}
32. 8.92×10^{-2}
33. 1.67×10^3
34. 3.95×10^3
35. 6.874×10^{-3}
36. 2.225×10^{-3}
37. 8.422×10^4
38. 7.985×10^4
39. 6.0073×10^{-4}
40. 9.0505×10^{-4}

Specify how many terminal zeros in the decimal form of each number are significant. See Example 4.

41. $4{,}870{,}000 = 4.870000 \times 10^6$
42. $9{,}540{,}000 = 9.5400 \times 10^6$
43. $24{,}000 = 2.40 \times 10^4$
44. $38{,}000 = 3.8000 \times 10^4$
45. $5500 = 5.5 \times 10^3$
46. $19{,}500 = 1.95 \times 10^4$
47. $7{,}570{,}000 = 7.570 \times 10^6$
48. $25{,}000{,}000 = 2.50 \times 10^7$

Exercises 49-60 are for [EE] calculators only. Enter each number into the calculator in scientific notation. See Example 7.

49. 6.875×10^3
50. 9.473×10^5
51. 5.437×10^{-3}
52. 2.4653×10^6
53. 4.743×10^6
54. 1.0503×10^4
55. 7.3333×10^{-1}
56. 3.4347×10^{-2}
57. 6×10^2
58. 5×10^5
59. 1.9×10^{-5}
60. 4.7×10^{-4}

Compute, using scientific notation. Express each answer in decimal form. For non-[EE] calculators, see Example 5; for [EE] calculators, see Example 8.

61. $4,876,000,000 \times .000000085$

62. $12,472,000,000 \times .000000043$

63. $25,000,000,000 \times .000000929$

64. $74,200,000,000 \times .0000000858$

65. $\dfrac{983,000,000 \times 342,000,000}{5,550,000,000,000}$

66. $\dfrac{645,000,000 \times 12,500,000}{1,340,000,000}$

67. $\dfrac{.00000246 \times 245,000,000}{185,000}$

68. $\dfrac{.00000369 \times 525,000,000}{24,600}$

Compute, using scientific notation. Express each answer in decimal form. For non-[EE] calculators, see Example 6; for [EE] calculators, see Example 9.

69. $4,725,000 \times 872,000$

70. $345,000 \times 6,423,000$

71. $368,000 \times 5,555,000$

72. $2,280,000 \times 999,000$

73. $\dfrac{684,200}{.00025}$

74. $\dfrac{7,840,000}{.0125}$

75. $.00045 \times .0038$

76. $.000246 \times .00045$

77. $\dfrac{.043 \times .00036 \times .0002}{90 \times .54}$

78. $\dfrac{.0055 \times .0008 \times .0059}{65 \times .0035}$

A-9 Order of Operations

OBJECTIVES

After completing this section, you should

1. Know that parentheses, fraction bars, and brackets can be used to group numbers and operations.
2. Know the correct order in which operations are to be performed when a computation includes more than one operation.

In this section we consider some mathematical concepts that are related to calculations combining two or more different operations. Because the emphasis is on the concepts rather than on the computations, we will use "simple" numbers that will not require the use of a calculator. In Section A-11 we consider calculator sequences for computations that involve combined operations.

GROUPING SYMBOLS

Parentheses and fraction bars can be used to group two or more numbers and operations. For example, the parentheses in the expression

$$(3 + 2) \times 4$$

indicate that the sum 3 + 2 is to be computed first, and the result is to be multiplied by 4. The parentheses in the expression

$$3 + (2 \times 4)$$

indicate that the product 2 × 4 is to be computed first and the result is to be added to 3. The fraction bar in the quotient

$$\frac{10 - 4}{3} \tag{1}$$

indicates that the difference 10 - 4 is to be computed first, and the result is to be divided by 3. More generally, given an expression that involves more than one operation, any calculations that are grouped by parentheses or fraction bars are to be done first.

EXAMPLE 1

For each expression, specify which operation is to be done first.

a. (18 - 6) ÷ 2 b. 18 - (6 ÷ 2) c. (9 × 5) + 8 d. 9 × (5 + 8)

Solutions

a. Subtract b. Divide c. Multiply d. Add

Recall from Section A-1 that a quotient can be rewritten in *on-line* form. In some cases we must use parentheses to indicate which numbers and operations were grouped by the fraction bar. For example, Quotient (1) above can be written in on-line form as

$$(10 - 4) \div 3$$

where the parentheses indicate that the subtraction 10 - 4 is to be done first.

EXAMPLE 2

Write the on-line form of each quotient. Use parentheses as needed.

a. $\frac{14}{9 - 2}$ b. $\frac{9 + 2}{14 - 3}$

Solutions

a. $14 \div (9 - 2)$ b. $(9 + 2) \div (14 - 3)$

If more than one set of grouping symbols are used in an expression, we use brackets, [ ], in the same manner as parentheses.

EXAMPLE 3

The on-line form of $\frac{4 \times (2 + 6)}{7}$ is

$$[4 \times (2 + 6)] \div 7$$

ORDER OF OPERATIONS

In the examples above, grouping symbols are used to indicate which operations are to be done first. In general, expressions may or may not include grouping symbols. Hence, we need the following rule. For all expressions that involve combined operations, the *operations are to be performed in the following order:*

1. Operations inside parentheses or above or below a fraction bar.
2. Raising to powers.
3. Multiplications and divisions in the order in which they appear, left to right.
4. Additions and subtractions in the order in which they appear, left to right.

The following examples show how the order of operations rules are used in various computations.

EXAMPLE 4

a. $(3 \times 2)^2$ b. 3×2^2

Solutions

a. Do the multiplication in the parentheses first, then raise the product to the second power.

$$(3 \times 2)^2 = 6^2 = 36$$

b. Compute the power 2^2 first, then multiply by 3.

$$3 \times 2^2 = 3 \times 4 = 12$$

EXAMPLE 5

a. $8 \div 4 \times 2$ b. $8 \div (4 \times 2)$

Solutions

a. Do the division first, then multiply the quotient by 2.

$$8 \div 4 \times 2 = 2 \times 2 = 4$$

b. Do the multiplication in the parentheses first, then divide 8 by the resulting quotient.

$$8 \div (4 \times 2) = 8 \div 8 = 1$$

EXAMPLE 6

a. $6 \times (5 - 2)^2$ b. $6 \times 5 - 2^2$

Solutions

a. Do the subtraction in the parentheses first, then raise the difference to the second power and multiply the result by 6.

$$6 \times (5 - 2)^2 = 6 \times 3^2 = 6 \times 9 = 54$$

b. First, compute the power 2^2. Next, find the product 6×5 and then subtract 2^2.

$$6 \times 5 - 2^2 = 6 \times 5 - 4 = 30 - 4 = 26$$

EXAMPLE 7

a. $3 \times 2 + 7 - 5$ b. $3 + 2 \times 7 - 5$

Solutions

a. Do the multiplication first.

$$3 \times 2 + 7 - 5 = 6 + 7 - 5 = 8$$

b. Do the multiplication first.

$$3 + 2 \times 7 - 5 = 3 + 14 - 5 = 12$$

In some cases involving combined operations you may want to group multiplications or divisions in parentheses as a reminder of which operations are to be done first.

EXAMPLE 8

$$8 + \frac{15}{3}$$

Solution

The on-line form is $8 + (15 \div 3)$. Do the division first.

$$8 + (15 \div 3) = 8 + 5 = 13$$

EXAMPLE 9

$$\frac{2 + 3 \times 4}{7}$$

Solution

The on-line form is $[2 + (3 \times 4)] \div 7$. Do the multiplication first.

$$[2 + (3 \times 4)] \div 7 = [2 + 12] \div 7 = 14 \div 7 = 2$$

EXERCISE SET A-9

For each expression, specify which operation is to be done first. See Example 1.

1. $(24 + 6) \times 2$
2. $24 + (6 \times 2)$
3. $(24 - 6) \div 2$
4. $24 - (6 \div 2)$
5. $5 \times (4 \div 2)$
6. $8 \div (4 \times 5)$
7. $17 + (5 \times 4)$
8. $10 - (8 + 4)$
9. $(10 - 8) + 4$
10. $(16 - 2) \times 5$
11. $(14 \times 5) + 6$
12. $(15 + 6) \div 7$

Write the on-line form for each quotient. Use parentheses as needed. See Examples 2 and 3.

13. $\frac{12}{8 - 4}$
14. $\frac{16}{6 + 2}$
15. $\frac{32}{12 + 4}$
16. $\frac{40}{10 - 5}$
17. $\frac{8 - 2}{12 + 3}$
18. $\frac{15 + 5}{16 - 6}$
19. $\frac{12 - 2}{19 - 14}$
20. $\frac{32 - 7}{20 + 5}$
21. $\frac{8 \times (6 + 3)}{12}$
22. $\frac{9 \times (15 - 3)}{36}$
23. $\frac{(18 - 3) \times 12}{20}$
24. $\frac{(75 + 5) \times 6}{60}$
25. $\frac{6 \times (15 + 12)}{12 - 3}$
26. $\frac{5 \times (18 - 12)}{3 + 7}$
27. $\frac{30 \div (12 + 4)}{16 - 4}$
28. $\frac{(16 - 4) \div 8}{3 + 7}$

Compute. Use a calculator only when you find it necessary. See Examples 4, 5, 6, and 7.

29. $(4 \times 2)^2$
30. $(6 \times 2)^2$
31. 4×2^2
32. 6×2^2
33. $(3 \times 2)^3$
34. $(2 \times 4)^3$
35. 3×2^3
36. 2×4^3

37. $12 \div 4 \times 3$
38. $18 \div 3 \times 2$
39. $12 \div (4 \times 3)$
40. $18 \div (3 \times 2)$
41. $3 \times (5 - 3)^2$
42. $4 \times (6 - 4)^2$
43. $3 \times 5 - 3^2$
44. $4 \times 6 - 4^2$
45. $(4 + 2)^2 \div 4$
46. $(6 + 2)^2 \div 4$
47. $4 + 2^2 \div 4$
48. $6 + 2^2 \div 4$
49. $4 \times 2 + 5 \times 2$
50. $3 \times 5 + 4 \times 2$
51. $5 \times 3 + 6 - 2$
52. $4 \times 3 - 2 + 7$
53. $5 + 4 \times 3 - 2$
54. $6 + 2 \times 4 - 5$
55. $4 \times 3 + 6 \div 2$
56. $9 \times 5 - 6 \div 3$
57. $4^2 + 15 \div 5 - 4$
58. $3^2 + 9 \times 2 \div 3 - 10$
59. $35 \div 7 + 5^2 - 21 \div 3$
60. $12 \times 3 + 2^2 - 14 \div 7$

Compute. Use a calculator only when you find it necessary. See Examples 7 and 8.

61. $4 + \frac{12}{4}$
62. $9 - \frac{16}{8}$
63. $10 - \frac{16}{4}$
64. $12 + \frac{20}{5}$
65. $\frac{24}{8} + 2$
66. $\frac{28}{4} - 3$
67. $\frac{20 - 3 \times 4}{2}$
68. $\frac{30 + 2 \times 5}{10}$
69. $\frac{4 \times 5 - 5}{3}$
70. $\frac{4 \times 3 + 8}{5}$
71. $\frac{4 \times 2 + 6 \times 4}{4}$
72. $\frac{3 \times 2 + 9 \times 3}{11}$
73. $\frac{4 \times 9 - 12 \times 2}{6}$
74. $\frac{8 \times 5 - 4 \times 6}{4}$
75. $\frac{20 \div 5 + 4 \times 2}{4 + 2}$
76. $\frac{36 \div 9 + 5 \times 2}{9 - 2}$

A-10 Use of Calculator Memory

OBJECTIVES

After completing this section, you should know

1. Whether or not your calculator provides memory capability.
2. Which type of memory capability your calculator provides.

(Refer to the instruction booklet for your calculator to determine whether memory capability is provided. *If your calculator has no memory capability, omit this section.*)

Many calculators have a *memory* register (which cannot be seen) in which numbers, including results of calculations, can be recorded separately from the display. Different calculators may have different labels on the keys used to operate the memory. Hence, the symbols that we shall use in this section may not be exactly the same as those that appear on your calculator. (Refer to your instruction booklet to resolve any doubts about labels on keys.) The two types of memory capabilities most often used are described below. For [=] calculators, read both descriptions in order to determine which type of capability is provided on your calculator. For [ENT] calculators, read only the *storage-recall* type. Each of the sequences shown in the following examples is designed mainly to demonstrate use of the memory; the sequence itself may or may not be the most "efficient" sequence for the particular computation being done.

THE STORAGE-RECALL MEMORY

The simplest kind of memory is the *storage-recall* type, sometimes called the "scratch-pad" memory, which enables the user to store a number in the memory and recall it for later use. We shall use the symbols [STO] and [RCL] to name the keys that operate the storage-recall memory as follows:

[STO] enters the number from the display into the memory.

[RCL] enters a number from the memory into the display.

EXAMPLE 1

(18 × 25) + (9 × 47) = 873, as computed by

18 [×] 25 [=] [STO], 9 [×] 47 [+] [RCL] [=] → 873

or

18 [ENT] 25 [×] [STO], 9 [ENT] 47 [×] [RCL] [+] → 873

In each case, note that the [RCL] key recalls 450 (the product 18 × 25) from the memory and enters it into the display so that the computation can be completed.

Storage-recall memories do *not* clear when the [RCL] key is pressed. However, entering a new number into the memory will clear a number previously entered. The memory can be cleared completely by pressing the sequence [0] [STO] or by turning the calculator *off* and then *on*.

Sometimes, advance planning can help to avoid extra steps in a computation. On [=] calculators, in particular, when computing a *difference*, it may be more efficient to first compute the number to be subtracted and store it in the memory; when computing a *quotient*, it may be more efficient to first compute the divisor and store it in the memory.

EXAMPLE 2

$(26 \times 32) - (4 \times 52) = 624$, as computed by

4 [×] 52 [=] [STO] ;   26 [×] 32 [−] [RCL] [=] → 624

EXAMPLE 3

$(26 \times 32) \div (4 \times 52) = 4$, as computed by

4 [×] 52 [=] [STO] ;   26 [×] 32 [÷] [RCL] [=] → 4

THE FULLY ADDRESSABLE MEMORY

This second type of memory provides the capability of computing *within* the memory register. For example, numbers can be added to, or subtracted from, numbers already in the memory, without the need for recalling results to the display. (Some calculators can also multiply or divide a number already in the memory.) In this kind of memory, called the *fully addressable* type, the following keys (or their equivalents) are used as follows:

[M+] *enters* a number from the display to the memory or *adds* a number in the display to a number in the memory.

[M−] subtracts a number in the display from a number in the memory.

[MR] recalls a number from the memory to the display.

[MC] clears the memory.

It is important to remember that the [MR] key does *not* clear the memory—the [MC] key is used for this purpose.

EXAMPLE 4

$(18 \times 25) + (9 \times 47) = 873$, as computed by

[MC] 18 [×] 25 [=] [M+] ,   9 [×] 47 [=] [M+] [MR] → 873

EXAMPLE 5

$(26 \times 32) - (4 \times 52) = 624$, as computed by

[MC] 26 [×] 32 [=] [M+] ,   4 [×] 52 [=] [M-] [MR] → 624

When computing a quotient, if the memory capability does not include division, then it may be more efficient to compute the *divisor* first and store it in the memory, as in Example 3.

EXERCISE SET A-10

Write a calculator sequence that makes use of the memory capability of your calculator, and follow it to do each calculation. Use the symbols that appear on your calculator.

1. $(16 \times 32) + (56 \times 22)$
2. $(19 \times 48) + (82 \times 55)$
3. $(38 \times 27) - (36 \times 19)$
4. $(74 \times 34) - (66 \times 23)$
5. $(108 \times 67) - (47 \times 73)$
6. $(216 \times 59) - (132 \times 62)$
7. $(54 \times 72) \div (18 \times 24)$
8. $(136 \times 96) \div (17 \times 16)$
9. $(68 \times 108) \div (51 \times 12)$
10. $(142 \times 297) \div (213 \times 33)$

A-11 Combined Operations

OBJECTIVE

After completing this section, you should be able to do a computation involving combined operations either as a chain calculation or in steps that require the recording of intermediate results.

In previous sections we showed sequences for [=] calculators and [ENT] calculators in the same examples. In this section we consider these two types of calculators separately. If you have an [ENT] calculator, read only that part of the text headed [ENT] CALCULATORS (page 72).

[=] CALCULATORS

Because calculators differ in some of their capabilities, different types of calculators will sometimes be considered separately. Hence, once again you will have to classify your calculator. Press the sequence

2 [×] 3 [+] 4 [×] 5 [=]

1. If your answer is 50 and your calculator does *not* have parentheses keys, your calculator will be referred to as a B-TYPE calculator. In this section read only that part of the text headed B-TYPE CALCULATORS (see below)
2. If your answer is 50 and your calculator has parentheses keys such as

   [[(] and [)]] or [(] and [)]

   your calculator will be referred to as a P-TYPE calculator. In this section read only that part of the text headed P-TYPE CALCULATORS (page 64).
3. If your answer is 26, your calculator will be referred to as an H-TYPE calculator. In this section read that part of the text headed H-TYPE CALCULATORS (page 68). However, if your H-TYPE calculator has parentheses keys, it will be useful for you to study the section headed P-TYPE CALCULATORS (page 64).

B-TYPE CALCULATORS

If the operations in an expression can be entered in your calculator in the order in which the expression is read (left to right) so that the order of operations rules are followed (see Section A-9) without the need to record intermediate results, the expression is a *chain calculation* for your calculator. If an expression is not immediately a chain calculation, we can sometimes change it so that it will be.

EXAMPLE 1

Show a calculator sequence for a chain calculation and complete the computations.

a. (87.3 + 5.9) ÷ 6.4 b. 87.3 + (5.9 ÷ 6.4)

Solutions

The order of operations rules require that:

a. The addition is to be done first. Hence, the expression is a chain calculation. Compute by the sequence

87.3 [+] 5.9 [÷] 6.4 [=] → 14.5625

b. The division is to be done before the addition. Hence, use commutativity of addition to change the expression to the chain calculation

$$(5.9 \div 6.4) + 87.3$$

Compute by the sequence

5.9 [÷] 6.4 [+] 87.3 [=] → 88.221875

EXAMPLE 2

Show a calculator sequence for a chain calculation and complete the computations.

a. $(31 \times 42.9) - 11.7$ b. $31 \times (42.9 - 11.7)$

Solutions

The order of operations rules require that:

a. The multiplication is to be done first. Hence, the expression is a chain calculation. Compute by the sequence

31 [×] 42.9 [-] 11.7 [=] → 1318.2

b. The subtraction is to be done first. Hence, use commutativity of multiplication to change the expression to the chain calculation

$$(42.9 - 11.7) \times 31$$

Compute by the sequence

42.9 [-] 11.7 [×] 31 [=] → 967.2

EXAMPLE 3

Compute: a. $24 \times 3.9 + 18 - 14.6$ b. $24 + 3.9 \times 18 - 14.6$

Solutions

The order of operations rules require that:

a. The multiplication is to be done first. Hence, the expression is a chain calculation.

24 [×] 3.9 [+] 18 [-] 14.6 [=] → 97

b. Because the multiplication is to be done first, use commutativity of addition to change the expression to the chain calculation

$$(3.9 \times 18) + 24 - 14.6$$

Compute by the sequence

3.9 [×] 18 [+] 24 [-] 14.6 [=] → 79.6

EXAMPLE 4

Compute: $4.98 + \frac{23.6}{3.2} - 2.75$

Solution

The on-line form is

$$4.98 + (23.6 \div 3.2) - 2.75$$

Because the division is to be done first, use commutativity of addition to change the expression to the chain calculation

$$(23.6) \div 3.2) + 4.98 - 2.75$$

Compute by the sequence

23.6 [÷] 3.2 [+] 4.98 [-] 2.75 [=] → 9.605

Recall from Section A-7 that a number (the base) can be raised to a power either by repeated multiplications, by K-MULT, or by the [y^x] key. (In the following examples we show the K-MULT and [y^x] sequences.) If the base is in a form that involves one or more operations, some calculators require that the [=] key be pressed to complete these operations *before* the [y^x] key is pressed, others do not. For either type, it is acceptable to press the [=] key, as in the next example.

EXAMPLE 5

Compute: $(2.6 \times 1.7)^3$

Solution

Do the multiplication in the parentheses first, press the [=] key, then raise the product to the third power.

(K-MULT) 2.6 [×] 1.7 [=] [×] [=] [=] → 86.350888

([y^x]) 2.6 [×] 1.7 [=] [y^x] 3 [=] → 86.35089*

---

*Recall that answers may differ slightly when the [y^x] key is used.

Combined Operations

A computation may require that we compute a power of a number at the start of, or during, the computation, rather than at the end of the computation. In such cases, some calculators require that the [=] key be pressed *after* entering the exponent so that the base is raised to the power; others do not. For either type, it is acceptable to press the [=] key. Hence, in this book we will show the [=] symbol after the exponent has been entered.

EXAMPLE 6

a. 2.6×1.7^3 b. $8.2^4 - 2483$

Solutions

a. Because the power is to be computed first, use commutativity of multiplication to change the expression to the chain calculation

$$1.7^3 \times 2.6$$

Compute by one of the sequences

(K-MULT) 1.7 [×] [=] [=] [×] 2.6 [=] → 12.7738

([y^x]) 1.7 [y^x] 3 [=] [×] 2.6 [=] → 12.7738

b. This expression is a chain calculation.

(K-MULT) 8.2 [×] [=] [=] [=] [-] 2483 [=] → 2038.2176

([y^x]) 8.2 [y^x] 4 [=] [-] 2483 [=] → 2038.2176

Recall from Section A-9 that brackets can be used like parentheses if more than one set of grouping symbols are needed in an expression.

EXAMPLE 7

Compute: $\dfrac{2.15 + 43.7 \times .089}{3}$

Solution

The on-line form is

$$[2.15 + (43.7 \times .089)] \div 3$$

where the parentheses are used to indicate that the multiplication $43.7 \times .089$ is to be done first. Use commutativity of addition to change the expression to the chain calculation

$$[(43.7 \times .089) + 2.15] \div 3$$

Compute by the sequence

43.7 [×] .089 [+] 2.15 [÷] 3 [=] → 2.0131

Computations in the form of a quotient of products are frequently encountered and can be done in different ways. On a calculator, a convenient method is to first compute the product in the numerator and then *divide* the result successively *by each factor* in the denominator.

EXAMPLE 8

Compute the following quotient of products. Round off the answer according to the rule for products and quotients of approximate numbers.

$$\frac{1.15 \times 39.8}{.70 \times 46.2}$$

Solution

Compute the product in the numerator first, then divide the result in turn by each of the factors in the denominator. Use the sequence

1.15 [×] 39.8 [÷] .7 [÷] 46.2 [=] → 1.4152752

The answer is 1.4, to two significant digits.

RECORDING INTERMEDIATE RESULTS

In the preceding examples we were able to obtain chain calculations by using commutativity of addition or multiplication. Such procedures are not always possible. For example,

$$(5 \times 8) + (3 \times 4) \qquad (1)$$

is not a chain calculation because, if you enter the sequence

5 [×] 8 [+] 3 [×] 4 [=]

in your B-TYPE calculator, the operations would be done as follows:

$$\underbrace{5 \times 8} + 3 \times 4$$

$$\underbrace{40 \quad + 3} \times 4$$

$$43 \quad \times 4 = 172$$

But, the parentheses in (1) indicate that *both* products within the parentheses are to be computed before the addition is done. Hence, the correct calculation (without using a calculator) is

$$\underbrace{5 \times 8} + \underbrace{3 \times 4}$$

$$40 \quad + \quad 12 \quad = 52$$

Thus, it is sometimes necessary to do computations in steps, *writing* intermediate results as needed or storing them in the *memory* capability of the calculator, if available.

The symbols [STO] and [RCL] were introduced in Section A-10. In this book we shall also use the following extended meaning for each of these symbols:

[STO] Store a number in the memory *or* write it.

[RCL] Recall a number from the memory *or* from where it was written.

In the calculator sequences of this section, we will show an intermediate result (being stored or recalled) directly below the symbols [STO] and [RCL]. For example, the computation

$$(3 \times 5) + (8 \div 2)$$

can be done by the sequence

3 [×] 5 [=] [STO] (↓ 15), 8 [÷] 2 [+] [RCL] (↓ 15) [=] → 19

Note that the multiplication is done first and the intermediate result (the product 15) is stored in the memory or written. The division is done next, and the intermediate result 15 is added to the quotient when the [RCL] key is pressed.

EXAMPLE 9

Compute: $(17.6 + 3.5) \times (13.41 - 9.8)$

Solution

Do the calculation in steps.

17.6 [+] 3.5 [=] [STO] (↓ 21.1), 13.41 [-] 9.8 [×] [RCL] (↓ 21.1) [=] → 76.171

EXAMPLE 10

$(14 \times 5.6) + (7 \times 3.5) = 102.9$, as computed by

14 [×] 5.6 [=] [STO] (↓ 78.4), 7 [×] 3.5 [+] [RCL] (↓ 78.4) [=] → 102.9

EXAMPLE 11

Compute: $14.1^3 + 2.6 \times 3.5$

Solution

Compute the power first, then compute the product and add the result to the power. Use either of the sequences:

14.1 [×] [=] [=] [STO] → 2803.221, 2.6 [×] 3.5 [+] [RCL] → 2803.221 [=] → 2812.321

14.1 [y^x] 3 [=] [STO] → 2803.221, 2.6 [×] 3.5 [+] [RCL] → 2803.221 [=] → 2812.321

If you do a computation involving subtraction, and write intermediate results, it is convenient to *first compute the number to be subtracted.*

EXAMPLE 12

Compute: (14 × 5.6) - (7 × 3.5)

Solution

Compute 7 × 3.5 first.

7 [×] 3.5 [=] [STO] → 24.5, 14 [×] 5.6 [-] [RCL] → 24.5 [=] → 53.9

If you do a computation involving division and write intermediate results, it is convenient to *first compute the divisor.*

EXAMPLE 13

Compute: $\dfrac{13.7 - 8.9}{.7 + .5}$

Solution

The on-line form is (13.7 - 8.9) ÷ (.7 + .5). Compute .7 + .5 first.

.7 [+] .5 [=] [STO] → 1.2, 13.7 [-] 8.9 [÷] [RCL] → 1.2 [=] → 4

The examples of this section show that some computations can be rewritten as chain calculations; others cannot. If you have doubts about rewriting a particular computation, you should do the calculations in steps and record intermediate results as needed.

P-TYPE CALCULATORS

Different calculators may use different symbols to label the parentheses keys. In this book we will use [(] and [)].

If the operations in an expression can be entered in your calculator in the order in which the expression is read (left to right) so that the order of operations rules are followed (see Section A-9) without the need to record intermediate results, the expression is a *chain calculation* for your calculator. If an expression is not immediately a chain calculation, we can sometimes change it so that it is a chain calculation.

The parentheses keys, [(] and [)], instruct the calculator to complete the operations within the parentheses before doing other operations. For example, the calculation

$$26 - (64 \div 8)$$

as computed by the sequence

26 [-] [(] 64 [÷] 8 [)] [=] → 18

is a chain calculation. The parentheses instruct the calculator to complete the division before doing the subtraction.

EXAMPLE 1

a. $87.3 + (5.9 \div 6.4) = 88.221875$, as computed by the sequence

87.3 [+] [(] 5.9 [÷] 6.4 [)] [=] → 88.221875

b. $31 \times (42.9 - 11.7) = 967.2$, as computed by the sequence

31 [×] [(] 42.9 [-] 11.7 [)] [=] → 967.2

If an expression is a chain calculation without using parentheses keys, then it is not necessary to use them. However, they can be used, if you wish.

EXAMPLE 2

Compute: a. $(87.3 + 5.9) \div 6.4$ b. $(31 \times 42.9) - 11.7$

Solutions

In each case the expression is a chain calculation, and the computations can be done with or without the parentheses keys.

a. Compute by the sequence

87.3 [+] 5.9 [÷] 6.4 [=] → 14.5625

b. Compute by the sequence

31 [×] 42.9 [-] 11.7 [=] → 1318.2

Because operations within parentheses are completed when the "close" parenthesis key [)] is pressed, there is no need to press the [=] key after the [)] key. However, if the [)] key is being used to complete the *last* operation in a sequence, the [=] key must then be pressed in order to complete the entire sequence of operations.

EXAMPLE 3

Compute: a. (17.6 + 3.5) × (13.41 - 9.8) b. 24 + 3.9 × 18 - 14.6

Solutions

a. The expression is a chain calculation. Parentheses keys *may* be used for (17.6 + 3.5) but *must* be used for (13.41 - 9.8). Compute by the sequence

17.6 [+] 3.5 [×] [(] 13.41 [-] 9.8 [)] [=] → 76.171

b. Because the multiplication is to be completed before the addition and subtraction, group the product 3.9 × 18 in parentheses to obtain the chain calculation

$$24 + (3.9 \times 18) - 14.6$$

Compute by the sequence

24 [+] [(] 3.9 [×] 18 [)] [-] 14.6 [=] → 79.6

EXAMPLE 4

Compute: $4.98 + \frac{23.6}{3.2} - 2.75$

Solution

The on-line form is

$$4.98 + (23.6 \div 3.2) - 2.75$$

a chain calculation. Compute by the sequence

4.98 [+] [(] 23.6 [÷] 3.2 [)] [-] 2.75 [=] → 9.605

Recall from Section A-9 that brackets can be used like parentheses if more than one set of grouping symbols are needed in an expression.

EXAMPLE 5

Compute: $\dfrac{2.15 + 43.7 \times .089}{3}$

Solution

The on-line form is

$$[2.15 + (43.7 \times .089)] \div 3$$

where the parentheses indicate that the multiplication 43.7 × .089 is to be completed before the addition. Compute by the sequence

2.15 [+] [(] 43.7 [×] .089 [)] [÷] 3 [=] → 2.0131

In some cases that involve parentheses within brackets, care must be taken to press the parentheses keys, especially the close parenthesis key [)], the correct number of times.

EXAMPLE 6

The on-line form of $\dfrac{21.46 + 2.3}{13.6 - 32.2 \div 7}$ is

$$(2.46 + 2.3) \div [13.6 - (32.2 \div 7)]$$

a chain calculation. Compute by the sequence

21.46 [+] 2.3 [÷] [(] 13.6 [-] [(] 32.2 [÷] 7 [)] [)] [=] → 2.64

Computations in the form of a quotient of products are frequently encountered and can be done in different ways. On a calculator, a convenient method is to first compute the product in the numerator and then *divide* the result successively *by each* factor in the denominator.

EXAMPLE 7

Compute the following quotient of products. Round off the answer according to the rule for products and quotients of approximate numbers.

$$\frac{1.15 \times 39.8}{.70 \times 46.2}$$

Solution

Compute the product in the numerator first, then divide the result in turn by each of the factors in the denominator. Use the sequence

1.15 [×] 39.8 [÷] .7 [÷] 46.2 [=] → 1.4152752

The answer is 1.4, to two significant digits.

Recall from Section A-7 that the [y^x] key is used to raise a number (base) to a power. If the base is in a form that requires one or more operations, some calculators require that the [=] key be pressed to complete those operations *before* the [y^x] key is pressed, others do not. For either type it is acceptable to press the [=] key, as in the next example.

EXAMPLE 8

Compute: $(2.6 \times 1.7)^3$

Solution

This expression is a chain calculation with or without the use of parentheses keys. Do the multiplication in the parentheses first, press the [=] key, then raise the product to the third power.

2.6 [×] 1.7 [=] [y^x] 3 [=] → 86.35089

In Example 8 we used the [=] key to complete the operation of raising a base to a power. In some computations it is more convenient to use the [)] key to complete such an operation.

EXAMPLE 9

Compute: a. 2.6×1.7^3 b. $2.6 + 14.1^3 - 3.5$

Solutions

a. The expression is *not* a chain calculation as given. However, you can enclose 1.7^3 in parentheses to obtain the chain calculation

$$2.6 \times (1.7^3)$$

Then, compute by the sequence

2.6 [×] [(] 1.7 [y^x] 3 [)] [=] → 12.7738

b. Enclose 14.1^3 in parentheses to obtain the chain calculation

$$2.6 + (14.1^3) - 3.5$$

Compute by the sequence

2.6 [+] [(] 14.1 [y^x] 3 [)] [-] 3.5 [=] → 2802.321

RECORDING INTERMEDIATE RESULTS

The preceding examples indicate that parentheses keys are very useful for obtaining chain calculations. However, if you have any doubts about obtaining a chain calculation for a particular expression, you should do the calculations in steps, *writing* intermediate results as needed or storing them in the *memory* capability of the calculator, if available. The symbols [STO] and [RCL] were introduced in Section A-10. In this book we shall also use the following extended meaning for each of these symbols:

[STO] Store a number in the memory *or* write it.

[RCL] Recall a number from the memory *or* from where it was written.

In calculator sequences in this section we will show an intermediate result (being stored or recalled) directly below the symbols [STO] and [RCL].

If you do a computation involving a division and write intermediate steps, it is convenient to *first compute the divisor*. For example, the calculations of Example 6

$$\frac{21.46 + 2.3}{13.6 - 32.2 \div 7}$$

can be done as follows. Compute the divisor first:

13.6 [-] [(] 32.2 [÷] 7 [)] [=] [STO] (↓ 9), 21.46 [+] 2.3 [÷] [RCL] (↓ 9) [=] → 2.64

Note that the intermediate result, 9, is stored in the memory or written. Note also that the sum in the numerator is divided by the intermediate result, 9, when the [RCL] key is pressed.

H-TYPE CALCULATORS

If the operations in an expression can be entered in your calculator in the order in which the expression is read (left to right) so that the order of operations rules are followed (see Section A-9) without the need to record intermediate results, the expression is a *chain calculation.*

In an expression involving combined operations, H-TYPE calculators are designed to compute products, quotients, and powers *before* sums and differences are computed. For example, the calculation

$$2 \times 8 - 15 \div 3 + 5^2$$

as computed by the sequence

2 [×] 8 [-] 15 [÷] 3 [+] 5 [y^x] 2 [=] → 36

is a chain calculation. The calculator completes the multiplication, division, and squaring before adding and subtracting.

EXAMPLE 1

Compute: $24 \times 3.9 - 14.6 \div 2$

Solution

The expression is a chain calculation because the calculator will do the multiplication, 24 × 3.9, and the division, 14.6 ÷ 2, before the subtraction. Compute by the sequence

24 [×] 3.9 [-] 14.6 [÷] 2 [=] → 86.3

The use of the power key [y^x] varies on different models of H-TYPE calculators. In our examples we shall use sequences that can be applied regardless of which calculator model you are using.

EXAMPLE 2

Compute: a. $2.6 \times 3.5 + 14.1^3$ b. $8.2^4 - 2483$

Solutions

a. The expression is a chain calculation because the H-TYPE calculator will do the multiplication, 2.6 × 3.5, and the raising to a power, 14.1^3, before doing the addition. Compute by the sequence

2.6 [×] 3.5 [+] 14.1 [y^x] 3 [=] → 2812.321

b. The expression is a chain calculation because the calculator will raise 8.2 to the fourth power before doing the subtraction. Compute by the sequence

8.2 [y^x] 4 [-] 2483 [=] → 2038.2176

When addition or subtraction is to be done before multiplication or division, the addition or subtraction must be completed by pressing the [=] key before continuing with the computation.

EXAMPLE 3

Compute: (87.3 + 5.9) ÷ 6.4

Solution

The parentheses indicate that the addition is to be done before the division. Hence, first complete the addition (87.3 + 5.9) by pressing the [=] key. Compute by the sequence

87.3 [+] 5.9 [=] [÷] 6.4 [=] → 14.5625

In Example 3, if you do *not* press the [=] key to complete the addition, the calculator will first do the division, 5.9 ÷ 6.4, which will lead to an incorrect answer.

If an expression is not immediately a chain calculation, we may sometimes be able to change it to a chain calculation.

EXAMPLE 4

Compute: $31 \times (42.9 - 11.7)$

Solution

The parentheses indicate that the subtraction is to be done first. Use commutativity of multiplication to change the expression to the chain calculation

$$(42.9 - 11.7) \times 31$$

Complete the subtraction by pressing the [=] key. Compute by the sequence

42.9 [-] 11.7 [=] [×] 31 [=] → 967.2

Computations in the form of a quotient of products are frequently encountered and can be done in different ways. On a calculator, a convenient method is to first compute the product in the numerator, and then *divide* the result successively *by each* factor in the denominator.

EXAMPLE 5

Compute the following quotient of products. Round off the answer according to the rule for products and quotients of approximate numbers.

$$\frac{1.15 \times 39.8}{.70 \times 46.2}$$

Solution

Compute the product in the numerator first, then divide the result, in turn, by each of the factors in the denominator. Use the sequence

1.15 [×] 39.8 [÷] .7 [÷] 46.2 [=] → 1.4152752

The answer is 1.4, to two significant digits.

Sometimes a base that is to be raised to a power consists of an expression involving one or more operations. In such cases we shall complete the operations in the base by pressing the [=] key before raising to a power.

EXAMPLE 6

Compute: $(2.6 \times 1.7)^3$

Solution

Complete the multiplication, 2.6×1.7, by pressing the [=] key; then raise the product to the third power. Compute by the sequence

2.6 [×] 1.7 [=] [y^x] 3 [=] → 86.350888

In an expression involving only products, quotients, and powers, we shall change the expression (if necessary) so as to compute powers first.

EXAMPLE 7

Compute: $\dfrac{2.6 \times 1.7^3}{8}$

Solution

The on-line form is $(2.6 \times 1.7^3) \div 8$. Because the power must be computed first, use commutativity of multiplication to change the expression to the chain calculation

$$(1.7^3 \times 2.6) \div 8$$

Compute by the sequence

1.7 [y^x] 3 [=] [×] 2.6 [÷] 8 [=] → 1.596725

Recall from Section A-9 that brackets can be used like parentheses if more than one set of grouping symbols are needed in an expression.

EXAMPLE 8

Compute: $\dfrac{(2.15 + 43.7) \times .089}{3}$

Solution

The on-line form is

$$[(2.15 + 43.7) \times .089] \div 3$$

which is a chain calculation. The addition in the parentheses must be completed by pressing the [=] key before the multiplication is done. Compute by the sequence

2.15 [+] 43.7 [=] [×] .089 [÷] 3 [=] → 1.3602167

RECORDING INTERMEDIATE RESULTS

Some expressions cannot readily be changed to chain calculations for H-TYPE calculators. Thus, it may sometimes be preferable to do the computations in steps, writing intermediate results as needed or storing them in the memory capability of the calculator. The symbols [STO] and [RCL] were introduced in Section A-10. In this book we shall also use the following extended meaning for each of the symbols:

[STO] Store a number in the memory *or* write it.

[RCL] Recall a number from the memory *or* from where it was written.

In calculator sequences in this section we will show an intermediate result (being stored or recalled) directly below the symbols [STO] and [RCL].

EXAMPLE 9

Compute: (17.6 + 3.5) × (13.41 - 9.8)

Solution

Do the calculation in steps.

17.6 [+] 3.5 [=] [STO], 13.41 [-] 9.8 [=] [×] [RCL] [=] → 76.171

([STO] ↓ 21.1; [RCL] ↓ 21.1)

Note that the difference 13.41 - 9.8 is multiplied by the intermediate result 21.1 when the [RCL] key is pressed.

If you do a computation that requires a division and you use intermediate results, it is convenient to *first compute the divisor.*

EXAMPLE 10

Compute: $\frac{13.7 - 8.9}{.7 + .5}$

Solution

The on-line form is

$$(13.7 - 8.9) \div (.7 + .5)$$

Do the calculation in steps. Compute .7 + .5 first.

.7 [+] .5 [=] [STO], 13.7 [-] 8.9 [=] [÷] [RCL] [=] → 4

([STO] ↓ 1.2; [RCL] ↓ 1.2)

The examples in this section show that some computations can be rewritten as chain calculations; others cannot. If you have any doubts about rewriting a particular computation, you should do the calculation in steps and record intermediate results as needed. Furthermore, if you have any doubts as to which sequence of cperations your calculator will follow when doing combined operations, you can press the [=] key after each individual operation. Such a procedure will usually increase the number of key presses in a given computation. However, with practice and experience, you can expect to become familiar enough with your calculator to take greater advantage of its built-in capabilities.

[ENT] CALCULATORS

If the operations in an expression can be entered in your calculator in the order in which the expression is read (left to right) so that the order of operations rules are followed (see Section A-9) without the need to write intermediate results, the expression is a *chain calculation*. For example, the expression

$$31 \times 42.9 - 11.7$$

computed by the sequence

31 [ENT] 42.9 [×] 11.7 [-] → 1318.20

is a chain calculation because the multiplication is done before the subtraction.

EXAMPLE 1

Compute: $(42.9 - 11.7) \times 31$

Solution

This is a chain calculation because the subtraction is to be done first, as indicated by the parentheses. Use the sequence

42.9 [ENT] 11.7 [-] 31 [×] → 967.2

If an expression is not immediately a chain calculation, we can sometimes change it so that it is a chain calculation. For example,

$$87 + (162 \div 6)$$

is not a chain calculation because the division is to be done first. We can use commutativity of addition to rewrite the expression as

$$(162 \div 6) + 87$$

which is a chain calculation and can be computed by

162 [ENT] 6 [÷] 87 [+] → 114

A second, and much better, method for doing the calculation above (without rewriting it) depends upon the capability of [ENT] calculators to automatically store and recall intermediate results during a computation. These results are stored in a "memory stack," which we shall refer to more simply as the "stack." Consider again

$$87 + (162 \div 6)$$

and let us see how we can use the stack to treat this as a chain calculation. Begin by pressing

87 [ENT]

The number 87 is now in the display, but at the same time it has automatically been stored in the stack. Now, it would be incorrect to press 162 [+] because we do not want to add

162 to 87. Instead, we compute the quotient 162 ÷ 6 by the sequence

162 [ENT] 6 [÷] → 27

At this stage, 87 is in the stack and 27 is in the display. That is, two numbers (87 and 27) are now in the calculator. Hence, we can complete the computation by pressing the [+] key, at which point the calculator will add 27 (in the display) to 87 (in the stack) to obtain the final result, 114. The entire sequence may be written as

87 [ENT] ,   162 [ENT] 6 [÷] [+] → 114

where the comma (,) indicates that a result has been automatically stored in the stack until needed.

EXAMPLE 2

Compute: 18 - 14.6 + 24 × 3.9

Solution

The product 24 × 3.9 must be added to the difference 18 - 14.6. Reading from left to right, compute 18 - 14.6, which result is now automatically in the stack. Compute the product 24 × 3.9 and add it to the number in the stack. Use the sequence

18 [ENT] 14.6 [-],   24 [ENT] 3.9 [×] [+] → 97

EXAMPLE 3

Compute: $4.98 + \frac{23.6}{3.2} - 2.75$

Solution

The on-line form is

4.98 + (23.6 ÷ 3.2) - 2.75

Store 4.98 in the stack. Compute the quotient, add the result to 4.98, and complete the calculation by subtracting 2.75. Use the sequence

4.98 [ENT] ,   23.6 [ENT] 3.2 [÷] [+] 2.75 [-] → 9.605

EXAMPLE 4

The on-line form of

$$\frac{13.7 - 8.9}{.7 + .5}$$

is (13.7 - 8.9) ÷ (.7 + .5). Use the sequence

13.7 [ENT] 8.9 [-], .7 [ENT] .5 [+] [÷] → 4

A useful property of the stack is that it can be used more than once, as needed, in a given computation.

EXAMPLE 5

Compute: (13 × 8) + (5.7 × 11.4) - (1.6 × 7.43)

Solution

Use the sequence

13 [ENT] 8 [×], 5.7 [ENT] 11.4 [×] [+], 1.6 [ENT] 7.43 [×] [-] → 157.092

Computations in the form of a quotient of products are frequently encountered. The following example suggests two different methods for such computations.

EXAMPLE 6

Compute the following quotient of products. Round off the answer according to the rule for products and quotients of approximate numbers.

$$\frac{1.15 \times 39.8}{.70 \times 46.2}$$

Solution

a. The on-line form is (1.15 × 39.8) ÷ (.70 × 46.2). Use the sequence

1.15 [ENT] 39.8 [×], .7 [ENT] 46.2 [×] [÷] → 1.4152752

b. Compute the product in the numerator first, then *divide* the result *by each* of the factors in the denominator. Use the sequence

1.15 [ENT] 39.8 [×] .7 [÷] 46.2 [÷] → 1.4152752

In each case, the answer is 1.4, to two significant digits.

Recall from Section A-7 that the [y^x] key is used to raise a number (the base) to a power.

EXAMPLE 7

Compute: a. $(2.6 \times 1.7)^3$ b. 2.6×1.7^3

Solutions

a. Use the sequence

2.6 [ENT] 1.7 [×] 3 [y^x] → 86.35089

b. Store 2.6. Raise 1.7 to the power 3 and then multiply the result by 2.6. Use the sequence

2.6 [ENT], 1.7 [ENT] 3 [y^x] [×] → 12.7738

EXERCISE SET A-11

For Exercises 1-16, compute and round off the answers to two significant digits.

1. $(3.1 + 5) \times 7.3$
2. $(8.3 + 9) \times 4.5$
3. $6.5 \div (6 + 10.3)$
4. $8 \div (7.3 + 6.1)$
5. $(22 - 5.7) \times 1.7$
6. $(30 - 1.5) \times 2.3$
7. $4.2 + (5.7 \times 1.2)$
8. $8 + (1.5 \times 3.9)$
9. $12 + (10.3 \div 6)$
10. $27 + (2.9 \div 9)$
11. $(2.9 \times .3) - .34$
12. $(5.7 \times .7) - 1.91$
13. $7.8 - 1.2 + 6.2 \times 4.3$
14. $9.6 - 3.1 + 5.9 \times 2.1$
15. $8.2 + \frac{7.4}{3.6} - 6.4$
16. $6.8 + \frac{5.1}{2.4} - 3.1$

For Exercises 17-34, compute and round off the answers to four significant digits.

17. $(3 \times 2.7)^4$
18. $(4 \times 8.1)^3$
19. $(.6 \times 3.4)^5$
20. $(.5 \times 7.1)^4$
21. 7.2×1.06^6
22. 9.04×1.02^5
23. 4.7×6.1^3
24. 3.1×1.4^4
25. $(8.1 - 2.8)^4$
26. $(6.4 - 3.01)^5$
27. $1.2^6 - 4.3$
28. $1.05^5 - 1.7$
29. $9.3 \div 2.01^3$
30. $1.2^6 - 2.3$
31. $(10.3 + 1.2)^2$
32. $(.06 + 2.13)^5$
33. $5 \times (8.4 + .9)^4$
34. $6.1 \times (7.2 + .81)^3$

For Exercises 35-50, compute and round off the answers to three significant digits.

35. $\frac{9 + 4.3 \times 2.9}{7}$
36. $\frac{2.6 + .76 \times 15}{8}$
37. $\frac{5.7 \times 3.4 - 7.2}{9}$
38. $\frac{8.3 \times 3.5 - 4.7}{11}$
39. $(12 \times 6.09) + (1.6 \times 11)$
40. $(7.3 \times .5) + (4.2 \times 6)$
41. $(6.9 \times 2.6) + 5.7 \times 4$
42. $(5.4 \times 1.4) + 6 \times 3.8$
43. $(38.8 \times 5.7) - (2.4 \times 1.3)$
44. $(3.4 \times 7.8) - (8.1 \times 2.4)$
45. $(9.8 \times 4.8) - (3.2 \times 2.7) + (8.3 \times 4.5)$
46. $(4.6 \times 6.5) - (1.3 \times 6.1) + (7.3 \times 5.5)$

47. $\frac{8.1 - 2.9}{7.4 + .57}$

48. $\frac{9.2 - 4.1}{1.4 + 7.7}$

49. $\frac{3.9 + 4.7}{6.9 - 3.8}$

50. $\frac{3.3 + 3.9}{1.6 - .72}$

For Exercises 51-62, compute and write the answers under floating decimal point operation.

51. $3.3 \times 2.5 + 1.6^3$

52. $7.4 \times 1.5 + .8^4$

53. $1.5^4 + 7.3 \times 5.9$

54. $1.9^4 + 6.7 \times 8.3$

55. $2.7^3 - 6.99$

56. $1.1^5 - 1.062$

57. $3.1^4 - 25.3$

58. $1.5^5 - 2.9$

59. $(3 + 2.7) \times (4 + 8.1)$

60. $(6 + 3.4) \times (5 + 7.1)$

61. $(9.3 + 2.01) \times (6.5 - .82)$

62. $(7.2 + 1.7) \times (9.8 - 6.1)$

For Exercises 63-68, compute and round off the answers according to the rule for products and quotients of approximate numbers.

63. $\frac{42.6 \times 6.80}{4.70 \times 15.66}$

64. $\frac{37.1 \times 8.764}{1.80 \times 134.7}$

65. $\frac{246.70 \times 64.70 \times 3.950}{11.80 \times 1.750 \times 12.95}$

66. $\frac{24.6 \times 16.8 \times .075}{.096 \times 1.9 \times 34.3}$

67. $\frac{34.9 \times 185}{3.9 \times 16.8 \times 1.92}$

68. $\frac{1.47 \times 196}{2.90 \times .0170 \times 83.1}$

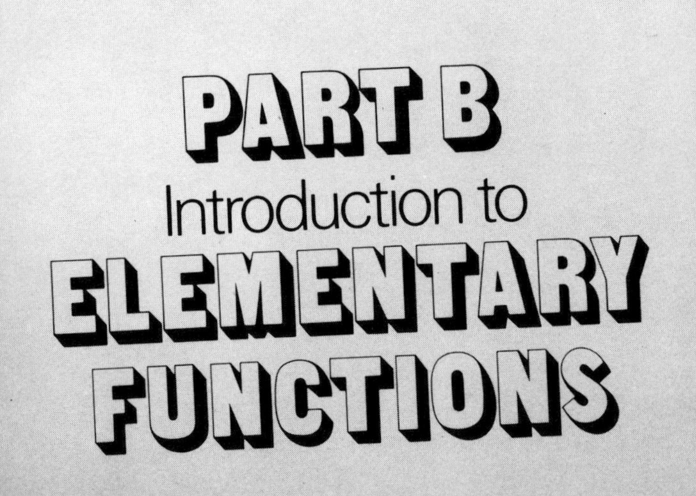
PART B
Introduction to
ELEMENTARY
FUNCTIONS

B-1 Writing Sequences, Evaluating Expressions

OBJECTIVES

After completing this section, you should be able to

1. Write and check calculator sequences appropriate for your calculator.
2. Evaluate expressions in x.

In this section and some of the following sections in this book, we shall show calculator sequences designed for different types of calculators. It is understood that you will *consider only those sequences appropriate for your calculator,* which you can identify by looking first for an [=] symbol or an [ENT] symbol.

Recall that to *evaluate an expression in x* means "Replace x by a given number and then perform the resulting calculations." For example, to evaluate the expression

$$3x + 5$$

for $x = 4.3$, we can replace x by 4.3 and obtain

$$3(4.3) + 5 = 17.9$$

To evaluate the same expression for $x = -4.3$, we replace x by -4.3 and obtain

$$3(-4.3) + 5 = -7.9$$

When the same expression is to be evaluated more than once, it is often helpful to write a calculator sequence to use as a guide. For example, the following sequences can be used for the computations shown above:

3 [×] x [+] 5 [=]   or   3 [ENT] x [×] 5 [+]

where x is to be replaced by a given number each time the sequence is used. We can *check* a sequence for correctness as follows:

1. Replace x in the given expression by an arbitrarily chosen "simple" number such as 2, 3, or 4, and do the resulting computations in steps, without following the sequence. (Because 0 and 1 have special properties, it is not usually wise to use 0 or 1 as check numbers.)
2. Using the same replacement for x as in Step 1, follow the sequence and compare the results. If both answers are the same, assume that the sequence is correct. If they are not the same, check the work of both steps again.

For example, to check the sequence for evaluating $3x + 5$, we can replace x by 2 to obtain

$$\underbrace{3 \times 2}_{6} + 5$$

$$6 \quad + 5 = 11$$

For $x = 2$, each of the sequences listed above results in the same answer, 11. (Use the sequence appropriate for your calculator to verify this result.)

EXAMPLE 1

Write and check a sequence to evaluate

$2.8x - 3.9$

Solution

Two possible sequences are

2.8 [×] x [-] 3.9 [=] or 2.8 [ENT] x [×] 3.9 [-]

Check: Replace x by 3. Then

$$\underbrace{2.8 \times 3}_{8.4} - 3.9 = 4.5$$

For $x = 3$, each of the listed sequences results in the same answer, 4.5. (Verify this result on your calculator.)

For the computations in the next example, you may find it helpful to read Appendices A and B.

EXAMPLE 2

Some possible sequences for evaluating the expression $\sqrt{9 - x^2}$ are:

x [×] x [=] [STO], 9 [-] [RCL] [=] [√]

9 [-] x [x^2] [=] [√]

9 [-] [(] x [×] x [)] [=] [√]

9 [ENT], x [ENT] x [×] [-] [√]

Check: Replace x by 2. Then

$$\sqrt{9 - 2^2} = \sqrt{5} = 2.2360679$$

For $x = 2$, each of the sequences above results in the same answer, 2.2360679. (Verify this result on your calculator.)

Occasionally, an arbitrarily chosen check number may not be appropriate for a given sequence. For example, if we choose 4 to check the sequence in Example 2, we obtain

$$\sqrt{9 - 16} = \sqrt{-7}$$

However, most calculators do not compute square roots of negative numbers. Hence, if we replace x by 4 in the sequence being checked, the calculator will signal "error." In such cases, we try another number, or recheck the sequence, or both.

If x appears more than once in an expression to be evaluated, it is efficient to store ([STO]) a given number replacement for x in the memory and then recall ([RCL]) that number as needed (see Section A-10).

EXAMPLE 3

a. Write and check a sequence to evaluate the expression

$$x^4 - \sqrt{x} + x$$

b. Evaluate the given expression for $x = 2.345$.

Solutions

a. Two possible sequences are:

x [y^x] 4 [=] [-] x [$\sqrt{\ }$] [+] x [=]

x [ENT] 4 [y^x] x [$\sqrt{\ }$] [-] x [+]

Check: Replace x by 4. Then

$$4^4 - \sqrt{4} + 4 = 256 - 2 + 4 = 258$$

For $x = 4$, each of the sequences above results in the same answer, 258. (Verify this result on your calculator.)

b. Begin by storing 2.345 in the memory: 2.345 [STO]. Now, after pressing 2.345 [STO], the number 2.345 is not only in the memory but is also in the display. Hence, you can immediately proceed with the computation, as indicated by the following sequences.

2.345 [STO] [y^x] 4 [=] [-] [RCL] [$\sqrt{\ }$] [+] [RCL] [=] → 31.052937

2.345 [STO] [ENT] 4 [y^x] [RCL] [$\sqrt{\ }$] [-] [RCL] [+] → 31.052937

When a given expression in x is evaluated for several replacements for x, we sometimes list the results in the form of a table. We shall use the symbol "y" to name computed values.

EXAMPLE 4

Evaluate $x^4 - \sqrt{x} + x$ for $x = 4.50, 4.51, 4.52, 4.53$. Round off the answers to the nearest hundredth, and list the results in a table.

Solution

Use one of the sequences of Example 3.

x	4.50	4.51	4.52	4.53
y	412.44	416.11	419.80	423.51

Admittedly, expressions such as $3x + 5$ can readily be evaluated without a written sequence to follow. However, practice is necessary in order to develop the ability to write and check calculator sequences. Hence, in the following exercise set, write and check sequences for your calculator, even for the very "simple" expressions.

EXERCISE SET B-1

(Note: Because more than one correct calculator sequence can be written for a given computation, we do not show sequences in the answers to exercises in this book.)

Write and check a calculator sequence to evaluate each expression, then use your sequence for each given value of x. Round off answers to all exercises to *two decimal places*.

For Exercises 1-8, see Examples 1 and 2.

1. $3.2x - 4.3$; $x = 1.8$
2. $6.5x - 2.7$; $x = 4.1$
3. $1.3x^2 + 5.2$; $x = 3.5$
4. $2.7x^2 + 8.4$; $x = 5.4$
5. $\sqrt{16 + x^2}$; $x = 2.3$
6. $\sqrt{36 + x^2}$; $x = 1.9$
7. $13.5 + \sqrt{12.1x^2 - 3.6}$; $x = .85$
8. $23 - \sqrt{43.9x^2 + 7.8}$; $x = .55$

For Exercises 9-18, use the memory capability of your calculator and list the answers in a table. See Examples 3 and 4.

9. $x^2 + \frac{1}{x} - x$; $x = 1.30, 1.32, 1.34, 1.36$
10. $x^2 - \frac{1}{x} + x$; $x = 2.40, 2.44, 2.48, 2.52$
11. $x^3 - \frac{2}{x} + \sqrt{x}$; $x = .56, .60, .64, .68$
12. $x^3 + \sqrt{x} + \frac{2}{x}$; $x = .75, .80, .85, .90$
13. $x^4 - 2x^2 - \frac{3}{x} - 1.5$; $x = .25, .50, .75, 1.25$
14. $x^4 + 3x^3 - \frac{4}{x} - 3.8$; $x = .18, .42, .62, 1.8$
15. $3x^3 - \frac{1.6}{x^2} + x$; $x = .25, .75, 1.5, 2.5$
16. $5x^3 + \frac{3.5}{x^2} - x$; $x = .4, 1.4, 2.4, 3.4$
17. $\frac{3.5}{x^2} + \frac{5.2}{x} - \sqrt{3.8 + x}$; $x = -.50, -.25, .25, .50$
18. $\frac{6.2}{x} - \frac{4.3}{x^2} + \sqrt{5.5 - x}$; $x = -1.60, -.85, .85, 1.60$

B-2 The Function Concept, Graphing

OBJECTIVES

After completing this section, you should

1. Know the meaning of *ordered pair of numbers, first component, and second component.*
2. Be familiar with the concept of a function defined by an equation.
3. Be able to prepare a table of ordered pairs of numbers from a given equation.
4. Be able to graph ordered pairs of numbers and draw graphs that consist of smooth curves.

A symbol such as (2,4) is called an *ordered pair* of numbers— the first number is called the *first component* and the second number is called the *second component*. Using x to name first components and y to name second components, the symbol (x,y) names any ordered pair of numbers. (In this book we shall use only x and y.) We shall refer to first components as *x-values* and to second components as *y-values*.

FUNCTIONS

A set of ordered pairs in which each x-value is paired with exactly one y-value is called a *function*. For example, the set of ordered pairs

$$(2,4),\ (3,6),\ (5,10),\ (-7,-14)$$

is a function. Now, note that each of the ordered pairs above satisfies the *rule* "The y-value is two times the x-value"; that is, each x-value is paired with twice itself. This rule can be given in the form of an equation

$$y = 2x$$

and we say that the equation "defines the function." For example:

1. The function specified by the rule "Each y-value is equal to three times the x-value" can be defined by the equation

$$y = 3x$$

2. The function specified by the rule "Each y-value is equal to the square root of the x-value" can be defined by the equation

$$y = \sqrt{x}$$

3. The function specified by the rule "Each y-value is equal to one-half the x-value, plus 11" can be defined by the equation

$$y = \frac{1}{2}x + 11$$

More generally, a function can be defined by specifying a set of x-values, together with a rule that enables us to compute the paired y-values. (Y-values are also referred to as *function values*.) Although there are many ways to give a rule for defining a function, we will define functions by means of equations only.

EXAMPLE 1

Given the set of x-values: 3.8, 16, 21.7, 31.5. For the function defined by each equation, compute the y-value for each of the given x-values, and write the resulting set of ordered pairs.

a. $y = 3x$ b. $y = \sqrt{x}$ c. $y = \frac{1}{2}x + 11$

Solutions

a. $y = 3x$: Multiply each x-value by 3.

(3.8,11.4), (16,48), (21.7,65.1), (31.5,94.5)

b. $y = \sqrt{x}$: Take the square root of each x-value (to the nearest tenth).

(3.8,1.9), (16,4.0), (21.7,4.7), (31.5,5.6)

c. $y = \frac{1}{2}x + 11$: Divide each x-value by 2, then add 11.

(3.8,12.9), (16,19.0), (21.7,21.9), (31.5,26.8)

GRAPHS OF FUNCTIONS

Ordered pairs of numbers can be associated with points in a plane. The point is called the *graph* of the ordered pair, the components of the ordered pair are called the *coordinates* of the point. The usual procedure for graphing ordered pairs is as follows. First, draw a horizontal line (called the *x-axis*), and a vertical line (called the *y-axis*), intersecting at a point called the *origin*, as in Figure B-2.1a. Next, introduce a *scale* on each axis, as in Figure B-2.1b. (The scales need not be the same on both axes.*) On the x-axis, *positive* scale numbers are located *to the right* of the origin, *negative* scale numbers are located *to the left* of the origin. On the y-axis, *positive* scale numbers are located *above* the origin, *negative* scale numbers are located *below* the origin.

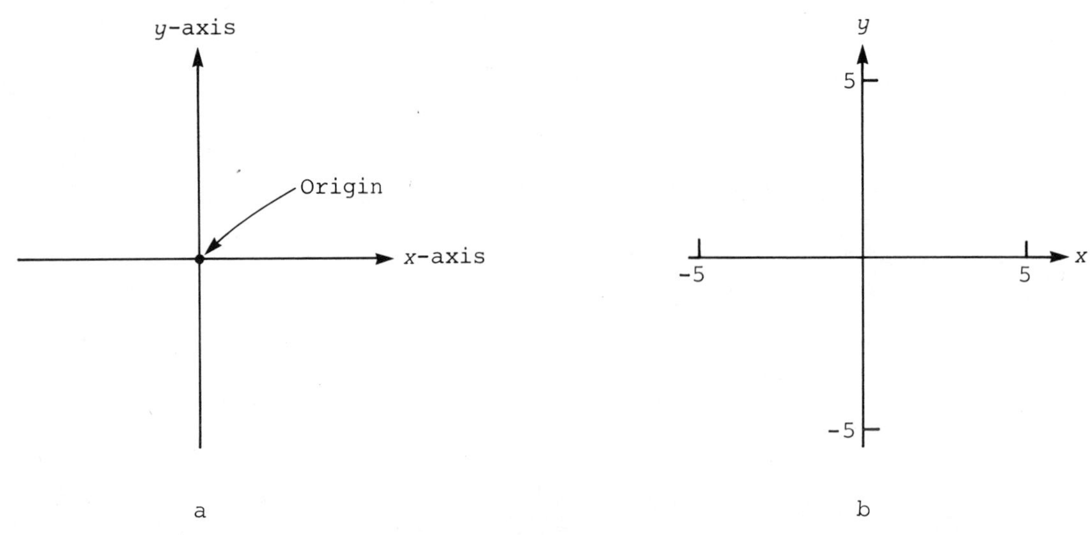

FIGURE B-2.1

---

*In the examples in the text and in the exercises we will suggest a choice of scales.

Figure B-2.2a shows several points the coordinates of which are integers. When the coordinates of points are not integers, we estimate the position of the graph, as shown in Figure B-2.2b.

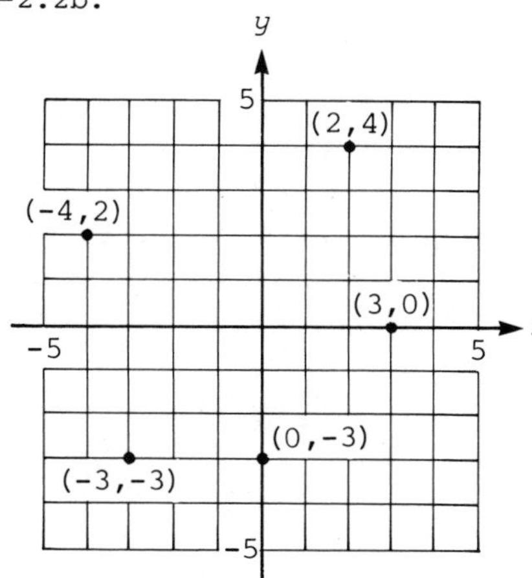

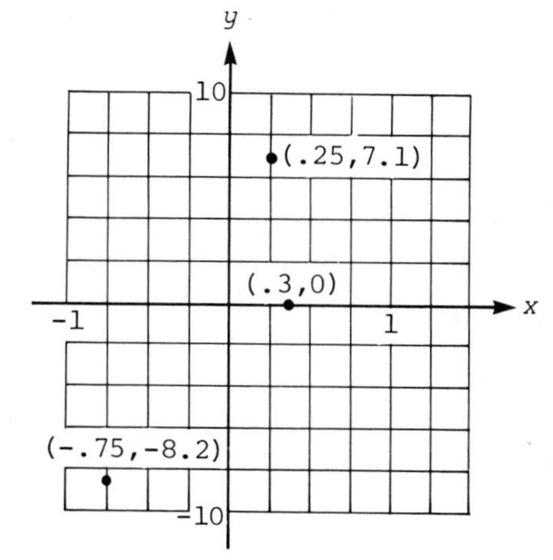

FIGURE B-2.2

EXAMPLE 2

On graph paper, graph each set of ordered pairs on a separate set of axes.

a. (3,4), (-3,4), (3,-4), (-3,-4)

b. (0,8), (-.25,7.2), (1.75,-6), (-.5,-9.1)

Solutions

a. Scale each axis from -5 to 5. Use 1 square* to equal 1 unit on each axis. Graph each ordered pair, as shown in Figure B-2.3

b. Scale the *x*-axis from -1 to 2, using 4 squares to equal 1 unit. Scale the *y*-axis from -10 to 10, using 1 square to equal 2 units. Graph each ordered pair, as shown.

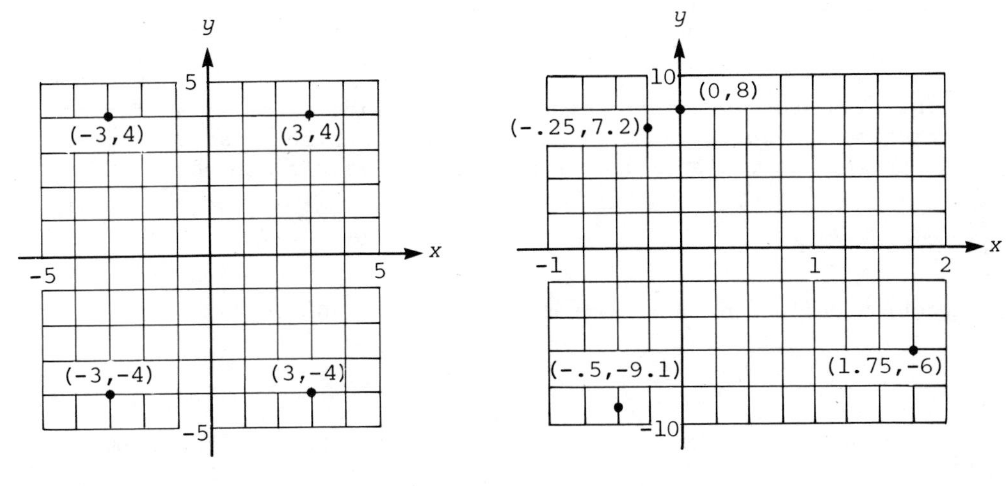

FIGURE B-2.3

* By "square" we mean the length of a side of a small square on graph paper that lies on the specified axis.

When constructing a graph, it is sometimes convenient to list the x-values, together with their paired y-values in the form of a *table* rather than as a set of ordered pairs.

EXAMPLE 3

Given the function defined by $y = \sqrt{x}$ and the set of x-values 0, 5, 10, 15, 20, 25, 30

a. Compute the associated y-values, to the nearest tenth, and list the resulting ordered pairs in a table.

b. Graph the ordered pairs of numbers of the table.

Solution

x-scale: 1 sq = 2 units $\qquad$ y-scale: 2 sq = 1 unit

a.

x	0	5	10	15	20	25	30
y	0	2.2	3.2	3.9	4.5	5.0	5.5

b.

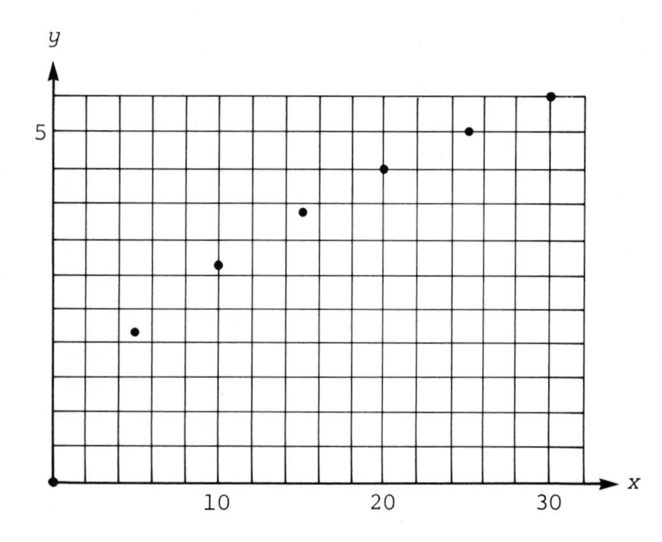

FIGURE B-2.4

In the examples above we constructed graphs consisting of sets of disconnected points. Most of the graphs with which we shall be concerned consist of *smooth curves* that are drawn through the points the coordinates of which we have computed.

EXAMPLE 4

Graph the function defined by $y = \sqrt{x}$ from $x = 0$ to $x = 30$.

Solution

Draw a smooth curve through the points of the graph constructed for Example 3.

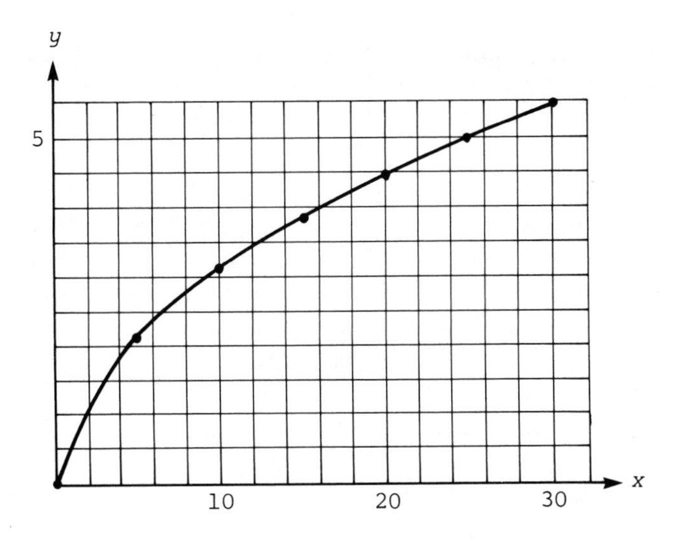

FIGURE B-2.5

EXERCISE SET B-2

For each given x-value compute, to the nearest tenth, the y-value for the function defined by the given equation, and write the resulting ordered pairs. See Example 1. Write sequences as needed.

1. $y = 5x$; x-values: 4.2, 12.5, 22, 38.6
2. $y = 12x + 5$; x-values: 1.9, 8.7, 16.4, 25.9
3. $y = 2.5x - 1.8$; x-values: .6, 2.4, 6.9, 11.5
4. $y = 7.1x - 3.3$; x-values: .2, 1.6, 4.9, 8.2
5. $y = \frac{1}{4}x + 10$; x-values: 1.5, 14.2, 24.3, 35.7
6. $y = \frac{1}{8}x - 15$; x-values: 8.6, 18.2, 32.3, 41.5
7. $y = \sqrt{2x} - 6$; x-values: 4.7, 10.4, 21.7, 38.4
8. $y = \sqrt{5x} + 4.2$; x-values: 7.5, 15.6, 23.4, 43.1
9. $y = x^2 + 4x - 3$; x-values: .8, 2.3, 5.9, 9.3
10. $y = 2x^2 - 3x + 7$; x-values: .5, 4.7, 12.6, 26.9

Graph each set of ordered pairs on the axes provided. See Example 2.

11. (4,8), (-3,2), (3,-4), (-2,-5)

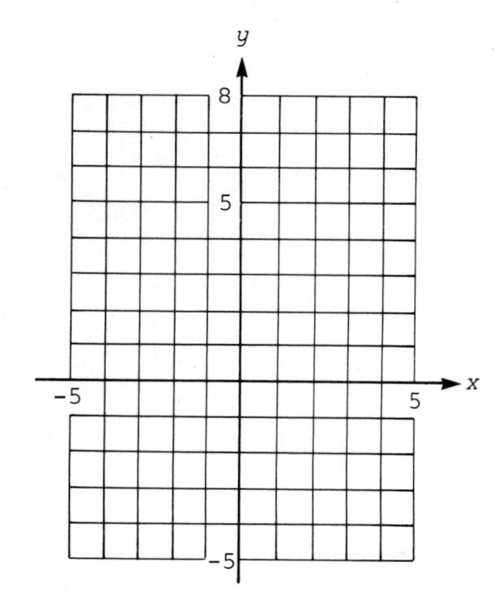

12. (1,-3), (-3,1), (-1,-3), (1,3)

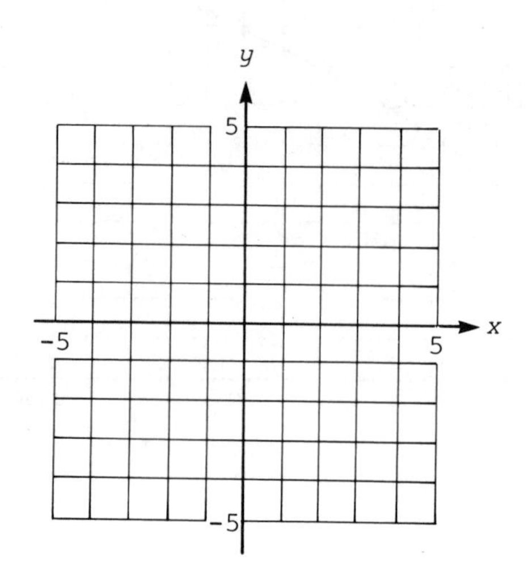

13. (-5,-4), (6,-2), (-2,-8), (9,4)

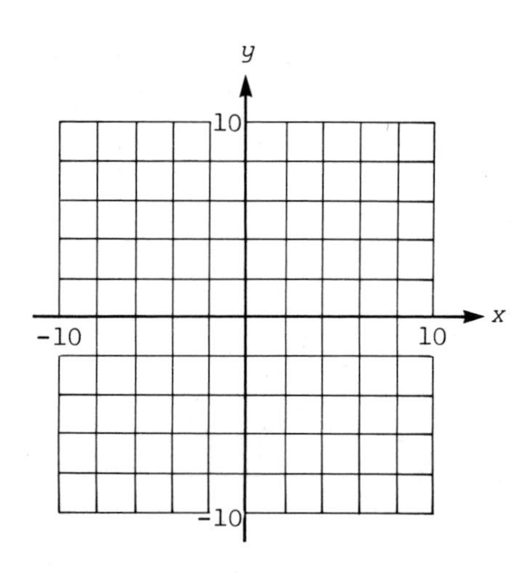

14. (-6,9), (-4,-7), (6,10), (-6,-4)

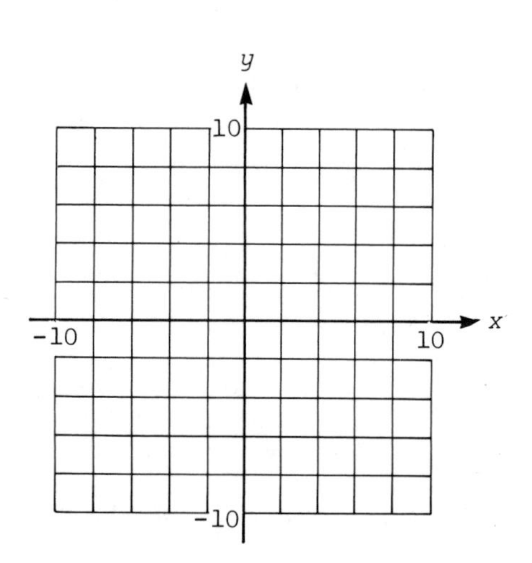

15. (0,0), (1.1,2.5), (-2.8,1.7), (-2.3,-2.4)

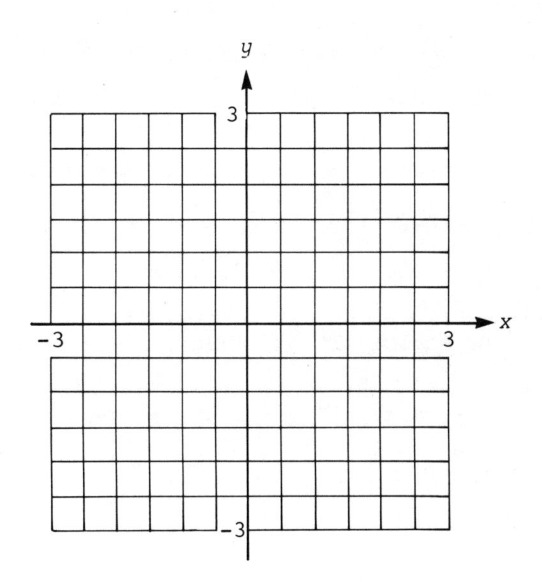

16. (0,1.2), (-2.4,0), (2.8,-2.5), (-2.6,-2.1)

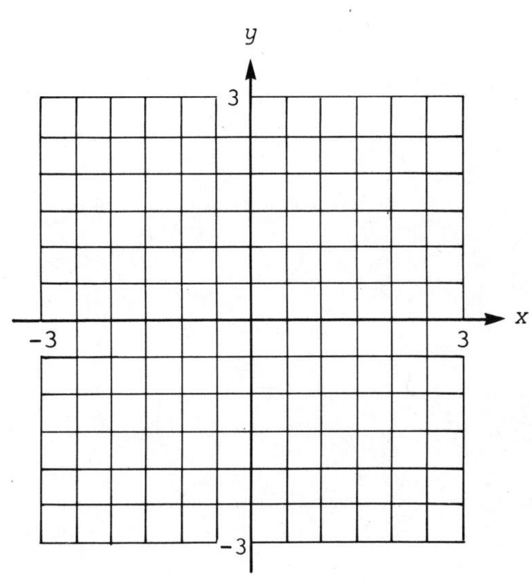

For the function defined by each equation and set of x-values

a. Compute the associated y-values and list the resulting ordered pairs in a table. For y-values that are not whole numbers, round off to the nearest tenth.

b. Graph each ordered pair.

c. Graph each function from the least x-value to the greatest x-value by drawing a smooth curve through the resulting points.

See Examples 3 and 4. (Write sequences as needed.)

17. $y = 2x - 20$; x-values: 0, 5, 10, 15, 20, 25, 30
(x-scale: 1 sq = 2 units; y-scale: 1 sq = 5 units)

18. $y = 3x - 40$; x-values: 0, 4, 8, 12, 16, 20, 24, 28
(x-scale: 1 sq = 2 units; y-scale: 1 sq = 5 units)

19. $y = \frac{2}{5}x + 8$; x-values: 0, 5, 10, 15, 20, 25, 30
(x-scale: 1 sq = 2 units; y-scale: 1 sq = 5 units)

20. $y = \frac{3}{8}x - 12$; x-values: 0, 2, 4, 6, 8, 10
    (x-scale: 1 sq = 1 unit; y-scale: 1 sq = 1 unit)

21. $y = 4\sqrt{x}$; x-values: 0, 5, 10, 15, 20, 25, 30
    (x-scale: 1 sq = 2 units; y-scale: 1 sq = 2 units)

22. $y = \frac{1}{2}\sqrt{x + 2}$; x-values: 0, 5, 10, 15, 20, 25, 30
    (x-scale: 1 sq = 2 units; y-scale: 5 sq = 1 unit)

23. $y = x^2 - 7x - 10$; x-values: 0, 2, 4, 6, 8, 10
    (x-scale: 1 sq = 1 unit; y-scale: 1 sq = 2 units)

24. $y = x^2 - 5x - 35$; x-values: 0, 2, 4, 6, 8, 10
    (x-scale: 1 sq = 1 unit; y-scale: 1 sq = 5 units)

B-3 Polynomial Functions

OBJECTIVES

After completing this section, you should be able to

1. List the coefficients of a polynomial.
2. Compute ordered pairs of numbers from an equation that defines a polynomial function.

Expressions such as

$$5x^2 - 6x - 9 \quad \text{and} \quad 2x^4 - 2.7x^3 + x^2 + 1.8x - 7.5$$

are called *polynomials in one variable*, x. (Variables other than x are also used.) The numerical factors that appear in the terms of a polynomial are called the *coefficients* of the polynomial.

EXAMPLE 1

List the coefficients of each polynomial.

a. $5x^2 + 6x - 9$ b. $2x^4 - 2.7x^3 + x^2 + 1.8x - 7.5$

Solutions

The *sign* of each coefficient must be included.

a. 5, 6, -9 b. 2, -2.7, 1, 1.8, -7.5

Note that if no numerical factor appears before the variable, as in the x^2 term of Example 1b, the coefficient is 1. In a term such as $-x^2$, the coefficient is -1.

In each polynomial of Example 1, observe that the term with the highest power of x (the greatest exponent) is written first and is followed by a succession of terms each of whose powers is decreased by 1. We shall always write polynomials in this form. If a particular power of x does not appear in a given polynomial, we assume that the coefficient for the "missing" power is zero. For example, the polynomial $x^3 - 19$ may be viewed as

$$x^3 + 0x^2 + 0x - 19$$

EXAMPLE 2

List the coefficients of $x^4 + 3.1x^2 - x + 14.5$.

Solution

Note that there is no x^3 term. The coefficients are:

1, 0, 3.1, -1, 14.5

Polynomial functions are defined by equations of the form

$$y = \text{a polynomial}$$

For example, $y = x^3 - 6x^2 + 11x + 4$ defines a polynomial function. An efficient calculator sequence for computing y-values of a polynomial function is based upon identification of the coefficients of the polynomial. Consider

$$y = ax^3 + bx^2 + cx + d$$

where a, b, c, and d are the coefficients. It can be shown that

$$ax^3 + bx^2 + cx + d \qquad (1)$$

can be written in the form

$$[(ax + b)x + c]x + d \qquad (2)$$

Expression (2) is a chain calculation because the computations can be done in the order in which the expression is read. Thus, y-values of polynomial functions can be computed by sequences suggested by Expression (2).

B-TYPE and P-TYPE:

a [×] x [+] b [×] x [+] c [×] x [+] d [=]

H-TYPE (Press the [=] key after each addition or subtraction):

a [×] x [+] b [=] [×] x [+] c [=] [×] x [+] d [=]

[ENT] calculators:

a [ENT] x [×] b [+] x [×] c [+] x [×] d [+]

If any of the coefficients after the first (b, c, or d) are *negative*, press the [-] key instead of the [+] key in the sequence.

The sequences above may appear to be complicated. With practice, however, they can be mastered and followed readily. The following examples show each of the three sequences — it is understood that you will read the sequence that is appropriate to your calculator.

EXAMPLE 3

If $y = x^3 - 6x^2 + 11x + 4$, find y for $x = 5$.

Solution

The coefficients are 1, -6, 11, and 4. Compute as follows.

B-TYPE and P-TYPE:

1 [×] 5 [-] 6 [×] 5 [+] 11 [×] 5 [+] 4 [=] → 34

H-TYPE:

1 [×] 5 [-] 6 [=] [×] 5 [+] 11 [=] [×] 5 [+] 4 [=] → 34

[ENT] calculators:

1 [ENT] 5 [×] 6 [-] 5 [×] 11 [+] 5 [×] 4 [+] → 34

The sequences listed above can be extended to polynomials that include terms involving x^4, x^5, and so forth.

EXAMPLE 4

If $y = 2x^4 + 3.1x^2 - 7x + 9$, find y for $x = 3$.

Solution

The coefficients are: 2, 0, 3.1, -7, 9.

B-TYPE and P-TYPE:

2 [×] 3 [+] 0 [×] 3 [+] 3.1 [×] 3 [-] 7 [×] 3 [+] 9 [=] → 177.9

H-TYPE:

2 [×] 3 [+] 0 [=] [×] 3 [+] 3.1 [=] [×] 3 [-] 7 [=] [×] 3 [+] 9 [=] → 177.9

[ENT] calculators:

2 [ENT] 3 [×] 0 [+] 3 [×] 3.1 [+] 3 [×] 7 [-] 3 [×] 9 [+] → 177.9

To compute y-values for negative values of x or for x-values that require several key presses to enter, it is convenient to store the replacement value for x in the memory. This can be done efficiently by storing ([STO]) the replacement value for x as soon as it has been entered into the calculator for the first time.

EXAMPLE 5

If $y = x^3 - 6x^2 + 11x + 4$ and $x = -1.13$, use one of the following sequences to verify that $y = -17.534297$.

B-TYPE and P-TYPE:

1 [×] 1.13 [+/-] [STO] [-] 6 [×] [RCL] [+] 11 [×] [RCL] [+] 4 [=]

H-TYPE:

1 [×] 1.13 [+/-] [STO] [-] 6 [=] [×] [RCL] [+] 11 [=] [×] [RCL] [+] 4 [=]

[ENT] calculators:

1 [ENT] 1.13 [+/-] [STO] [×] 6 [-] [RCL] [×] 11 [+] [RCL] [×] 4 [+]

EXERCISE SET B-3

List the coefficients of each polynomial. See Examples 1 and 2.

1. $3x^2 + 5x - 2$
2. $4x^2 + 3x - 3$
3. $2x^2 - 3x + 1$
4. $5x^2 - 2x + 4$
5. $x^3 + 2x^2 + x - 1$
6. $2x^3 + x^2 + 2x - 1$
7. $2x^3 - x^2 + x + 2$
8. $3x^3 + x^2 - x - 2$
9. $x^4 + 2.1x^2 + 3.2x - 1$
10. $-x^4 + 1.1x^3 - 1.4x^2 + 2.2$
11. $x^4 - 3.3x - 2.4$
12. $-x^4 + 2.2x - 2.8$
13. $-2.1x^4 - 1.9x + 4.5$
14. $-1.2x^4 - 9.1x + 5.4$

For each polynomial function, find the y-value for each given x-value. See Examples 3, 4, and 5. Round off y-values to no more than two decimal places.

15. $y = x^2 - 3x + 3$; $x = 2$, $x = -2$
16. $y = x^2 + 3x - 2$; $x = 2$, $x = -2$
17. $y = -2x^2 - 2x + 1$; $x = 3$, $x = -3$
18. $y = -3x^2 + 2x - 1$; $x = 3$, $x = -3$
19. $y = -2x^3 + x^2 - x + 1$; $x = 2.1$, $x = -2.1$, $x = 1.95$, $x = -1.95$
20. $y = -3x^3 - x^2 - 4$; $x = 1.8$, $x = -1.8$, $x = 2.45$, $x = -2.45$
21. $y = 1.2x^3 - 2.1x + 3.1$; $x = .45$, $x = -.45$, $x = 1.68$, $x = -1.68$
22. $y = 2.1x^3 - 1.2x + 1.3$; $x = .54$, $x = -.54$, $x = 2.04$, $x = -2.04$
23. $y = 1.2x^4 + 3.1x^3 - 1.8x^2 + 2.2x - .9$; $x = .4$, $x = -.4$
24. $y = 2.3x^4 - 1.8x^3 - 3.5x^2 + .9x + 1.7$; $x = .7$, $x = -.7$
25. $y = 3x^4 + 1.2x - 4.3$; $x = 2.15$, $x = -2.15$
26. $y = 2x^4 - 3.2x + 5.6$; $x = 1.86$, $x = -1.86$
27. $y = 1.4x^4 - 2.2x + 1.3$; $x = .25$, $x = -.25$, $x = .35$, $x = -.35$
28. $y = 4.1x^4 - 3.2x + 3.1$; $x = .25$, $x = -.25$, $x = .35$, $x = -.35$

B-4 Graphing Polynomial Functions

OBJECTIVES

After completing this section, you should be able to

1. Construct a graph of a polynomial function.
2. Estimate the zeros of a polynomial function from its graph.
3. Read coordinates of points of intersection of graphs.

The graphing techniques introduced in Section B-2 can be used to draw graphs of polynomial functions. The procedure is:

1. Compute a table of ordered pairs.
2. Plot the point corresponding to each such ordered pair.
3. Draw a smooth curve through the plotted points.

EXAMPLE 1

Graph the polynomial function defined by

$$y = x^4 - x^3 - 4x^2 - 5x + 5$$

from $x = -1$ to $x = 3$. Use intervals of .25 unit for x, and round off y-values to the nearest tenth. On the x-axis, use 4 squares to equal 1 unit; on the y-axis, use 1 square to equal 1 unit.

Solution

Use one of the calculator sequences introduced in Section B-3 to prepare a table of ordered pairs. The meaning of "intervals of .25 unit" will be clear to you after inspecting the following table.

x	-1.00	-.75	-.50	-.25	0	.25	.50	.75	1.00
y	8.0	7.2	6.7	6.0	5.0	3.5	1.4	-1.1	-4.0

x	1.25	1.50	1.75	2.00	2.25	2.50	2.75	3.00
y	-7.0	-9.8	-12.0	-13.0	-12.3	-9.1	-2.6	8.0

Figure B-4.1a shows the set of points corresponding to the set of ordered pairs of numbers in the table. Figure B-4.1b shows the graph obtained by drawing a smooth curve through the points.

A *zero of a function* is an x-value for which the associated y-value is zero. For example, we can verify that 2 and 3 are zeros of the function defined by

$$y = x^2 - 5x + 6 \qquad (1)$$

by first replacing x by 2 and then by 3, and computing

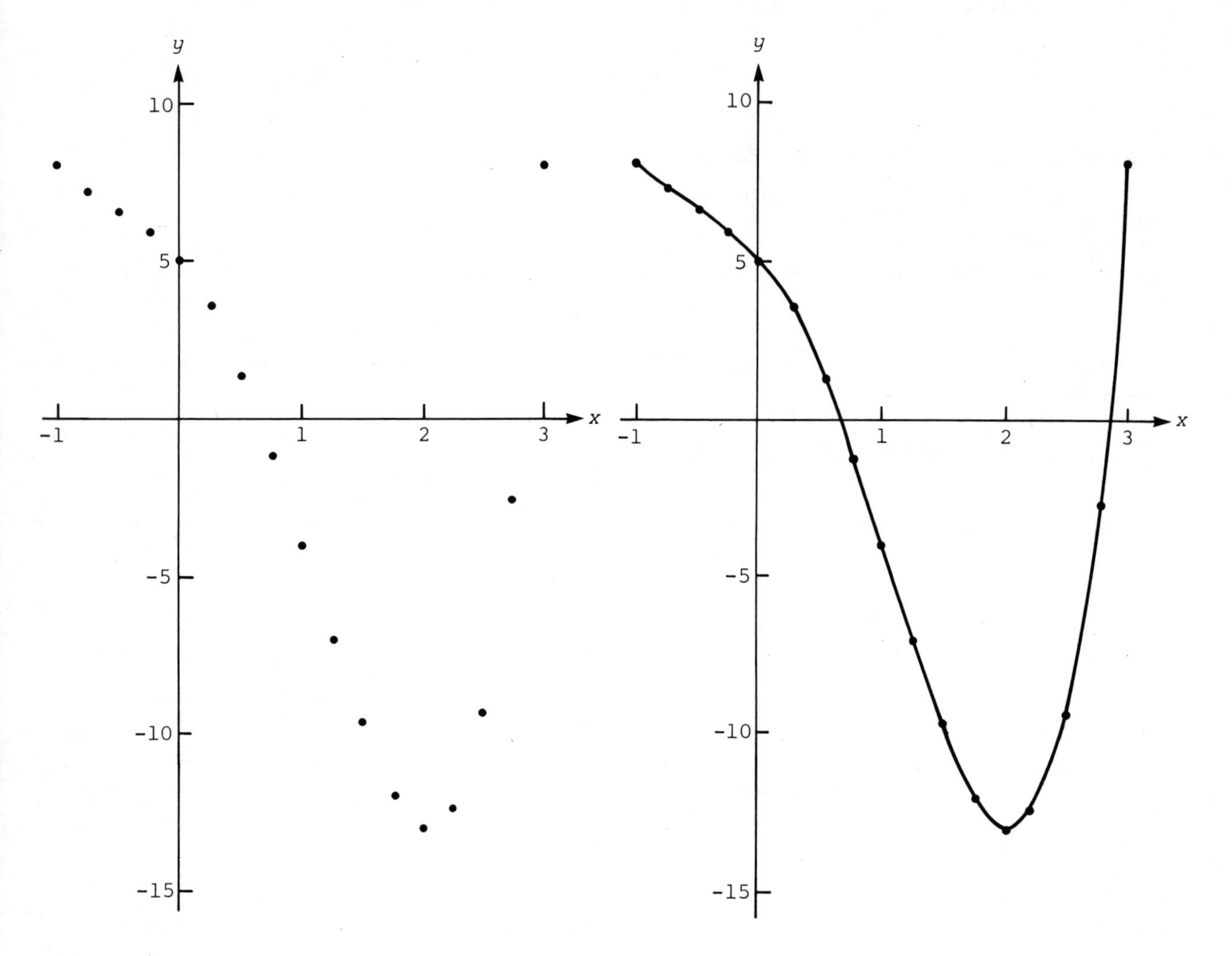

FIGURE B-4.1

$$y = 2^2 - 5(2) + 6 = 0 \quad \text{and} \quad y = 3^2 - 5(3) + 6 = 0$$

Now, in Figure B-4.2 consider the graph of the function defined by Equation (1), and note that we can read off the zeros of the function by reading the x-values of the points at which the graph crosses the x-axis. When a graph crosses the x-axis *between* two consecutive integers, we *estimate* the zeros of the function.

EXAMPLE 2

By reading from the graph shown in the solution of Example 1 (shown above), note that the function defined by

$$y = x^4 - x^3 - 4x^2 - 5x + 5$$

has a zero between 0 and 1 and a second zero between 2 and 3. The zeros of the function are (approximately) .7 and 2.8.

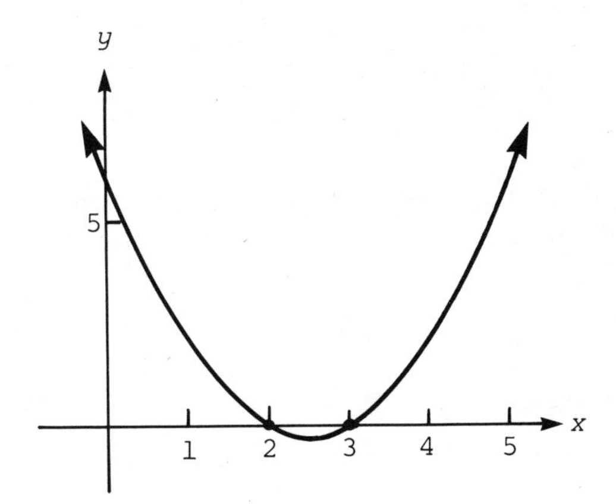

FIGURE B-4.2

In the next section we consider a method for obtaining better approximations of zeros of polynomial functions.

INTERSECTION OF GRAPHS

A useful technique in many areas of mathematics involves drawing more than one graph on the same set of axes and then reading the coordinates of points where the graphs intersect (*intersection points*).

EXAMPLE 3

From the graphs of

$$y = 3x^2 - 2$$

$$y = x^2 + 6$$

shown in the figure, note that there are two intersection points: (2,10) and (-2,10).

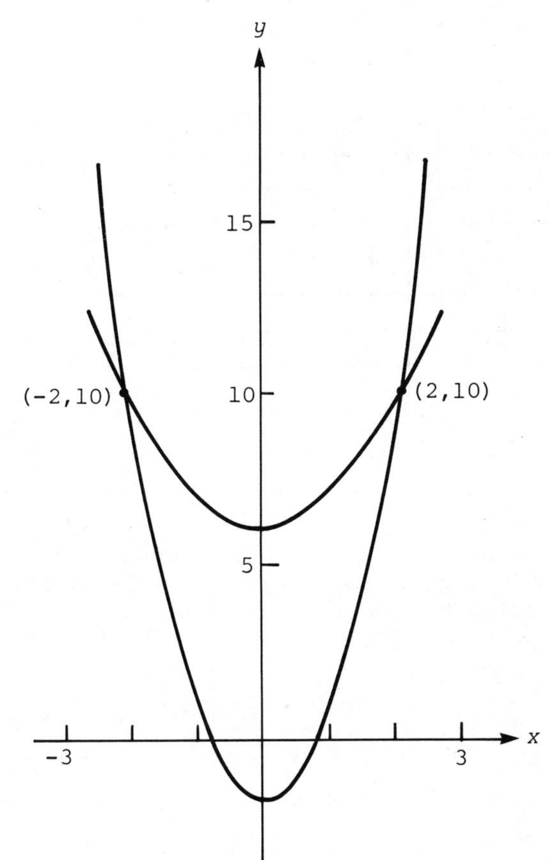

FIGURE B-4.3

EXERCISE SET B-4

For each polynomial function, (a) complete the table and round off the y-values to the nearest tenth. (b) Graph the resulting set of ordered pairs on the axes provided. (c) Specify any zeros of the function that appear on the graph.

1. $y = x^3 - x^2 - 4x + 4$

x	-.5	-.25	0	.25	.5	.75	1	1.25	1.5	1.75	2	2.25
y												

2. $y = 2x^3 - 11x^2 + 10x + 8$

x	-.5	-.25	0	.25	.5	.75	1	1.25	1.5	1.75	2	2.25
y												

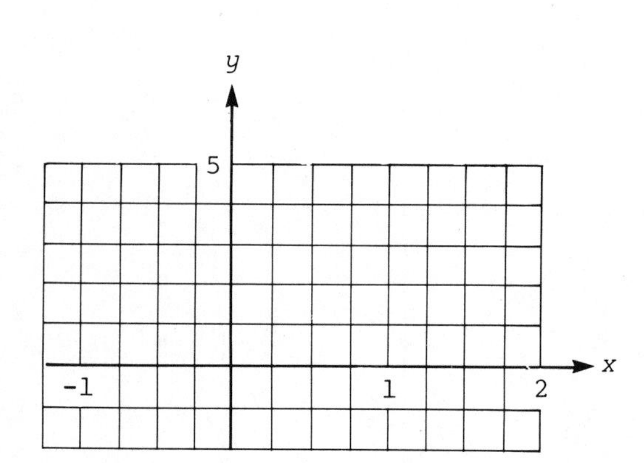

EXERCISE 1

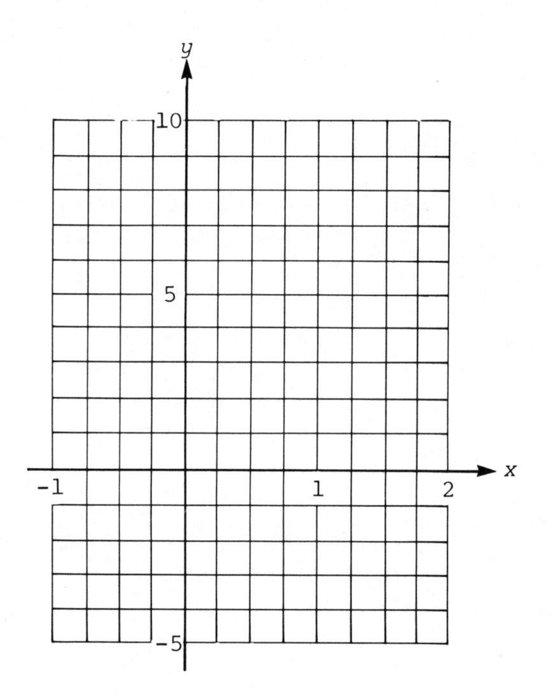

EXERCISE 2

Graph the polynomial function defined by each equation. Compute a table of values using intervals of .25 unit for x; round off the y-values to the nearest tenth. (x-scale: 4 sq = 1 unit, y-scale: 1 sq = 1 unit.) To the nearest tenth, estimate any zeros of the function that appear on the graph.

3. $y = 2x^3 + 9x^2 + 7x - 6$; from $x = -3$ to $x = .75$
4. $y = 3x^3 - 2x^2 - 3x + 2$; from $x = -1.25$ to $x = 1.75$
5. $y = 6x^4 - x^3 - 7x^2 + x + 1$; from $x = -1.25$ to $x = 1.25$
6. $y = 6x^4 + x^3 - 7x^2 - x + 1$; from $x = -1.25$ to $x = 1.25$
7. $y = 4x^4 - 5x^2 + 1$; from $x = -1.5$ to $x = 1.5$
8. $y = 9x^4 - 13x^2 + 4$; from $x = -1.5$ to $x = 1.5$

In each of Exercises 9-12, graph each pair of polynomial functions on the same set of axes, and specify the coordinates of the points of intersection. Use intervals of .5 for x-values; round off y-values to the nearest tenth. (x-scale: 2 sq = 1 unit; y-scale: 1 sq = 1 unit.) See Example 3.

9. $y = 2x^2 - 9$

   $y = \frac{1}{3}x^2 + 6$

   ($x = -3.5$ to $x = 3.5$)

10. $y = -2x^2 - 2$

    $y = -3x^2 + 2$

    ($x = -2.5$ to $x = 2.5$)

11. $y = 2x^2 + x - 1$

    $y = x^2 + 2x + 1$

    ($x = -2$ to $x = 2.5$)

12. $y = 2x^2 - x - 1$

    $y = x^2 - 2x + 1$

    ($x = -2.5$ to $x = 2$)

B-5 Solving Polynomial Equations

OBJECTIVES

After completing this section, you should be able to

1. Obtain solutions of a polynomial equation to a specified number of places.
2. Compute zeros of a polynomial function to a specified number of places.

Given an equation in x, if we replace x by a number and do the resulting indicated computations, we obtain either a false statement or a true statement. For example, given

$$x^2 + 3x - 4 = 0 \qquad (1)$$

if we replace x by 3, we obtain

$$3^2 + 3(3) - 4 = 0, \quad \text{or} \quad 14 = 0$$

which is a false statement. On the other hand, if we replace x by 1, we obtain

$$1^2 + 3(1) - 4 = 0, \quad \text{or} \quad 0 = 0$$

a true statement. For a given equation in x, any replacement number for x that results in a true statement is called a *solution* of the equation. Thus, 1 is a solution of Equation (1). We can verify that -4 is also a solution of Equation (1) by replacing x by -4 to obtain

$$(-4)^2 + 3(-4) - 4 = 0, \quad \text{or} \quad 0 = 0$$

and we now see that Equation (1) has two solutions, 1 and -4.

Recall from Section B-4 that a *zero* of a function is an x-value for which the associated y-value is zero. Now, consider the polynomial function defined by the equation

$$y = x^2 + 3x - 4 \qquad (2)$$

From the discussion above, we know that the polynomial $x^2 + 3x - 4$ is equal to zero if $x = 1$ or $x = -4$. Hence, 1 and -4 are the zeros of polynomial function (2). More generally, the zeros of a polynomial function defined by an equation in the form

$$y = \text{a polynomial}$$

are the same numbers as the solutions of the related polynomial equation

$$\text{polynomial} = 0$$

It follows that the problem of finding the zeros of a polynomial function can be solved if we can solve the related polynomial equation. Below we shall develop a calculator method for solving polynomial equations.

Figure B-5.1(a) shows a part of a graph of a function from $x = 1$ to $x = 3$. Observe that the y-value associated with 1 is negative (-1), the y-value associated with 3 is positive (+1), and there is a zero of the function (the number c) between 1 and 3. Figure B-5.1(b) shows a part of a graph of a function from $x = 2$ to $x = 3$. Observe that the y-value associated with 2 is positive (+1), the y-value associated with 3 is negative (-1),

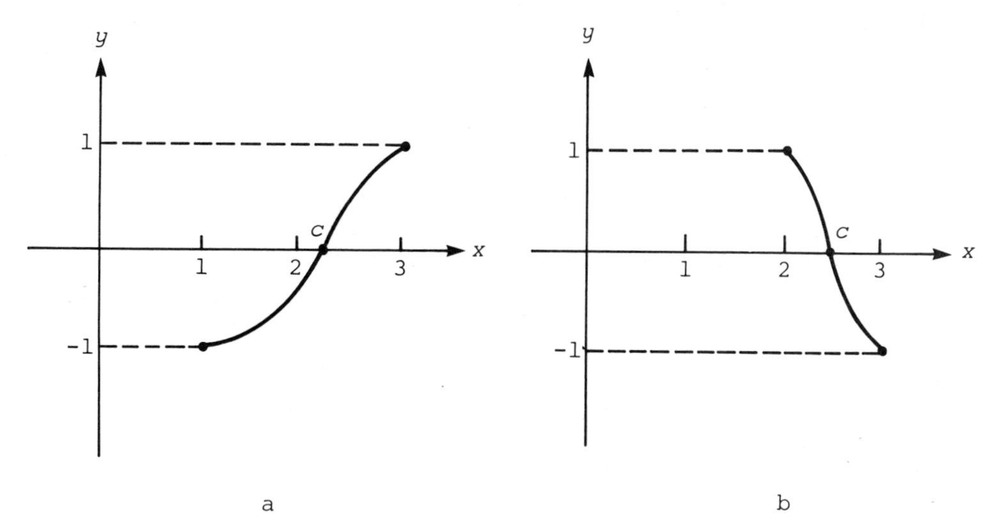

FIGURE B-5.1

and there is a zero (c) of the function between 2 and 3. Observations such as these suggest the following *sign-change principle:*

Let s and t be two x-values, with s less than t. For a given function, if the y-values associated with s and t, respectively, are opposite in sign, then there is at least one zero of the function between s and t.

Note that the sign-change principle specifies that there is *at least* one zero between s and t. The examples and exercises of this book are selected so that there will be *only one* zero between s and t.

To see how the sign-change principle is used in solving equations, let us find a solution (to two decimal places) of the equation

$$x^4 - x^3 - 4x^2 - 5x + 5 = 0 \tag{3}$$

From Example 1 of Section B-4 (page 95), we know that between 0 and 1 there is a zero of the function defined by the equation $y = x^4 - x^3 - 4x^2 - 5x + 5$. This zero is a solution of Equation (3). To find the solution, we compute tables in which we list x-values, and *signs only* of y-values, and watch for a change in sign. First, we compute for x-values between 0 and 1, as follows.

x	0	.1	.2	.3	.4	.5	.6	.7
y	+	+	+	+	+	+	+	-

There is a change in the sign (+ to -) from $x = .6$ to $x = .7$. Hence, by the sign-change principle, the required solution is between .6 and .7. Next, we compute the table

x	.60	.61	.62	.63	.64	.65
y	+	+	+	+	+	-

Because there is a change in sign (+ to -) from $x = .64$ to $x = .65$, we stop computing. The required solution is between .64 and .65. Now we must determine whether the solution is closer to .64 or closer to .65. If it is closer to .64, then it will be less than .645; if it is closer to .65, then it will be greater than .645 (see Figure B-5.2).

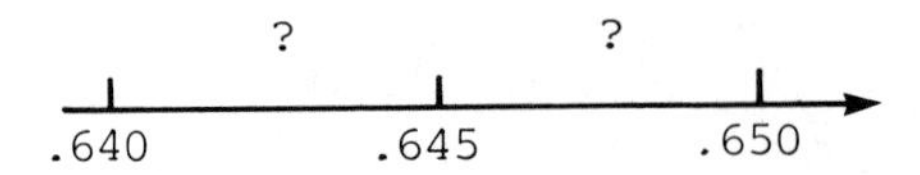

FIGURE B-5.2

We compute the table

x	.640	.645
y	+	+

(the + entry for .640 is taken from the computations above) and observe that there is *no sign change* between $x = .640$ and $x = .645$. Thus, the solution is greater than .645, and we conclude that the required solution is .65, to two decimal places.

EXAMPLE 1

The equation $x^4 - x^3 - 4x^2 - 5x + 5 = 0$ has a solution between 2 and 3. Find that solution (to two decimal places).

Solution

x	2.0	2.1	2.2	2.3	2.4	2.5	2.6	2.7	2.8	2.9
y	-	-	-	-	-	-	-	-	-	+

The required solution is between 2.8 and 2.9.

x	2.80	2.81	2.82	2.83
y	-	-	-	+

The required solution is between 2.82 and 2.83. Next, to determine whether the required solution is closer to 2.82 or 2.83, compute the table

x	2.820	2.825
y	-	+

Because there is a sign change between 2.820 and 2.825, the solution is less than 2.825, and therefore closer to 2.820. Hence, the required solution is 2.82, to two decimal places.

A little extra care may be needed when finding a negative solution of an equation to a specified number of decimal places. For example, the equation

$$x^2 - 1.36x - 10.6 = 0$$

has a solution between -2.65 and -2.64. If we want the solution to two decimal places, we will have to determine whether the solution is closer to -2.65 or to -2.64. If the solution is greater than -2.645, then it is closer to -2.640; if it is less than -2.645, then it is closer to -2.650 (see Figure B-5.3).

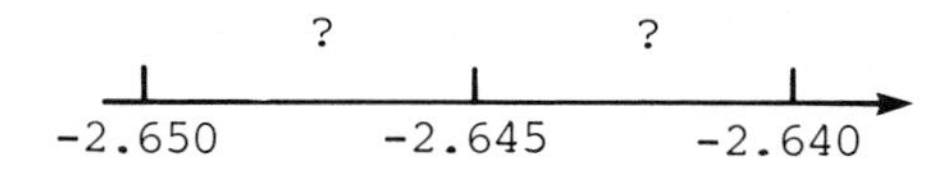

FIGURE B-5.3

In the table

x	-2.650	-2.645
y	+	-

we observe a sign change between -2.650 and -2.645. Hence, the solution is less than -2.645 and is therefore closer to -2.65 than to -2.64. We conclude that the required solution is -2.65, to two decimal places.

As stated earlier in this section, the zeros of a polynomial function are the same numbers as the solutions of the related polynomial equation. Hence, the calculator method for solving polynomial equations can also be used to compute the zeros of polynomial functions.

EXAMPLE 2

Given $y = x^2 + 1.2x - 5.6$

a. Graph the function from $x = -4$ to $x = 0$. Use intervals of .5 for x, round off the y-values to the nearest tenth.

b. From the graph, estimate a zero of the function and then compute it to two decimal places.

Solutions

a. Compute a table of values; draw the graph.

x	-4.0	-3.5	-3.0	-2.5	-2.0	-1.5	-1.0	-.5	0
y	5.6	2.5	-.2	-2.4	-4.0	-5.2	-5.8	-6.0	-5.6

b. From the graph (see page 104), the zero is approximately -3.2.

x	-3.2	-3.1	-3.0
y	+	+	-

The zero is between -3.1 and -3.0.

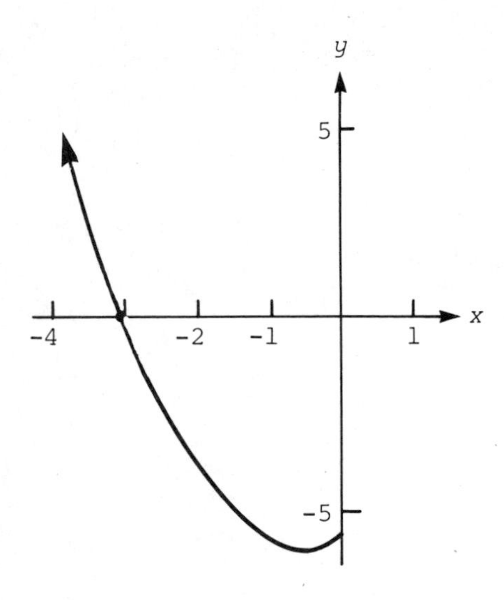

FIGURE B-5.4

x	-3.10	-3.09	-3.08	-3.07	-3.06	-3.05	-3.04
y	+	+	+	+	+	+	-

The zero is between -3.05 and -3.04. To determine whether the zero is closer to -3.05 or to -3.04, compute the table

x	-3.050	-3.045
y	+	+

Because there is no sign change between -3.050 and -3.045, the zero is greater than -3.045. Hence, the zero is -3.04, to two decimal places.

EXERCISE SET B-5

Each equation has a solution between the given numbers. Find that solution to two decimal places. See Example 1.

1. $x^2 - 12x + 31 = 0$; between 8 and 9
2. $x^2 - 12x + 31 = 0$; between 3 and 4
3. $x^2 - 4x - 3 = 0$; between 4 and 5
4. $x^2 - 4x - 3 = 0$; between -1 and 0
5. $3x^3 + 8x^2 - 7x - 14 = 0$; between 1 and 2
6. $3x^3 + x^2 - 8x - 14 = 0$; between 2 and 3
7. $x^3 + 9x^2 + 14x + 6 = 0$; between -8 and -7
8. $x^3 + 9x^2 + 14x + 6 = 0$; between -1 and 0
9. $x^3 + x^2 - 13 = 0$; between 2 and 3

10. $x^3 - 9x^2 + 13 - 0$; between 1 and 2

11. $x^4 + 10x^3 + 22x^2 - 10x - 23 = 0$; between -4 and -3

12. $x^4 + 10x^3 + 22x^2 - 10x - 23 = 0$; between -7 and -6

For each function (a) draw the graph for the specified x-values, using intervals of .5 for x, and (b) from the graph estimate a zero between the given numbers and compute it to two decimal places. See Example 2.

13. $y = x^2 - 2x - 1$; from $x = 0$ to $x = 3$

14. $y = x^2 - 2x - 2$; from $x = 0$ to $x = 3$

15. $y = x^3 + x^2 - 6x + 4$; from $x = -3.5$ to $x = 0$

16. $y = x^3 + 9x^2 + 13x - 23$; from $x = -5$ to $x = -3$

17. $y = x^3 + .2x^2 - 2.04x - 1.24$; from $x = 0$ to $x = 2.5$

18. $y = x^3 + .5x^2 - 1.2x - .7$; from $x = 0$ to $x = 2$

19. $y = x^3 + 2x^2 - 1.25x - 1.75$; from $x = -1$ to $x = 1$

20. $y = x^3 - 1.4x^2 - .16x + .56$; from $x = -1$ to $x = 1$

B-6 Angle Measure

OBJECTIVES

After completing this section, you should be able to

1. Change the measure of an angle from *degrees-minutes* form to *degrees-decimal* form or from *degrees-decimal* form to *degrees-minutes* form.
2. Change the measure of an angle from *degrees* to *radians* or from *radians* to *degrees*.
3. Compute the length of arc of a circle.

There are two commonly used units for measuring angles: degrees and radians.

DEGREE MEASURE

One *degree* (written 1°) is the measure of an angle in which one of the sides is rotated $\frac{1}{360}$ of one rotation about its endpoint (Figure B-6.1). The *degree measure* of an angle is the number of times that it contains a 1° angle. It is a *positive* number if the rotation is in the counterclockwise direction [Figure B-6.2(a)]; it is a *negative* number if the rotation is in the clockwise direction [Figure B-6.2(b)].

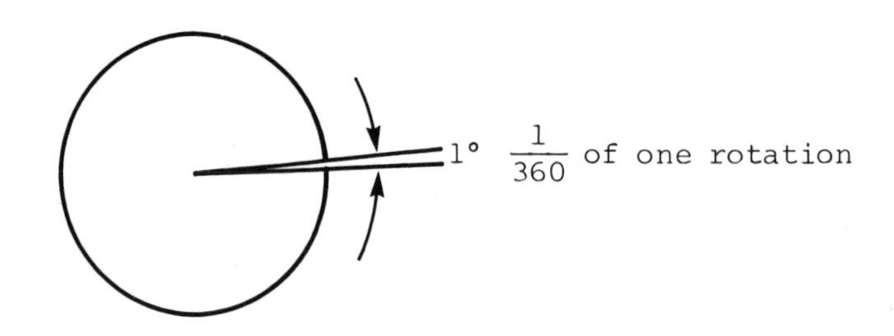

FIGURE B-6.1

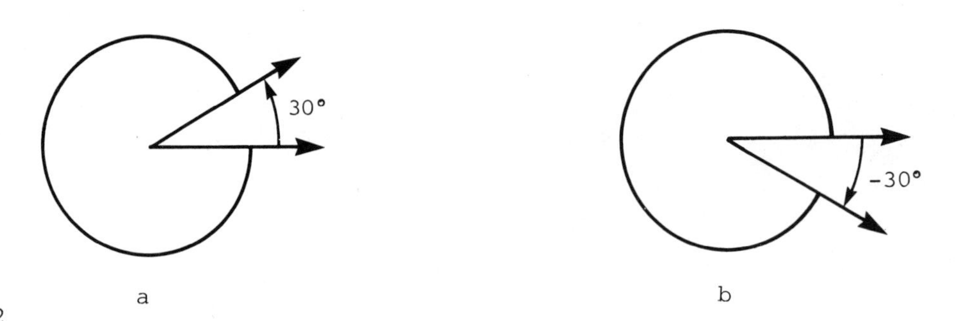

FIGURE B-6.2

For greater accuracy, we subdivide 1 degree into 60 minutes (written 60'). Thus,

$$1^\circ = 60' \quad \text{and} \quad 1' = \frac{1}{60}^\circ$$

Degree measure can be expressed in *degrees-minutes form* (abbreviated "deg-min") or in *degrees-decimal form* (abbreviated "deg-dec").

EXAMPLE 1

Change to deg-dec form, to the nearest hundredth.

a. 16' b. 39°16' c. -103°16'

Solutions

a. $16' = \frac{16^\circ}{60} = .26666667^\circ$

To the nearest hundredth, 16' = .27°.

b. 39°16' = 39° + 16' = (39 + .26666667)° = 39.26666667°

To the nearest hundredth, 39°16' = 39.27°.

c. -103°16' = -(103° + 16') = -(103 + .26666667)° = -103.26666667°

To the nearest hundredth, -103°16' = -103.27°.

EXAMPLE 2

Change to deg-min form, to the nearest whole number of minutes.

a. .81° b. 143.81° c. -21.81°

Solutions

a. $.81^\circ = (.81 \times 60)' = 48.6'$

To the nearest whole number of minutes, .81° = 49'.

b. 143.81° = (143 + .81)° = 143° + 48.6' = 143°48.6'

To the nearest whole number of minutes, 143.81° = 143°49'.

c. -21.81° = -(21 + .81)° = -(21° + 48.6') = -21°48.6'

To the nearest whole number of minutes, -21.81° = -21°49'.

RADIAN MEASURE

One *radian* (written "1 radian" or, simply, 1) is the measure of an angle in which one of the sides is rotated $\frac{1}{2\pi}$ (approximately $\frac{1}{6.28}$) of one rotation about its endpoint (Figure B-6.3). The *radian measure* of an angle is the number of times it contains a 1 radian angle.

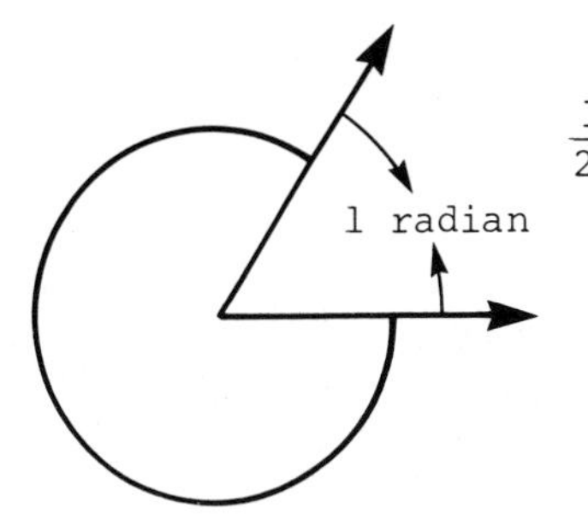

FIGURE B-6.3

It is a *positive* number if the rotation is in the counterclockwise direction (Figure B-6.4a); it is a *negative* number if the rotation is in the clockwise direction (Figure B-6.4b). When an angle is given as a number without a degree symbol, it is to be understood to mean a "number of radians." For example, an angle measure given as 2.6 means "2.6 radians."

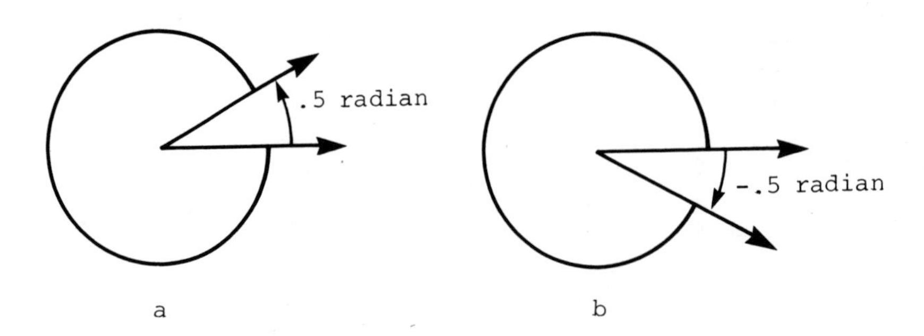

FIGURE B-6.4

Radian measures are often given in forms such as $\frac{\pi}{12}$, $\frac{5\pi}{6}$, and so forth, where π appears as a factor. We can use the [π] key* to change such forms to decimal form. (Some calculators require that you press the [F] key before the [π] key.)

EXAMPLE 3

Change each radian measure to decimal form, to the nearest thousandth.

a. $\frac{\pi}{12}$ b. $\frac{5\pi}{6}$

Solutions

a. $\frac{\pi}{12}$ = .262 to the nearest thousandth, as computed by

[π] [÷] 12 [=] → .26179939 or [π] [ENT] 12 [÷] → .26179939

b. $\frac{5\pi}{6}$ = 2.618 to the nearest thousandth, as computed by

5 [×] [π] [÷] 6 [=] → 2.617994

or

5 [ENT] [π] [×] 6 [÷] → 2.617994

---

*If your calculator has no [π] key, use 3.141593 for π.

DEGREE-RADIAN CONVERSIONS

Because 1 radian is $\frac{1}{2\pi}$ of one complete rotation, there are 2π radians, or 360° in one complete rotation, and π radians, or 180°, in one-half of one complete rotation. Therefore, the following formula can be used to convert radians to degrees, or degrees to radians.

$$\frac{\text{degrees}}{180} = \frac{\text{radians}}{\pi} \qquad (1)$$

From Formula (1) we obtain the following convenient Formulas (1a) and (1b):

$$\text{radians} = \frac{\text{degrees} \times \pi}{180} \qquad (1a)$$

$$\text{degrees} = \frac{\text{radians} \times 180}{\pi} \qquad (1b)$$

EXAMPLE 4

Change 72.6° to radians, to the nearest hundredth.

Solution

Substitute 72.6 for "degrees" in Formula (1a) and compute the number of radians.

$$\text{radians} = \frac{72.6 \times \pi}{180} = 1.267109$$

To the nearest hundredth, 72.6° = 1.27 radians.

EXAMPLE 5

Change -12°45' to radians, to the nearest thousandth.

Solution

First, change -12°45' to deg-dec form (-12.75°), as in Example 1. Next, substitute -12.75 for "degrees" in Formula (1a) and compute the number of radians.

$$\text{radians} = \frac{(-12.75) \times \pi}{180} = -.2225295$$

To the nearest thousandth, -12°45' = -.223 radians.

EXAMPLE 6

Change 1.9 radians to degrees in deg-dec form, to the nearest tenth.

Solution

Substitute 1.9 for "radians" in Formula (1b) and compute the number of degrees.

$$\text{degrees} = \frac{1.9 \times 180}{\pi} = 108.86198$$

To the nearest tenth, 1.9 radians = 108.9°.

EXAMPLE 7

Change $\frac{3\pi}{4}$ radians to degrees.

Solution

Substitute $\frac{3\pi}{4}$ for "radians" in Formula (1b), and compute the number of degrees.

$$\text{degrees} = \frac{\frac{3\pi}{4} \times 180}{\pi} = 135$$

Hence, $\frac{3\pi}{4}$ radians = 135°.

Some calculators can directly change degrees to radians and radians to degrees. If your calculator has such a capability, you should only use it *after* you understand the important relationship [Formula (1)] between degree measure and radian measure.

ARC LENGTH

The length, s, of an arc of a circle with radius, r, is related to the measure of the central angle, θ, of the arc (see Figure B-6.5) by either of two formulas. If the central angle is measured in degrees, then

$$s = \frac{\pi D^\circ r}{180} \qquad (2)$$

where D° is the degree measure of the central angle. If the central angle is measured in radians, then

$$s = r\theta \qquad (3)$$

where θ is the radian measure of the angle.

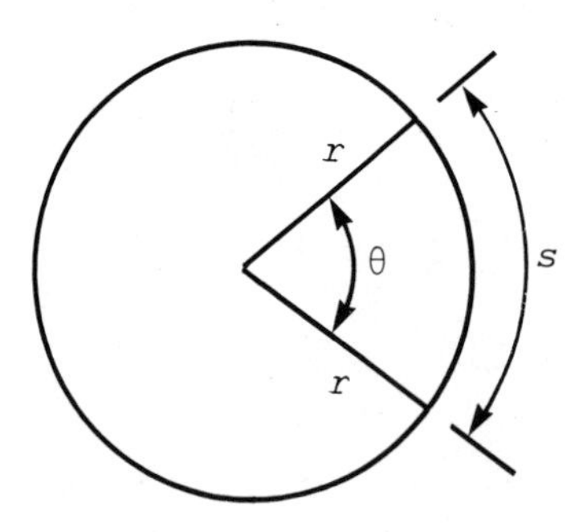

FIGURE B-6.5

EXAMPLE 8

To the nearest tenth, find the length of arc of a circle with radius 8.6 centimeters if the measure of the central angle is

a. 87.4°   b. 1.8

Solutions

a. Because the central angle is in degrees, use Formula (2).

$$s = \frac{\pi(87.4°)(8.6)}{180} = 13.118593$$

The arc length is 13.1 cm, to the nearest tenth.

b. Because the central angle is in radians, use Formula (3).

$$s = 8.6 \times 1.8 = 15.48$$

The arc length is 15.5 cm, to the nearest tenth.

EXERCISE SET B-6

Change each angle measure to deg-dec form, to the nearest hundredth. See Example 1.

1. 19'
2. 37'
3. 41'
4. 11'
5. 56°17'
6. 72°39'
7. 158°53'
8. 279°49'
9. -245°31'
10. -376°20'
11. -63°5'
12. -4°16'

Change each angle measure to deg-min form, to the nearest minute. See Example 2.

13. .6°
14. .3°
15. 8.54°
16. 9.73°
17. 38.15°
18. 49.35°
19. 172.47°
20. 256.92°
21. -356.09°
22. -300.61°
23. -42.90°
24. -75.75°

Change each radian measure to decimal form, to the nearest thousandth. See Example 3.

25. $\frac{\pi}{3}$
26. $\frac{\pi}{8}$
27. $\frac{3\pi}{4}$
28. $\frac{5\pi}{4}$
29. $\frac{7\pi}{12}$
30. $\frac{13\pi}{12}$
31. $-\frac{7\pi}{6}$
32. $-\frac{11\pi}{6}$

Change each angle measure to radians, to the nearest hundredth. See Example 4.

33. 60°
34. 90°
35. 52.7°
36. 73.6°
37. 236.3°
38. 348.5°
39. -68.4°
40. -127.2°

Change each angle measure to radians, to the nearest thousandth. See Example 5.

41. 17°48'
42. 81°25'
43. 241°42'
44. 356°36'
45. -8°47'
46. -65°21'
47. -307°40'
48. -189°9'

Change each angle measure to deg-dec form, to the nearest tenth. See Example 6.

49. 1.6
50. .9
51. .5
52. 1.9
53. 2.4
54. 4.6
55. -3.8
56. -5.3
57. -6.3
58. -7.5
59. .05
60. .005

Change each angle measure to degrees, to the nearest degree. See Example 7.

61. $\frac{5\pi}{4}$
62. $\frac{7\pi}{4}$
63. $\frac{5\pi}{12}$
64. $\frac{11\pi}{12}$
65. $\frac{7\pi}{9}$
66. $\frac{11\pi}{9}$
67. $-\frac{6\pi}{5}$
68. $-\frac{9\pi}{5}$

To the nearest tenth, find the length of arc of a circle for each central angle θ and radius r. See Example 8.

69. $\theta = 54.5°$, $r = 3.2$ in.
70. $\theta = 78.6°$, $r = 6.7$ ft
71. $\theta = 2.1$, $r = .75$ cm
72. $\theta = 3.7$, $r = 1.25$ cm
73. $\theta = \frac{2\pi}{5}$, $r = 1.2$ km
74. $\theta = \frac{5\pi}{12}$, $r = .85$ km
75. $\theta = 16°52'$, $r = 5.2$ ft
76. $\theta = 164°34'$, $r = 2.7$ in.

B-7 Trigonometric Functions

OBJECTIVES

After completing this section, you should be able to

1. Find the y-value associated with a given x-value (angle) for a given trigonometric function.
2. Find the angle associated with a given y-value for a given trigonometric function.

In this section we introduce six functions related to the field of mathematics called *trigonometry*.

THE SINE, COSINE, AND TANGENT FUNCTIONS

Recall from Section B-2 that an equation can be used to define a function. The three most used *trigonometric functions* are defined by the equations

$$y = \sin x, \qquad y = \cos x, \qquad y = \tan x$$

where *sin*, *cos*, and *tan* are abbreviations for *sine*, *cosine*, and *tangent*, respectively. The equation

$$y = \sin x$$

specifies the rule "Given the number x, pair with it the number *sine of* x." Similar remarks apply to the cosine and tangent equations. Although it is beyond the scope of this book to give a general description of the rule given by each of these equations, we shall consider some specific uses of these functions in Sections B-9 and B-10.

There is more than one method available for computing the function values $\sin x$, $\cos x$, and $\tan x$. For our purposes, given a trigonometric function and an x-value, we shall rely on a calculator to compute the associated y-value.

It is convenient to think of x-values used for trigonometric functions as angle measures or, more simply, as angles. Hence, it is important to distinguish between degree and radian measure of angles when computing associated y-values. As stated in Section B-6, when an angle measure is given as a number with a *degree symbol*, *degree measure* is indicated; if *no degree symbol* follows the number, *radian measure* is indicated.

Your calculator should have a [D-R] switch or key (or its equivalent) that sets the calculator to accept numbers either as degree measure or radian measure. We shall say "set to degree mode" to mean "set the calculator to compute with degree measure," and "set to radian mode" to mean "set the calculator to compute with radian measure."

THE [SIN], [COS], AND [TAN] KEYS

The trigonometric keys [SIN], [COS], and [TAN], (and the [F] key, if applicable) are used to compute y-values for trigonometric functions. The angle measure is entered *first*, then the appropriate trigonometric key is pressed. (In general, we shall round off trigonometric y-values to five places.)

Because certain calculator sequences require neither the [=] key nor the [ENT] key, these sequences can be applied to *both* [=] and [ENT] calculators. Example 1 includes examples of such sequences.

EXAMPLE 1

Compute to five decimal places.

a. sin 53°   b. cos 253°   c. tan(-53°)

Solutions

Because the angles are in degree measure, set to degree mode.

a. sin 53° = .79864, as computed by either of the sequences

53 [SIN] → .79863551   or   53 [F] [SIN] → .79863551

b. cos 253° = -.29237, as computed by either of the sequences

253 [COS] → -.29237171*   or   253 [F] [COS] → -.29237171*

c. tan(-53°) = -1.32704, as computed by either of the sequences

53 [+/-] [TAN] → -1.3270448   or   53 [+/-] [F] [TAN] → -1.3270448

As shown in Example 1, the [F] key is pressed *before* the trigonometric key. In the remaining examples of this section we will not specifically show the [F] key in a sequence, with the understanding that you will use the [F] key if your calculator requires it.

EXAMPLE 2

Compute sin 74°18' to five decimal places.

Solution

First, change 74°18' to 74.3°. Next, set to degree mode and use the sequence

74.3 [SIN] → .96269175

sin 74°18' = .96269, to five decimal places.

---

*If your calculator shows an "error" signal, see Appendix D.

EXAMPLE 3

Compute to five decimal places.

a. sin 3.43 b. cos(-2.1)

Solution

Because the angles are given in radian measure, set to radian mode.

a. sin 3.43 = -.28443, as computed by

3.43 [SIN] → -.28442571

b. cos(-2.1) = -.50485, as computed by

2.1 [+/-] [COS] → -.50484610

The [SIN], [COS], and [TAN] keys operate only on a number in the display (either a new entry or the result of a previous calculation). Hence, if we want to compute trigonometric values such as $\frac{2\pi}{3}$, the computation for $\frac{2\pi}{3}$ must be completed *before* pressing the [SIN] key. (On [=] calculators, this is done by pressing the [=] key, as shown in the next example.)

EXAMPLE 4

$\sin \frac{2\pi}{3}$ = .86603, to five places, as computed by one of the sequences (radian mode):

2 [×] [π] [÷] 3 [=] [SIN] → .86602541

or

2 [ENT] [π] [×] 3 [÷] [SIN] → .86602541

THE SECANT, COSECANT, AND COTANGENT FUNCTIONS

Three other trigonometric functions are defined in terms of reciprocals, as follows:

$$y = \sec x = \frac{1}{\cos x}, \qquad y = \csc x = \frac{1}{\sin x}, \qquad y = \cot x = \frac{1}{\tan x}$$

where *sec*, *csc*, and *cot* are abbreviations for *secant*, *cosecant*, and *cotangent*, respectively.

EXAMPLE 5

Compute to five decimal places.

a. sec(-35°) b. csc 1.3 c. cot 41.2°

Solutions

a. Set to degree mode: sec(−35°) = 1.22077, as computed by

35 [+/−] [COS] [1/x] → 1.2207746

b. Set to radian mode: csc 1.3 = 1.03782, as computed by

1.3 [SIN] [1/x] → 1.0378200

c. Set to degree mode: cot 41.2° = 1.14229, as computed by

41.2 [TAN] [1/x] → 1.1422908

FINDING AN ANGLE FROM A TRIGONOMETRIC FUNCTION VALUE

In the examples above, we were given an angle (x-value) and a trigonometric function, and asked to find the associated y-value. Next, we consider the inverse problem: Given a y-value and a trigonometric function, find the associated angle. For example, given that

$$\sin x = .89725 \tag{2}$$

find the angle, x (in degrees or in radians). This problem may also be stated in the form of an equation

$$x = \text{Arc sin } .89725 \tag{3}$$

read "x is the angle the sine of which is .89725." Calculator sequences for solving such problems differ in certain details. On some calculators, one of the keys [ARC] or [INV] is used, together with the [SIN], [COS], or [TAN] key (and the [F] key, if applicable). Other calculators use keys marked [SIN⁻¹], [COS⁻¹], or [TAN⁻¹], together with the [F] key. Following are four possible sequences for computing the right-hand side of Equation (3) in degrees or radians. By examining the keyboard of your calculator, you should be able to determine which sequence applies to your calculator. (We will use degree mode.)

.89725 [ARC] [SIN] → 63.798914

.89725 [INV] [SIN] → 63.798914

.89725 [F] [ARC] [SIN] → 63.798914

.89725 [F] [SIN⁻¹] → 63.798914

In the examples in the remainder of this text, we will use only the symbols

[SIN], [COS], [TAN], and [ARC]

with the understanding that you will use the appropriate sequence for your calculator.

EXAMPLE 6

Compute:

a. Arc tan 8.70218, to the nearest hundredth of a degree.

b. Arc cos(-.12359), to the nearest hundredth of a radian.

Solutions

a. Arc tan 8.70218 = 83.44°, as computed (in degree mode) by

8.70218 [ARC] [TAN] → 83.444682

b. Arc cos(-.12359) = 1.69, as computed (in radian mode) by

.12359 [+/-] [ARC] [COS] → 1.6947031

INVERSE OPERATIONS

On your calculator (or mentally) you can verify that

$$25 + 5 - 5 = 25 \quad \text{and} \quad 25 - 5 + 5 = 25$$

and thus note that the operations *add 5* and *subtract 5* have the effect of "reversing" each other; that is, if either of the two operations is applied to a given number and the other operation is applied immediately after, the result is the same given number. We say that *add 5* and *subtract 5* are "inverse" operations. More generally, for any numbers x and N,

$$x + N - N = x \quad \text{and} \quad x - N + N = x$$

and we say that *addition* and *subtraction* are *inverse operations*. Similarly, note that

$$25 \times 5 \div 5 = 25 \quad \text{and} \quad 25 \div 5 \times 5 = 25$$

or, more generally,

$$x \cdot N \div N = x \quad \text{and} \quad x \div N \cdot N = x$$

Thus, *multiplication* and *division* are also called *inverse operations*. Still another example of inverse operations is provided by the operations *square* and *square root*. You can verify that

$$\sqrt{25^2} = 25 \quad \text{and} \quad (\sqrt{25})^2 = 25$$

With a calculator, it is not difficult to verify that the operations *compute the sine* and *compute the Arc sine* are inverse operations. For example, let us compute sin 60° and then compute Arc sine of the result:

$$\sin 60° = .8660254$$

$$\text{Arc sin } .8660254 = 59.999999°$$

The result 59.999999° is certainly close enough to 60° to indicate that

$$\text{Arc sin}(\sin 60°) = 60°$$

and we see that the operations *sine* and *Arc sine* "reverse" each other. Note also that

$$\sin(\text{Arc sin } .6138052) = .6138052$$

as you can verify by the sequence

.6138052 [ARC] [SIN] [SIN] → .6138052

In general,

$$\text{Arc sin}(\sin x) = x \quad \text{and} \quad \sin(\text{Arc sin } x) = x$$

Two other pairs of inverse trigonometric operations are: *compute the cosine* and *compute the Arc cosine*, and *compute the tangent* and *compute the Arc tangent*. That is,

$$\text{Arc cos}(\cos x) = x \quad \text{and} \quad \cos(\text{Arc cos } x) = x$$

$$\text{Arc tan}(\tan x) = x \quad \text{and} \quad \tan(\text{Arc tan } x) = x$$

EXERCISE SET B-7

Compute to five decimal places. See Examples 1 and 2. (Set to degree mode.)

1. sin 72°
2. sin 27°
3. cos 32°
4. cos 107°
5. tan 87°
6. tan 71°
7. sin(-19°)
8. cos(-108°)
9. tan(-122°)
10. tan 234°36'
11. sin 317°52'
12. cos 241°41'
13. tan(-200°27')
14. cos(-335°19')

Compute to five decimal places. See Examples 3 and 4. (Set to radian mode.)

15. sin .51
16. cos .95
17. tan .63
18. cos 1.58
19. sin 2.56
20. tan 3.59
21. tan(-2.42)
22. cos(-5.01)
23. sin(-6.42)
24. tan(-3.33)
25. $\sin \frac{\pi}{3}$
26. $\cos \frac{\pi}{6}$
27. $\tan \frac{3\pi}{4}$
28. $\tan \frac{5\pi}{6}$
29. $\sin \frac{2\pi}{3}$
30. $\cos \frac{11\pi}{6}$
31. $\cos(-\frac{5\pi}{6})$
32. $\tan(-\frac{7\pi}{6})$

Compute to five decimal places. See Example 5.

33. sec 15°
34. csc 75°
35. cot 68.4°
36. sec 118°
37. csc(-130°)
38. cot(-207°)
39. sec .25
40. sec .49
41. cot(-1.96)
42. cot(-2.49)
43. csc 1.05
44. csc 2.22

Find each angle to the nearest hundredth in (a) degrees and (b) radians. See Example 6.

45. Arc Sin .3456
46. Arc Sin .4392
47. Arc Tan 5.6724
48. Arc Tan 3.4141
49. Arc Cos .5423
50. Arc Cos .7145
51. Arc Sin(-.1977)
52. Arc Sin(-.2468)
53. Arc Tan(-4.4130)
54. Arc Tan(=2.6815)
55. Arc Cos(-.2797)
56. Arc Cos(-.7596)

For each value of x, verify that, to five decimal places, sin(Arc sin x) = x, cos(Arc cos x) = x, and tan(Arc tan x) = x. (Hint: Determine the value of the expression in the parentheses first.)

57. x = .92745
58. x = .05677
59. x = -.34784
60. x = -.68310
61. x = .75433
62. x = .80015

For each angle measure x, verify that, to two significant digits, Arc sin(sin x) = x and Arc tan(tan x) = x.

63. 75°
64. 60°
65. .85
66. .44
67. -30°
68. -45°

For each angle measure x, verify that, to the nearest whole number, Arc cos(cos x) = x.

69. 76°
70. 45°
71. 120°
72. 135°

B-8 Computations with Trigonometric Function Values

OBJECTIVE

After completing this section, you should be able to do combined operations that include trigonometric function values.

The operation of computing a trigonometric function value is *unary*; that is, each such operation is performed on *one* number. Thus, when a trigonometric key on a calculator is pressed, the operation is applied only to the number in the display (either a new entry or the result of a previous calculation). Consequently, pressing the [SIN], [COS], or [TAN] keys during a computation will *not* affect any previous calculations. Similar comments apply to the [ARC] [SIN], [ARC] [COS], and [ARC] [TAN] sequences.

The following paragraph is for [=] calculators only. If you have an [ENT] calculator, read only Examples 1c and 2c, and then proceed with the remainder of this section.

On many calculators, trigonometric function values can be entered as any part of a chain calculation; on others they cannot. To test your calculator, set to degree mode and press

4 [×] 30 [SIN] [=]

If your answer is 2 (which is correct), then your calculator can chain trigonometric functions. If your answer to the sequence is not 2, then your calculator does not chain all calculations involving trigonometric functions. For such calculators, commutativity of multiplication can be used on certain simple products to obtain a chain calculation. For example, if you change 4 *sin* 30°* to *sin* 30° × 4, the computation is a chain calculation using the sequence

30 [SIN] [×] 4 [=] → 2

For more complicated calculations, you may have to record intermediate results.

EXAMPLE 1

To three significant digits, 9.37 cos 38° = 7.38, as computed by one of the following sequences. (Set to degree mode.)

a. If your calculator chains trigonometric functions:

9.37 [×] 38 [COS] [=] → 7.3836608

---

*If *A* is a number, then "*A* sin *x*" means "*A* × sin *x*," "*B* cos *x*" means "*B* × cos *x*," and so forth.

b. If your calculator does not chain trigonometric functions, rewrite the product as cos 38° × 9.37. Then,

38 [COS] [×] 9.37 [=] → 7.3836608

c. If you have an [ENT] calculator:

9.37 [ENT] 38 [COS] [×] → 7.3836608

EXAMPLE 2

To three significant digits, $\frac{36.2}{\tan 48°} = 32.6$, as computed by one of the following sequences. (Set to degree mode.)

a. If your calculator chains trigonometric functions:

36.2 [÷] 48 [TAN] [=] → 32.594627

b. If your calculator does not chain trigonometric functions, compute the divisor first, and store it.

48 [TAN] [STO] , 36.2 [÷] [RCL] [=] → 32.594627

c. If you have an [ENT] calculator:

36.2 [ENT] 48 [TAN] [÷] → 32.594627

In the remaining examples of this book we will show sequences that chain trigonometric functions. It is understood that you will use the sequences appropriate to your calculator.

Examples 1 and 2 require a single multiplication or division. Calculations involving trigonometric functions frequently require more than a single operation.

In the following examples, unless specified otherwise we will compute answers to three significant digits, except for angle measures which will be computed to the nearest tenth of a degree or radian.

EXAMPLE 3

$\frac{47.3 \sin 79.6°}{21.5} = 2.16$, as computed by

47.3 [×] 79.6 [SIN] [÷] 21.5 [=] → 2.1638573

or

47.3 [ENT] 79.6 [SIN] [×] 21.5 [÷] → 2.1638573

EXAMPLE 4

$\frac{18 \sin .91}{\sin .65} = 23.5$, as computed by one of the following sequences. (Because no degree symbol appears on the angle measures, set to radian mode.)

18 [×] .91 [SIN] [÷] .65 [SIN] [=] → 23.482132

or

18 [ENT] .91 [SIN] [×] .65 [SIN] [÷] → 23.482132

SEQUENCES WITH THE [ARC] KEY

Recall from Section B-7 that we can use the [ARC] key (or the equivalent key on your calculator) to find the angle associated with a given trigonometric function.

EXAMPLE 5

If $B = \text{Arc tan } \frac{46.8}{9.7}$, find B in (a) degrees and (b) radians. (Round off to the nearest tenth.)

Solutions

a. Set to degree mode. Use one of the sequences

46.8 [÷] 9.7 [=] [ARC] [TAN] → 78.290391

or

46.8 [ENT] 9.7 [÷] [ARC] [TAN] → 78.290391

To the nearest tenth, $B = 78.3°$.

b. Set to radian mode and use one of the sequences of Part a. Verify that, to the nearest tenth, $B = 1.4$.

In Section B-7 we saw that, given a y-value of a trigonometric function, we can use the [ARC] trigonometric sequence to find the associated angle. That is, if N is a y-value and

$$\sin x = N$$

then

$$x = \text{Arc sin } N$$

In some problems the number N may have to be computed first.

EXAMPLE 6

If $\sin C = \dfrac{12.6 \sin 42.5°}{14.4}$, find C to the nearest tenth.

Solution

Think of $\dfrac{12.6 \sin 42.5°}{14.4}$ as N. Then,

$$\sin C = N \quad \text{or} \quad C = \text{Arc} \sin N$$

or

$$C = \text{Arc} \sin \frac{12.6 \sin 42.5°}{14.4}$$

First, compute the quotient (N), then apply the [ARC] [SIN] sequence. (Set to degree mode.)

12.6 [×] 42.5 [SIN] [÷] 14.4 [=] [ARC] [SIN] → 36.23805

or

12.6 [ENT] 42.5 [SIN] [×] 14.4 [÷] [ARC] [SIN] → 36.23805

To the nearest tenth, $C = 36.2°$.

SEQUENCES INVOLVING SQUARES OF NUMBERS

Trigonometric computations often include squares of numbers. For such calculations, the [x^2] key on [=] calculators is particularly useful (see Appendix B). (If your B-TYPE calculator has no such key, do the computations of the following example in steps, recording intermediate results as needed.)

EXAMPLE 7

If $c = \sqrt{4.2^2 + 3.5^2 - 2(4.2)(3.5) \cos 54°}$, find c to the nearest tenth.

Solution

Set to degree mode. Use one of the following sequences.

B-TYPE (First compute the number to be subtracted.)

2 [×] 4.2 [×] 3.5 [×] 54 [COS] [=] [STO], 4.2 [x^2] [+] 3.5 [x^2] [-] [RCL] [=] [$\sqrt{\ }$] → 3.5509314

P-TYPE

4.2 [x^2] [+] 3.5 [x^2] [-] [(] 2 [×] 4.2 [×] 3.5 [×] 54 [COS] [)] [=] [$\sqrt{\ }$] → 3.5509314

H-TYPE

4.2 [x^2] [+] 3.5 [x^2] [=] [-] 2 [×] 4.2 [×] 3.5 [×] 54 [COS] [=] [$\sqrt{\ }$] → 3.5509314

ENT calculators

4.2 ENT ×; 3.5 ENT × +;

2 ENT 4.2 × 3.5 × 54 COS × - √ → 3.5509314

Thus, c = 3.6, to the nearest tenth.

EXERCISE SET B-8

Exercises 1-20, round off to three significant digits.

Compute. See Examples 1 and 2.

1. 25 sin 65°
2. 65 cos 95°
3. 96 cos 15°37'
4. 12.2 tan 117°42'
5. 75 tan .68
6. 34 sin 1.59
7. $\frac{48.3}{\sin 37.2°}$
8. $\frac{68.3}{\cos 15.3°}$
9. $\frac{125}{\cos(-145°53')}$
10. $\frac{247}{\tan(-71°27')}$
11. $\frac{17.6}{\tan(-.74)}$
12. $\frac{31.9}{\sin(-1.68)}$

Compute. See Examples 3 and 4.

13. $\frac{56.2 \sin 87.4°}{33.7}$
14. $\frac{16.9 \sin 152.5°}{13.2}$
15. $\frac{15.5 \tan 18°45'}{42.3}$
16. $\frac{17.7 \tan 23°16'}{27.3}$
17. $\frac{24 \sin .64}{\sin .23}$
18. $\frac{86 \sin .98}{\sin .16}$
19. $\frac{68.3 \cos(-1.17)}{\tan(.83)}$
20. $\frac{75.2 \tan(-2.36)}{\cos(1.66)}$

In Exercises 21-28, each expression represents an angle B. Compute angle B in (a) degrees and (b) radians. Round off to the nearest tenth. See Examples 5 and 6.

21. Arc cos $\frac{16.7}{21.4}$
22. Arc cos $\frac{41.9}{62.5}$
23. Arc tan $\frac{32.4}{18.2}$
24. Arc tan $\frac{43.6}{33.7}$
25. Arc sin $\frac{15.3 \sin 48.2°}{16.3}$
26. Arc sin $\frac{37.7 \sin 112.7°}{56.5}$
27. Arc cos $\frac{75.3 \tan(-.56)}{127.6}$
28. Arc cos $\frac{55.5 \tan(-1.33)}{245.8}$

Compute to the nearest tenth. See Example 7.

29. $\sqrt{3.2^2 + 6.8^2 - 2(3.2)(6.8) \cos 37°}$
30. $\sqrt{7.3^2 + 4.1^2 - 2(7.3)(4.1) \cos 100°}$
31. $\sqrt{1.9^2 + 2.7^2 - 2(1.9)(2.7) \cos .65}$
32. $\sqrt{12.3^2 + 10.5^2 - 2(12.3)(10.5) \cos .96}$
33. $\sqrt{5.7^2 + 6.9^2 - 2(5.7)(6.9) \cos 56°28'}$
34. $\sqrt{3.7^2 + 7.3^2 - 2(3.7)(7.3) \cos 42°17'}$

In Exercises 35-38, compute to the nearest thousand. The distance, R, (in miles) between the sun and the planet Mercury is given by

$$R = \frac{3.442 \times 10^7}{1 - .206 \cos \theta}$$

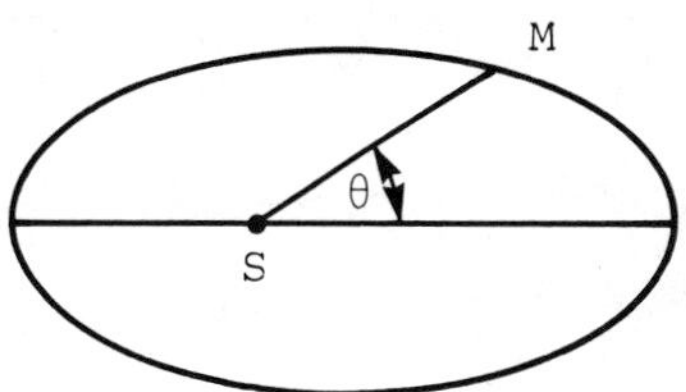

35. Find R for $\theta = \frac{\pi}{6}$.

36. Find R for $\theta = \frac{\pi}{3}$.

37. Find R for $\theta = 0$. (This is the greatest distance between Mercury and the sun.)

38. Find R for $\theta = \pi$. (This is the least distance between Mercury and the sun.)

B-9 Right Triangle Trigonometry

OBJECTIVES

After completing this section, you should be able to

1. Find the measure of one acute angle of a right triangle when the measure of the other acute angle is known.
2. Use trigonometric ratios to find the length of a side, or the measure of an acute angle, of a right triangle.
3. Use the Pythagorean rule to find the length of a side of a right triangle if the lengths of the other two sides are known.

A *right triangle* is a triangle with one *right* angle (90°). The other two angles are *acute* angles (angle measure between 0° and 90°). Throughout this section we will use A, B, C, and a, b, c to denote the angles and sides of right triangles, as indicated in Figure B-9.1. Capital letters A and B name—and represent the measures of—the acute angles of triangle ABC. Lowercase letters a and b name—and represent the lengths of—the sides *opposite* angles A and B, respectively. The letter c names—and represents the length of—the *hypotenuse* (the side opposite right angle C). Side a is said to be *adjacent* to angle B; side b is said to be *adjacent* to angle A. Under the heading Right Triangle Trigonometry we consider methods for computing lengths of sides and measures of angles of right triangles.

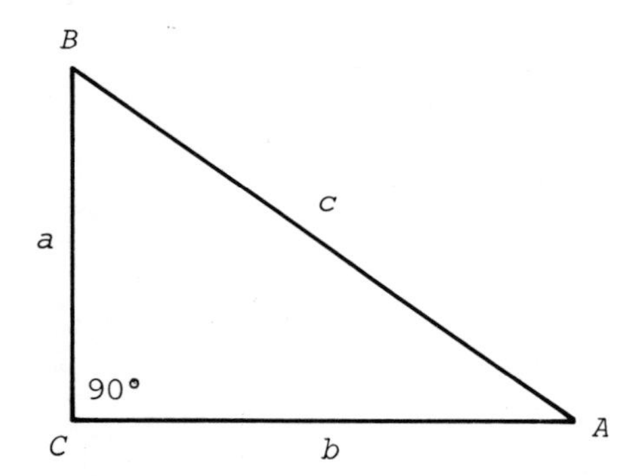

FIGURE B-9.1

Given the measure of one acute angle of a right triangle, we can find the measure of the other acute angle of the triangle by using a concept from geometry: "The acute angles of a right triangle are *complementary*"; that is, the sum of the measures of the acute angles is 90°.

EXAMPLE 1

In right triangle ABC, angles A and B are complementary. If $A = 32.8°$, then

$$32.8° + B = 90°$$

$$B = (90 - 32.8)° = 57.2°$$

TRIGONOMETRIC RATIOS

The acute angles of a right triangle are related to the sides and hypotenuse of the triangle by the sine, cosine, and tangent functions, as follows (see Figure B-9.1):

$$\sin A = \frac{\text{side opposite } A}{\text{hypotenuse}} \quad \text{or} \quad \sin A = \frac{a}{c} \tag{1}$$

$$\cos A = \frac{\text{side adjacent to } A}{\text{hypotenuse}} \quad \text{or} \quad \cos A = \frac{b}{c} \tag{2}$$

$$\tan A = \frac{\text{side opposite } A}{\text{side adjacent to } A} \quad \text{or} \quad \tan A = \frac{a}{b} \tag{3}$$

$$\sin B = \frac{\text{side opposite } B}{\text{hypotenuse}} \quad \text{or} \quad \sin B = \frac{b}{c} \tag{4}$$

$$\cos B = \frac{\text{side adjacent to } B}{\text{hypotenuse}} \quad \text{or} \quad \cos B = \frac{a}{c} \tag{5}$$

$$\tan B = \frac{\text{side opposite } B}{\text{side adjacent to } B} \quad \text{or} \quad \tan B = \frac{b}{a} \tag{6}$$

We shall refer to the right-hand equations listed above as *trigonometric ratios*.

Trigonometric ratios can be used to find the length of a side of a right triangle. In general, unless specified otherwise we shall *find lengths of sides of triangles to as many significant digits as in the length of the side with the least number of significant digits*.

EXAMPLE 2

a. If 12 cm is the given length of a side of a triangle, the other two sides are computed to two significant digits.

b. If 12.2 cm and 14.60 cm are the given lengths of two sides of a triangle, the third side is computed to three significant digits (12.2 has three significant digits).

EXAMPLE 3

In right triangle *ABC*, find sides *a* and *c*.

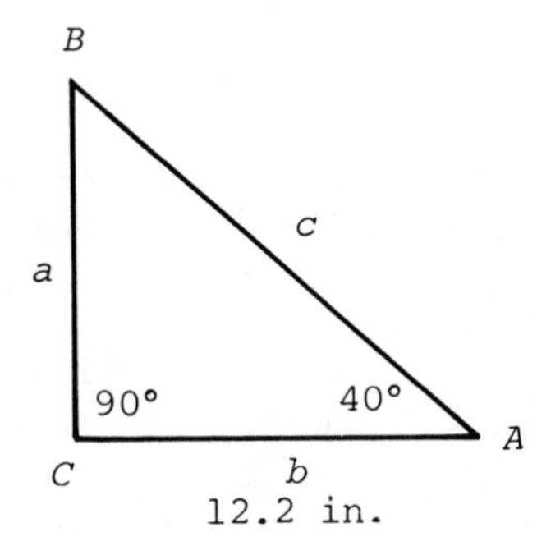

FIGURE B-9.2

Solutions

a. Note that side a is *opposite* angle A and the 12.2-in. side is *adjacent* to angle A. Hence, use the tangent ratio (3):

$$\tan A = \frac{a}{b} \longleftrightarrow \tan 40.0° = \frac{a}{12.2}$$

$$a = 12.2 \tan 40.0° = 10.237016$$

To three significant digits, $a = 10.2$ in.

b. Note that side c is the *hypotenuse* and the 12.2-in. side is *adjacent* to angle A. Hence, use the cosine ratio (2):

$$\cos A = \frac{b}{c} \longleftrightarrow \cos 40.0° = \frac{12.2}{c}$$

$$c = \frac{12.2}{\cos 40.0°} = 15.925969$$

To three significant digits, $c = 15.9$ in.

Trigonometric ratios can also be used to find the measure of an angle of a triangle. Because the length of a side and the measure of an angle of a triangle are measurements, they are approximate numbers. We shall use the following rule to relate the precision of the measure of an angle of a triangle to the number of significant digits in the lengths of the sides of the triangle.

Table B-9.1

Least number of significant digits in lengths of sides	Round off angle measure to the nearest
two	whole degree
three	tenth of a degree
four	hundredth of a degree
five	thousandth of a degree

EXAMPLE 4

Refer to Table B-9.1.

a. If 8.6, 9.21, and 12.45 are the lengths of three sides of a triangle, round off a computed angle measure to the nearest whole degree. (The least number of significant digits is *two*.)

b. If 8.6000, 9.21, and 12.456 are the lengths of three sides of a triangle, round off a computed angle measure to the nearest tenth of a degree. (The least number of significant digits is *three*.)

If a problem does not include a figure, it is helpful to sketch and label a figure with the given information. Use the notation of Figure B-9.1.

EXAMPLE 5

In right triangle *ABC*, if a = 8.40 cm and b = 4.90 cm, compute angle A.

Solution

Sketch and label triangle *ABC* as shown. Note that the 4.90 cm side is *adjacent* to angle A, and the 8.40 cm side is *opposite* angle A. Hence, choose the tangent ratio (3):

$$\tan A = \frac{a}{b} \longleftrightarrow \tan A = \frac{8.40}{4.90} = 1.7142857$$

$$A = \text{Arc tan } 1.7142857$$

$$A = 59.7436°$$

To the nearest tenth, A = 59.7°.

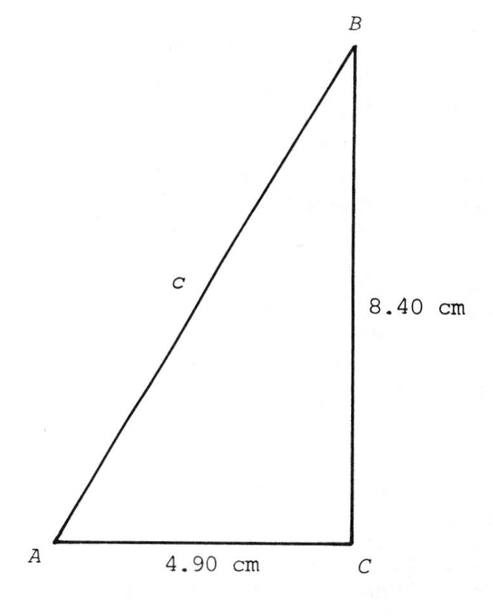

FIGURE B-9.3

THE PYTHAGOREAN RULE

The following relationship between the lengths (a, b, and c) of the sides of a right triangle, called the *Pythagorean rule* (or theorem), has been known for at least 2000 years.

$$c^2 = a^2 + b^2 \tag{7}$$

The following three formulas are derived from Equation (7).

$$c = \sqrt{a^2 + b^2}, \qquad a = \sqrt{c^2 - b^2}, \qquad b = \sqrt{c^2 - a^2}$$

These formulas enable us to find the length of one of the sides of a right triangle if we know the lengths of the other two sides.

EXAMPLE 6

In a right triangle, if a = 8.60 yd and b = 11.2 yd, find the length, c, of the hypotenuse.

Solution

Choose the formula that enables you to solve for c. Substitute appropriately, and compute.

$$c = \sqrt{a^2 + b^2} = \sqrt{8.6^2 + 11.2^2} = 14.120906$$

To three significant digits, c = 14.1 yd.

APPLICATIONS

Right triangle trigonometry can be used to solve many different types of applied problems.

EXAMPLE 7

A ladder 17.4 ft long rests against a wall. The foot of the ladder is 8.5 ft from the base of the wall. At what distance from the ground does the top of the ladder touch the wall?

Solution

Let a represent the required length. Draw and label a figure, as shown. Sides b and c are given. Hence, choose the formula that enables you to solve for a:

$$a = \sqrt{c^2 - b^2} = \sqrt{17.4^2 - 8.5^2} = 15.182555$$

Round off to two significant digits. The ladder touches the wall 15 ft up from the ground.

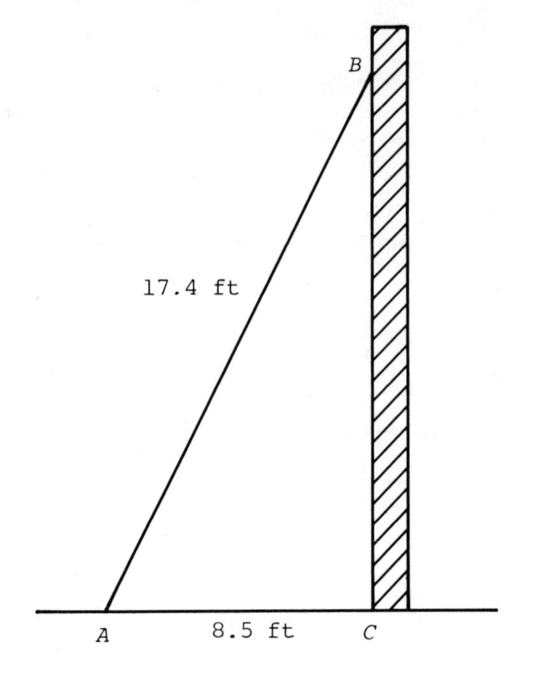

FIGURE B-9.4

EXAMPLE 8

A steel cable is to be tied from point A on the ground to point B at the top of a tower. A surveyor determines that point A is 113 ft from the base C of the tower, and $A = 73.1°$. If cable is sold only in whole numbers of feet, find the least number of feet of cable needed.

Solution

Note that the 113-ft side is *adjacent* to angle A and the required side c is the *hypotenuse*. Hence, choose the cosine ratio (2):

$$\cos A = \frac{b}{c} \longleftrightarrow \cos 73.1° = \frac{113}{c}$$

$$c = \frac{113}{\cos 73.1°} = 388.71421$$

The least amount of cable needed is 389 ft.

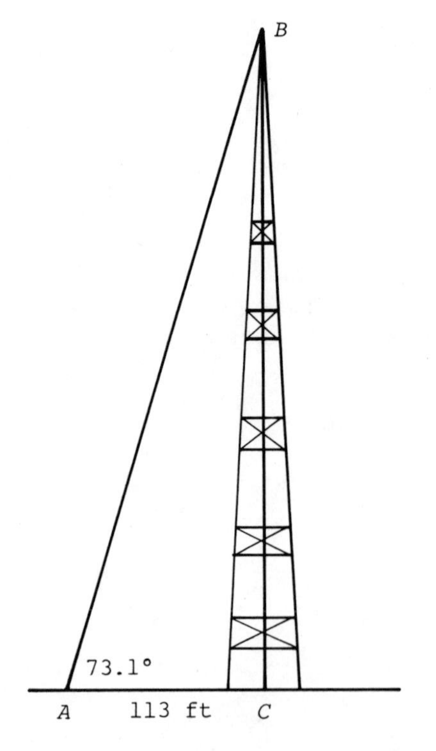

FIGURE B-9.5

EXERCISE SET B-9

Given the measure of one acute angle of a right triangle, find the measure of the other one. See Example 1.

1. $A = 73.4°$ 2. $B = 25.9°$ 3. $A = 42.3°$
4. $B = 17.1°$ 5. $A = 68.5°$ 6. $B = 81.6°$

Given the lengths of two sides of a triangle, specify the number of significant digits to which the third side is to be computed. See Example 2.

7. 25, 194 8. 47, 631 9. 25.0, 194.0 10. 47.0, 631.0
11. 8.4, 26.3 12. 19.5, 7.3 13. 1.0606, 1.080 14. 3.741, 3.8600

Find the length of each required side of right triangle *ABC*. Round off answers according to the rule illustrated in Example 2. See Example 3.

15. If $B = 42.6°$ and $c = 21.5$ ft, find (a) side b and (b) side a.
16. If $A = 67.4°$ and $c = 6.4$ in., find (a) side a and (b) side b.
17. If $A = 25.6°$ and $a = 17.1$ cm, find (a) side b and (b) side c.
18. If $B = 76.9°$ and $b = 35.6$ mm, find (a) side c and (b) side a.

Given the three sides of a triangle, specify the number of places to which an angle measure of the triangle is to be computed. See Table B-9.1 and Example 4.

19. 3.12, 4.0, 5.123 20. 3.0, 4.0, 5.00 21. 1123, 2000.8, 1917.24
22. 13.00, 14.123, 24.30 23. 1123.0, 2000.8, 1917.24 24. 123.45, 141.310, 200.94

In degrees, find (a) angle A and (b) angle B of right triangle *ABC*. See Examples 3 and 4.

25. If $a = 1.8$ yd and $b = 6.5$ yd, find (a) A and (b) B.
26. If $a = 6.2$ ft and $c = 9.6$ ft, find (a) A and (b) B.
27. If $b = 25$ cm and $c = 31$ cm, find (a) A and (b) B.
28. If $a = 35$ mm and $b = 98$ mm, find (a) A and (b) B.
29. If $a = 13.7$ in. and $c = 29.9$ in., find (a) A and (b) B.
30. If $a = 68.4$ mi and $c = 70.6$ mi, find (a) A and (b) B.

Find the length of the required side of right triangle *ABC*. See Examples 4 and 2.

31. $a = 12$ ft, $b = 18$ ft, $c = ?$ 32. $a = 72$ ft, $b = 25$ ft, $c = ?$
33. $b = 16.43$ m, $c = 29.86$ m, $a = ?$ 34. $b = 75.64$ cm, $c = 121.42$ cm, $a = ?$
35. $a = .56$ in., $c = .94$ in., $b = ?$ 36. $a = .19$ yd, $c = .33$ yd, $b = ?$

Solve each problem. See Examples 2, 4, 7, and 8.

37. A gate 4.3 ft wide and 6.4 ft high needs a brace between opposite corners. How long must the brace be?

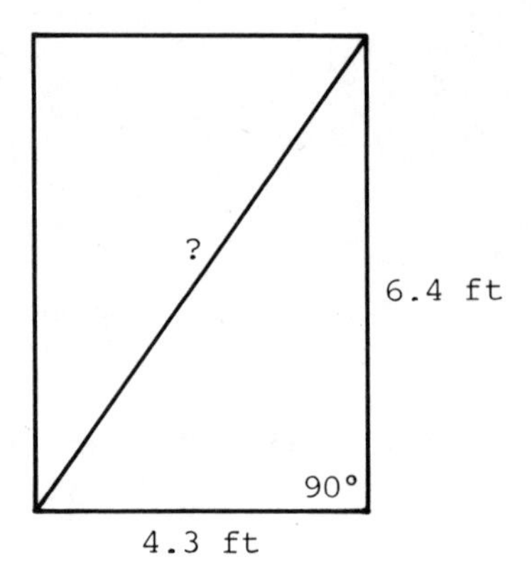

38. Solve Exercise 37 if the gate is 5.1 ft wide and 7.4 ft high.

39. At a distance of 46.0 ft from the base of a tower, the angle of elevation to the top of the tower is measured to be 68.9°. What is the height of the tower?

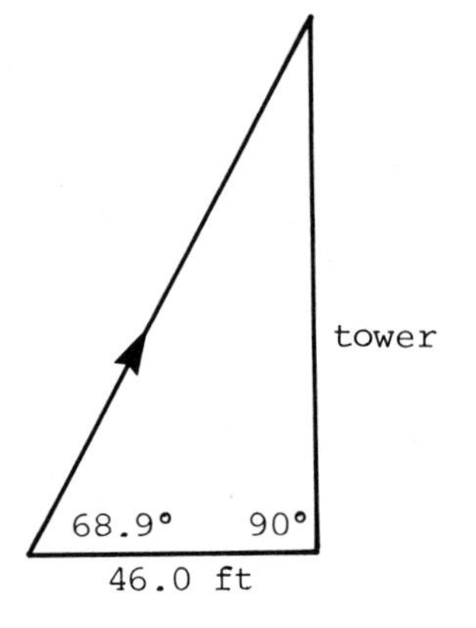

40. Solve Exercise 39 if, at a distance of 75.0 ft from the base of the tower, the angle of elevation to the top of the tower is 50.9°.

41. From the edge of a vertical cliff 96.8 yd high, the angle formed by the line of sight to the nearest point of an island in a lake and the face of the cliff, is measured to be 78.4°. How far is the island from the foot of the cliff?

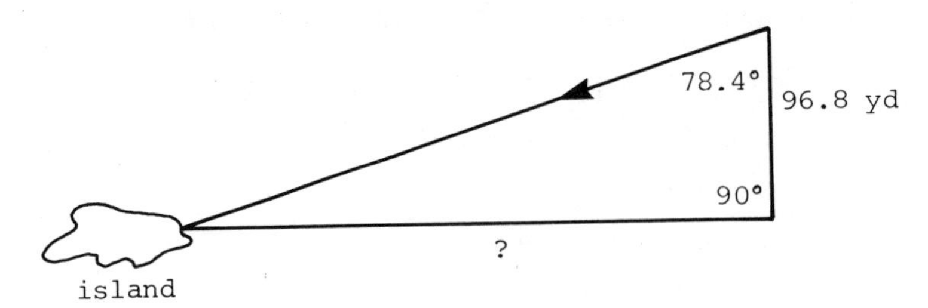

42. Solve Exercise 41 if the cliff is 68.6 yd high and the measured angle is 69.8°.

43. Two airplanes leave an airport at the same moment, one flying east, the other flying south. If the airplane flying east averages 352 mph and the airplane flying south averages 427 mph, how far apart are they after one hour?

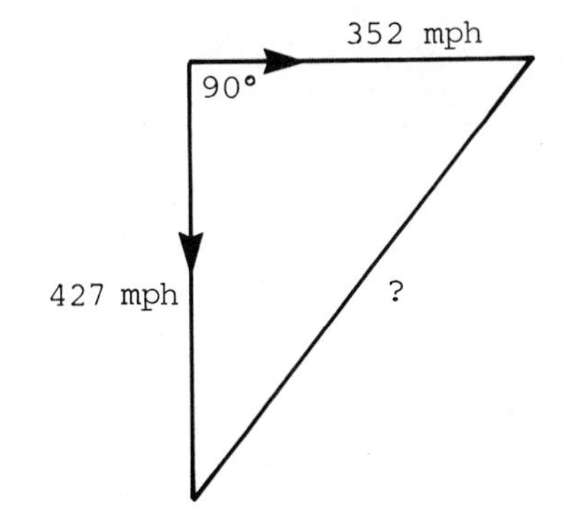

44. Solve Exercise 43 if the airplane flying east averages 415 mph and the airplane heading south averages 572 mph.

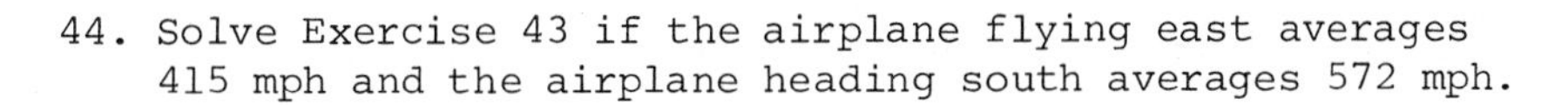

45. After crossing a straight river 257 yd wide, it is intended that a boat land at a point *P* directly across from its starting point *A*. However, the current causes the boat to land at a point *B*, 25.5 yd downstream from the intended landing point. What was the drift angle? How far did the boat actually travel?

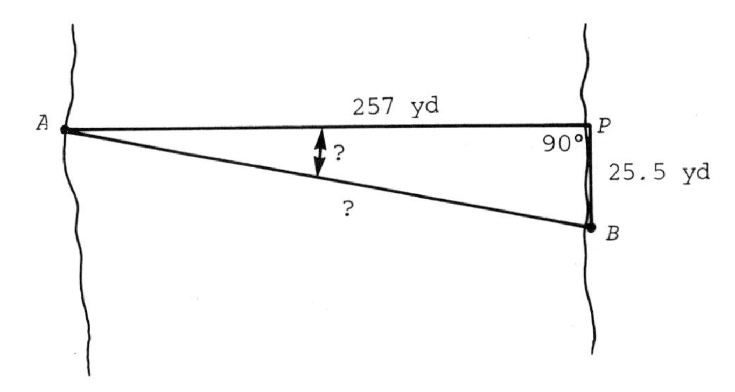

46. Solve Exercise 45 if the river is 798 ft wide and the boat lands at a point 92.6 ft downstream from the intended landing point, *P*.

B-10 Law of Sines, Law of Cosines

OBJECTIVES

After completing this section, you should be able to

1. Find the measure of an angle of a triangle, given the other two angles.
2. Use the law of sines to find the measure of an angle or the length of a side of a triangle.
3. Use the law of cosines to find the measure of an angle or the length of a side of a triangle.

In this section we will consider three rules that enable us to find the length of a side or the measure of an angle of a triangle. Throughout this section and in Exercise Set B-10, we will use the notation indicated in Figure B-10.1. This notation is the same as that introduced in Section B-9, except that angle C is not necessarily a right angle.

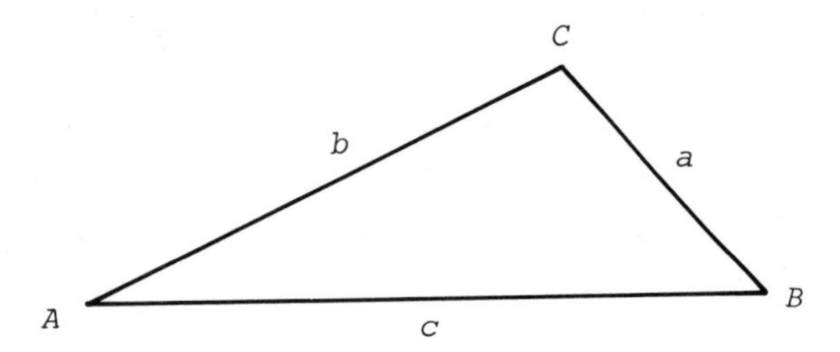

FIGURE B-10.1

The round-off rules introduced in Section B-9 are followed in the examples of this section.

1. *For the length of a side*: Round off to as many significant digits as in the length of the side with the least number of significant digits.
2. *For the measure of an angle*: See Table B-9.1, page 128.

SUM OF THE ANGLES OF A TRIANGLE

The first of the three rules states that "The sum of the measures of the angles of a triangle is 180° or π radians."

EXAMPLE 1

Find the third angle of a triangle (to the nearest hundredth of a degree or radian) if

a. $A = 82.67°$, $B = 39.51°$

b. $B = 1.21$, $C = .83$

Solutions

a. $C = (180 - 82.67 - 39.51)° = 57.82°$

b. $A = \pi - 1.21 - .83 = 1.1015927$

$A = 1.10$, to the nearest hundredth of a radian.

LAW OF SINES

The second of the three rules is called the *law of sines:*

$$\frac{a}{\sin A} = \frac{b}{\sin B} = \frac{c}{\sin C} \tag{1}$$

In a given problem we choose whichever two of the three fractions of Equation (1) form an equation in which *three* of the four terms are known. The law of sines may be used to find the length of a side or the measure of an angle of a triangle.

EXAMPLE 2

In a triangle, if $b = 4.610$ yd, $B = 26.25°$, and $A = 83.07°$, use the law of sines to find side a.

Solution

Because b, B, and A are given, select the two fractions that involve b, B, and A:

$$\frac{a}{\sin A} = \frac{b}{\sin B}$$

Substitute 4.610 for b, 26.25° for B, 83.07° for A, and solve for a. (Set to degree mode.)

$$\frac{a}{\sin 83.07°} = \frac{4.610}{\sin 26.25°} \longleftrightarrow a = \frac{\sin 83.07° \times 4.610}{\sin 26.25°} = 10.346909$$

To four significant digits, $a = 10.35$ yd.

EXAMPLE 3

In a triangle, if $b = 20.70$ cm, $B = 83.08°$, and $c = 19.68$ cm, use the law of sines to find angle C.

Solution

Because b, B, and c are given, select the two fractions that involve b, B, and c:

$$\frac{b}{\sin B} = \frac{c}{\sin C}$$

Substitute 20.70 for b, 83.08° for B, and 19.68 for c. (Set to degree mode.) Solve first for sin C, then for C.

$$\frac{20.70}{\sin 83.08°} = \frac{19.68}{\sin C} \longleftrightarrow \sin C = \frac{\sin 83.08° \times 19.68}{20.70}$$

$$\sin C = .94379894$$

Then,

$$C = \text{Arc } \sin .94379894 = 70.699651°$$

To the nearest hundredth of a degree, $C = 70.70°$.

LAW OF COSINES

The third rule is called the *law of cosines*, in any of the forms

$$a^2 = b^2 + c^2 - 2bc \cos A \tag{2}$$

$$b^2 = a^2 + c^2 - 2ac \cos B \tag{3}$$

$$c^2 = a^2 + b^2 - 2ab \cos C \tag{4}$$

Each of these equations may be used to find the length of a side of a triangle. In a particular problem, we choose the equation that has the desired length (a, b, or c) on the left-hand side. Because each equation leads to the *square* of the required length, the computation is completed by taking the *square root* of the right-hand side of the equation. (You may want to read Appendix A.)

EXAMPLE 4

In a triangle, if $a = 4.61$ m, $b = 10.35$ m, and $C = 70.68°$, use the law of cosines to find side c.

Solution

Because c is required, choose Equation (4):

$$c^2 = a^2 + b^2 - 2ab \cos C$$

Substitute 4.61 for a, 10.35 for b, 70.68° for C and set to degree mode.

$$c^2 = 4.61^2 + 10.35^2 - 2(4.61)(10.35)\cos 70.68°$$

$$c = 9.8388601$$

To three significant digits, $c = 9.84$ m.

The law of cosines is also used to solve for the measure of an angle of a triangle. The following equations are derived from Equations (2), (3), and (4), respectively.

$$\cos A = \frac{b^2 + c^2 - a^2}{2bc} \tag{5}$$

$$\cos B = \frac{a^2 + c^2 - b^2}{2ac} \tag{6}$$

$$\cos C = \frac{a^2 + b^2 - c^2}{2ab} \qquad (7)$$

Because each of these equations leads to the *cosine* of the required angle, the computation is completed by taking the *Arc cosine* of the answer.

EXAMPLE 5

In a triangle, if a = 9.32 ft, b = 7.92 ft, and c = 10.62 ft, use the law of cosines to find angle C.

Solution

Because angle C is required, select Equation (7):

$$\cos C = \frac{a^2 + b^2 - c^2}{2ab}$$

Substitute 9.32 for a, 7.92 for b, 10.62 for c, and compute cos C.

$$\cos C = \frac{9.32^2 + 7.92^2 - 10.62^2}{2(9.32)(7.92)} = .24930366$$

Then, set to degree mode, and

$$C = \text{Arc cos } .24930366 = 75.56369°$$

To the nearest tenth, C = 75.6°.

EXERCISE SET B-10

The notation used in this exercise set is that shown in triangle *ABC*.

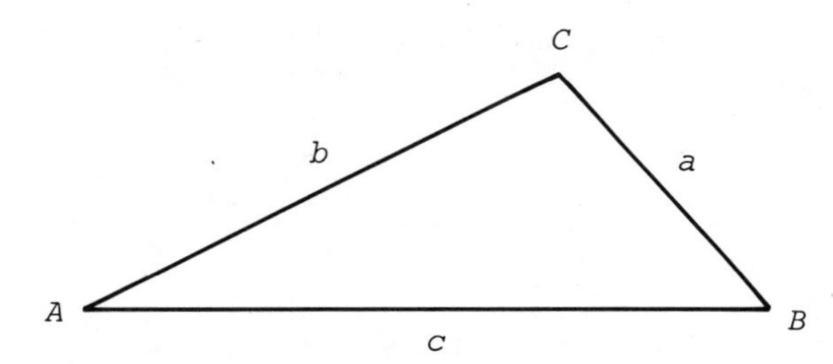

Find the measure of the third angle of each triangle. See Example 1.

1. A = 62.18°, B = 35.38°
2. A = 56.27°, B = 45.66°
3. A = 98.65°, C = 54.07°
4. A = 85.69°, C = 62.54°
5. B = 16°24', C = 75°34'
6. B = 25°45', C = 80°42'
7. A = 1.86, B = .64
8. A = 1.47, B = .96
9. A = 1.05, C = 1.16
10. A = 1.27, C = 1.15

In each of the following exercises, unless otherwise stated, round off each answer according to the round-off rules given in Section B-9.

For each triangle, use the law of sines to find (a) the length of the required side and (b) the measure of the third angle. See Example 2.

11. Find b if $a = 5.320$ ft, $A = 20.62°$, and $B = 75.43°$.
12. Find c if $a = 32.56$ in., $A = 26.67°$, and $C = 81.83°$.
13. Find a if $c = 58.45$ cm, $C = 98.34°$, and $A = 37.43°$.
14. Find a if $b = 1.91$ m, $A = 111.58°$, and $B = 6.08°$.
15. Find c if $a = 1.42$ m, $A = 35.67°$, and $C = 91.5°$.
16. Find b if $c = 76.85$ cm, $B = 62.25°$, and $C = 34.17°$.

For each triangle, (a) use the law of sines to find the measure of the required angle and (b) find the measure of the third angle. See Example 3.

For Exercises 17-22, set to degree mode.

17. Find A if $a = 12.15$ cm, $b = 15.32$ cm, and $B = 34.55°$.
18. Find A if $a = 3.25$ m, $c = 5.62$ m, and $C = 68.1°$.
19. Find B if $c = 18.7$ yd, $b = 10.5$ yd, and $C = 106.8°$.
20. Find B if $b = 24.64$ ft, $a = 53.62$ ft, and $A = 112.33°$.
21. Find C if $c = 16$ in., $b = 16.5$ in., and $B = 32.1°$.
22. Find C if $c = 74$ mm, $a = 94$ mm, and $A = 42.9°$.

Use the law of cosines to find the length of the required side of each triangle. See Example 4.

23. Find a if $b = 4.0$ in., $c = 3.5$ in., and $A = 71°$.
24. Find a if $b = 16$ mm, $c = 10$ mm, and $A = 85°$.
25. Find b if $a = 17.4$ cm, $c = 12.7$ cm, and $B = 8.6°$.
26. Find b if $a = 28.9$ in., $c = 53.4$ in., and $B = 12.9°$.
27. Find c if $b = 20.625$ in., $a = 16.375$ in., and $C = 105.5°$.
28. Find c if $b = 9.08$ ft, $a = 21.42$ ft, and $C = 118.6°$.

In Exercises 29-32, use the law of cosines to find the measure of each of the three angles of the given triangle. See Example 5. (Check your results by noting how "close" the sum of the three angle measures is to 180°.)

29. In a triangle with $a = 5$ m, $b = 9$ m, and $c = 7$ m, find A, B, and C, to the nearest tenth of a degree.
30. In a triangle with $a = 7.48$ cm, $b = 7.00$ cm, and $c = 5.00$ cm, find A, B, and C, to the nearest tenth of a degree.
31. In a triangle with $a = 1.2$ cm, $b = 9.0$ cm, and $c = 10$ cm, find A, B, and C in degree-minute form, to the nearest minute.
32. In a triangle with $a = 2.7$ ft, $b = 5.1$ ft, and $c = 4.4$ ft, find A, B, and C in degree-minute form, to the nearest minute.

B-11 Graphing Trigonometric and Inverse Trigonometric Functions

---

OBJECTIVES

After completing this section, you should be able to

1. Write calculator sequences for computations involving trigonometric and inverse trigonometric functions.
2. Draw graphs of trigonometric and inverse trigonometric functions.

In this section we shall use *radian* measure only. Set your calculator accordingly. In Section B-1 we stated that if the same set of calculations is to be repeated with different numbers, it is helpful to write and check a calculator sequence for this purpose. For repeated computations involving trigonometric functions, writing sequences is even more useful.

In Section B-8 we stated that when a trigonometric key on a calculator is pressed, the resulting operation is applied only to the number in the display (either a new entry or the result of a previous computation). Consequently, pressing the [SIN], [COS], [TAN] keys (or sequences that involve the [ARC] key) will *not* affect any previous calculations.

Let us see how we use this property when planning calculator sequences for trigonometric functions. Consider the expression

$$8 + \sin 2 \tag{1}$$

which can be viewed more simply as

$$8 + A$$

where A represents the number *sin* 2. Because the sequence 2 [SIN] has no effect on any previous entries, we can compute Expression (1) by one of the sequences (radian mode)

8 [+] 2 [SIN] [=] or 8 [ENT] 2 [SIN] [+]

You can verify that the result is 8.90930, to five decimal places.

We often have to compute trigonometric function values of a number N, where N is in a form that requires separate calculations. For example, we may want to compute sin $2x$ (note that N is equal to $2x$). In such cases, the computations required to compute N must be completed *before* pressing a trigonometric key. Thus, one of the following sequences can be used for sin $2x$:

2 [×] x [=] [SIN] or 2 [ENT] x [×] [SIN]

EXAMPLE 1

Write a calculator sequence for the expression

$$\sin 2x + \cos x$$

Solution

View the given expression as

$$A + B$$

where A equals $\sin 2x$ and B equals $\cos x$.

a. For [=] calculators: a sequence for A is 2 [×] x [=] [SIN]; a sequence for B is x [COS]. The two sequences can be "chained" by the [+] key to obtain

2 [×] x [=] [SIN] [+] x [COS] [=]

b. For [ENT] calculators: a sequence for A is 2 [ENT] x [×] [SIN]; a sequence for B is x [COS]. The two sequences can be "chained" as

2 [ENT] x [×] [SIN] x [COS] [+]

Check: For checking trigonometric sequences in radian mode, 1 is a convenient replacement. Replace x by 1. Then

$$\sin(2 \times 1) + \cos 1 = .90929742 + .54030231$$

$$= 1.4495997$$

For $x = 1$, either of the sequences shown above gives the same result, 1.4495997. (Use a sequence appropriate for your calculator to verify this result.)

EXAMPLE 2

To obtain a sequence for computing values of

$$\tan \frac{x}{2} - 4 \sin x$$

think of $\tan \frac{x}{2}$ as the number A, $\sin x$ as the number B, and the given expression as

$$A - 4B$$

Some suggested sequences are:

B-TYPE: x [SIN] [×] 4 [=] [STO], x [÷] 2 [=] [TAN] [-] [RCL] [=]

P-TYPE: x [÷] 2 [=] [TAN] [-] [(] 4 [×] x [SIN] [)] [=]

H-TYPE: x [÷] 2 [=] [TAN] [-] x [SIN] [×] 4 [=]

[ENT] calculators: x [ENT] 2 [÷] [TAN], 4 [ENT] x [SIN] [×] [-]

Check: Replace x by 1. Then

$$\tan \frac{1}{2} - 4 \sin 1 = .5463025 - 3.3658839$$

$$= -2.8195814$$

(Use a sequence appropriate to your calculator to verify this result.)

When planning calculator sequences for your calculator, it is not always essential to obtain chain calculations. The important idea is to have correct sequences—even if they call for recording intermediate results. (Of course, skill in writing chain calculations can be developed by practice.)

GRAPHING TRIGONOMETRIC FUNCTIONS

The graphing techniques introduced in Section B-2 can be used when drawing graphs of trigonometric functions.

1. Compute a table of ordered pairs. (Write calculator sequences as needed.)
2. Plot the point corresponding to each ordered pair, and draw a smooth curve through the resulting points.

The following examples will show an equation, a table, and a graph. The y-values in the table have been rounded off to the nearest hundredth. As you study the examples, you should verify the y-values shown in the tables.

For the graphs of some trigonometric functions, we frequently use x-values that include π as a factor. For such graphs, a convenient choice of scale on the x-axis is 12 squares to equal π units (1 square equal to $\frac{\pi}{12}$ unit). Then, because $\frac{\pi}{6}$ equals $2(\frac{\pi}{12})$, we have that $\frac{\pi}{6}$ corresponds to 2 squares; because $\frac{\pi}{3}$ equals $4(\frac{\pi}{12})$, we have that $\frac{\pi}{3}$ corresponds to 4 squares, and so forth.

EXAMPLE 3

$y = \sin x$, from $x = 0$ to $x = 2\pi$. (See page 142 for the graph.)

x	0	$\frac{\pi}{6}$	$\frac{\pi}{4}$	$\frac{\pi}{3}$	$\frac{\pi}{2}$	$\frac{2\pi}{3}$	$\frac{3\pi}{4}$	$\frac{5\pi}{6}$	π
y	0	.50	.71	.87	1.00	.87	.71	.50	0

x	$\frac{7\pi}{6}$	$\frac{5\pi}{4}$	$\frac{4\pi}{3}$	$\frac{3\pi}{2}$	$\frac{5\pi}{3}$	$\frac{7\pi}{4}$	$\frac{11\pi}{6}$	2π
y	-.50	-.71	-.87	-1.0	-.87	-.71	-.50	0

(x-scale: 1 sq = $\frac{\pi}{12}$ unit, y-scale: 10 sq = 1 unit)

You probably would not need a written calculator sequence for the calculations required in Example 3. For the next example, however, a calculator sequence is worthwhile.

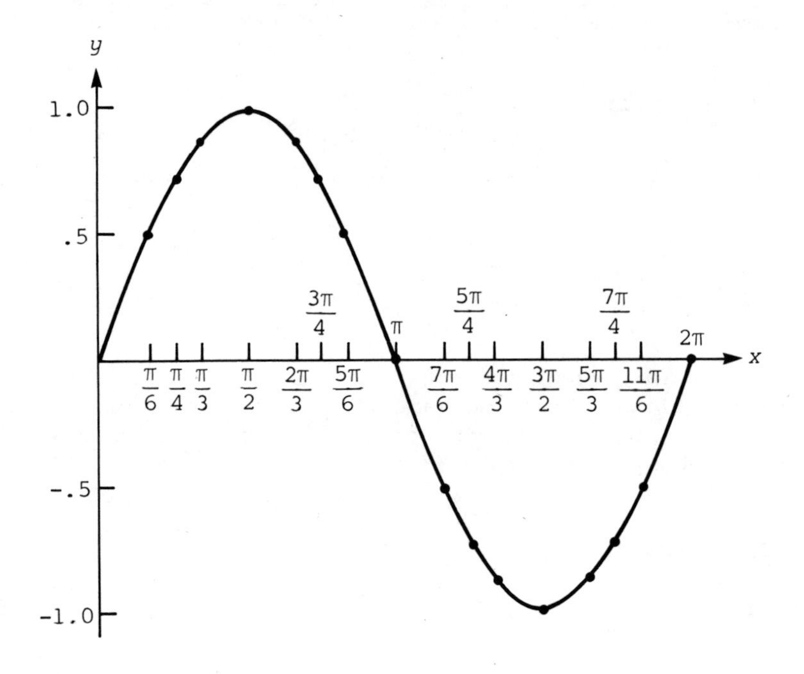

Figure B-11.1

EXAMPLE 4

$y = 2 \sin x + \cos x$, from $x = 0$ to $x = 4.5$. Use intervals of .25 for x-values.

x	0	.25	.5	.75	1	1.25	1.5	1.75	2	2.25
y	1	1.46	1.84	2.09	2.22	2.21	2.07	1.79	1.40	.93

x	2.5	2.75	3	3.25	3.5	3.75	4	4.25	4.5
y	.40	-.16	-.71	-1.21	-1.64	-1.96	-2.17	-2.24	-2.17

(x-scale: 4 sq = 1 unit, y-scale: 10 sq = 1 unit)

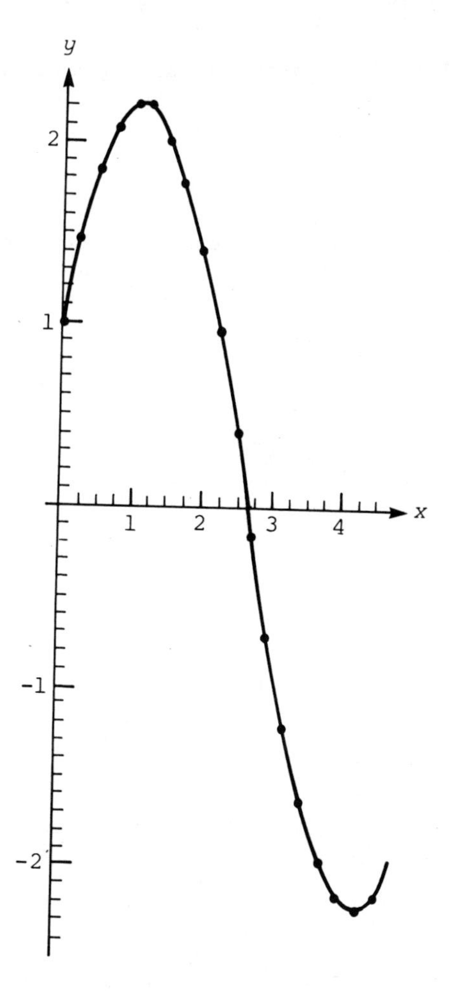

FIGURE B-11.2

GRAPHING INVERSE TRIGONOMETRIC FUNCTIONS

In Section B-7 we computed angles associated with expressions such as

$$\text{Arc sin } .89725$$

More generally, the equations

$$y = \text{Arc sin } x \quad \text{and} \quad y = \text{Arc cos } x$$

(read "y equals arc sine x" and "y equals arc cosine x") are said to define the *inverse sine function* and the *inverse cosine function*, respectively. There is a special restriction on the x-values for these two inverse trigonometric functions. Set your calculator to radian mode, press the sequence 2 [ARC] [SIN], then clear your calculator and press the sequence 2 [+/-] [ARC] [SIN]. In each case, note that the display shows an error signal. This results from the fact that y-values for the inverse sine and inverse cosine functions can be computed only for x-values from -1 to +1, inclusive. Thus, *when you check a calculator sequence that involves either Arc sin or Arc cos,* you must *choose a number between -1 and +1* as a replacement for x. (A convenient choice is .5.)

The graphing techniques used in the preceding examples can also be used for graphing inverse trigonometric functions.

EXAMPLE 5

Draw the graph of the inverse cosine function, y = Arc cos x, from $x = -1$ to $x = 1$. Use intervals of .25 unit.

x	-1	-.75	-.5	-.25	0	.25	.5	.75	1
y	3.14	2.42	2.09	1.82	1.57	1.32	1.05	.72	0

(x-scale: 4 sq = 1 unit, y-scale: 10 sq = 1 unit)

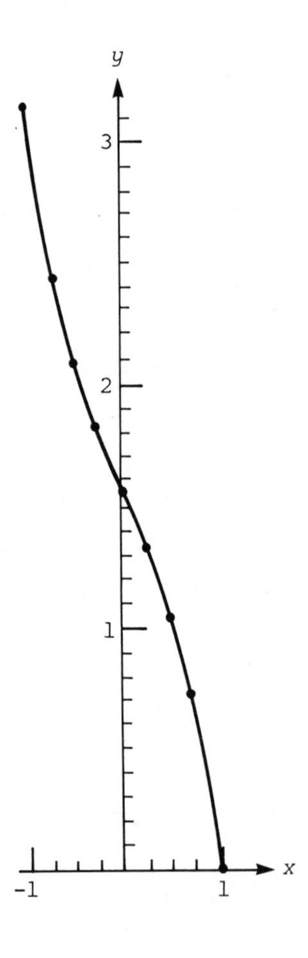

FIGURE B-11.3

EXERCISE SET B-11

For each expression, write and check a calculator sequence. See Examples 1 and 2. Use your sequence to evaluate each expression for (a) $x = .75$ and (b) $x = -.75$. Answers to the nearest hundredth.

1. $\cos 3x - \tan x$
2. $\sin 2x - \tan x$
3. $\sin \frac{x}{4} - 2 \cos x$
4. $\cos \frac{x}{3} - 5 \tan x$
5. $2 \tan x - 3 \cos \frac{x}{6}$
6. $3 \sin x - 2 \cos \frac{x}{12}$
7. $\sin \frac{x}{12} + \text{Arc} \tan x$
8. $\cos 3x + \text{Arc} \tan x$
9. $1.3 \cos \frac{x}{3} + 2 \text{ Arc} \cos x$
10. $2.4 \sin \frac{x}{6} + 3 \text{ Arc} \sin x$

Graph the function defined by each equation. See Example 3. (x-scale: 1 sq $= \frac{\pi}{12}$ unit, y-scale: 5 sq = 1 unit) For Exercises 11 and 12, use the axes provided. Compute for $x = 0, \frac{\pi}{6}, \frac{\pi}{4}, \frac{\pi}{3}, \frac{\pi}{2}, \frac{2\pi}{3}, \frac{3\pi}{4}, \frac{5\pi}{6}, \pi, \frac{7\pi}{6}, \frac{5\pi}{4}, \frac{4\pi}{3}, \frac{3\pi}{2}, \frac{5\pi}{3}, \frac{7\pi}{4}, \frac{11\pi}{6}, 2\pi$.

11. $y = \cos x$, from $x = 0$ to $x = 2\pi$

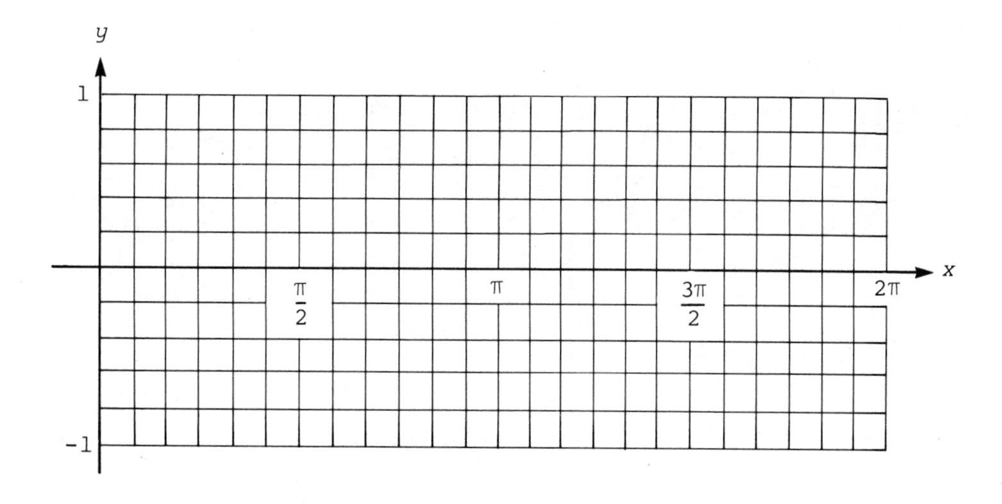

12. $y = \frac{1}{2} \sin x$, from $x = 0$ to $x = 2\pi$

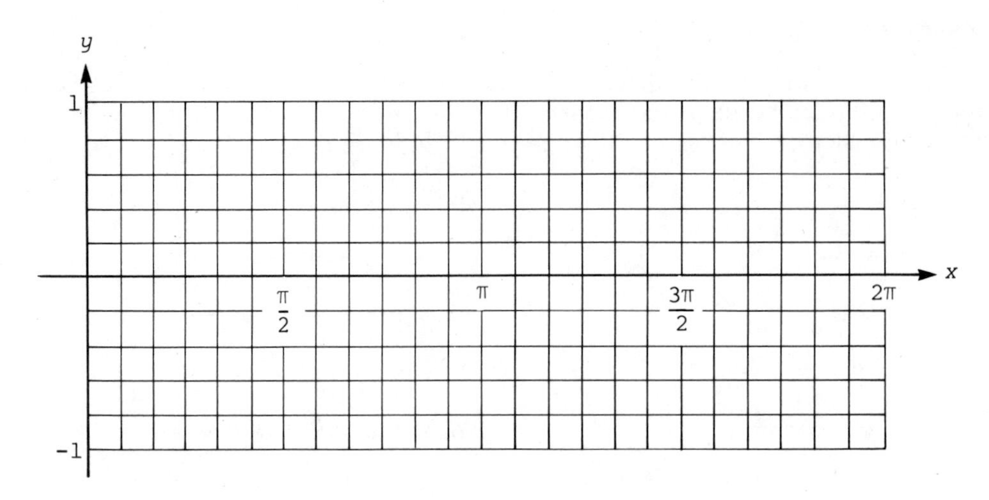

For Exercises 13 and 14, use the axes provided; compute for $x = -\pi, -\frac{5\pi}{6}, -\frac{3\pi}{4}, -\frac{2\pi}{3}, -\frac{\pi}{2}, -\frac{\pi}{3}, -\frac{\pi}{4}, -\frac{\pi}{6}, 0, \frac{\pi}{6}, \frac{\pi}{4}, \frac{\pi}{3}, \frac{\pi}{2}, \frac{2\pi}{3}, \frac{3\pi}{4}, \frac{5\pi}{6}, \pi$.

13. $y = \sin \frac{1}{2} x$, from $x = -\pi$ to $x = \pi$

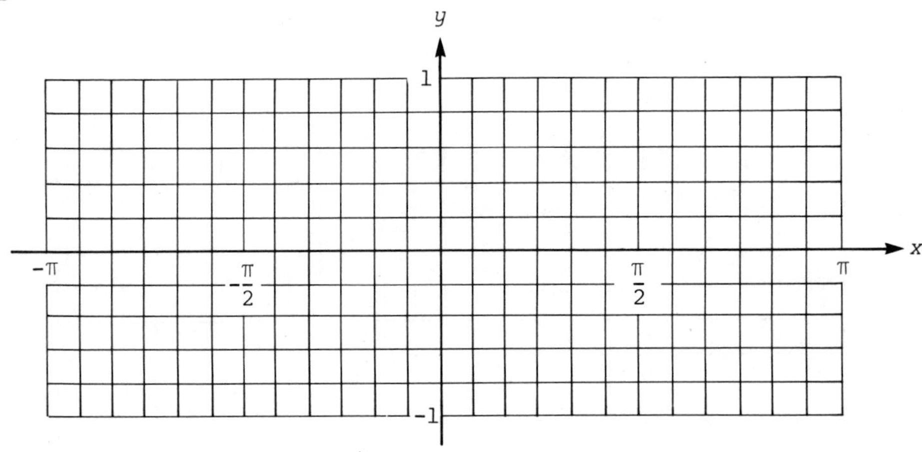

14. $y = \cos \frac{1}{2} x$, from $x = -\pi$ to $x = \pi$

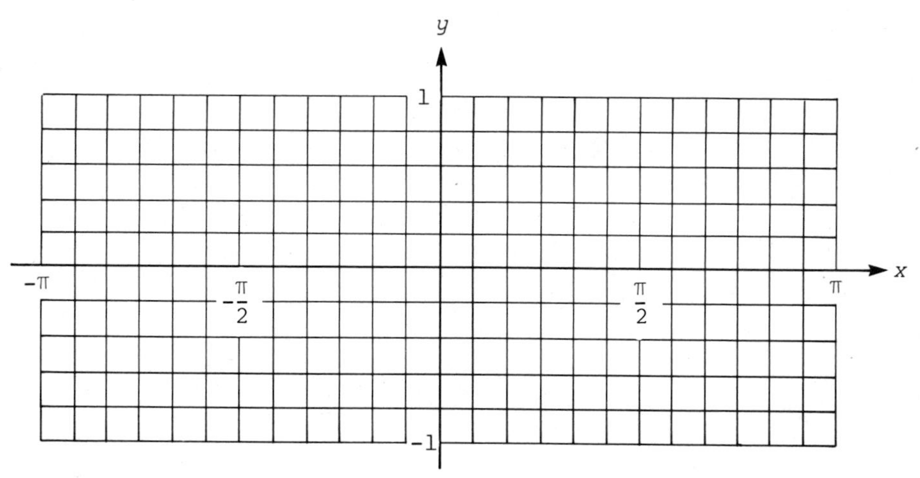

For Exercises 15 and 16, use $x = -\frac{5\pi}{12}, -\frac{\pi}{3}, -\frac{\pi}{4}, -\frac{\pi}{6}, -\frac{\pi}{12}, 0, \frac{\pi}{12}, \frac{\pi}{6}, \frac{\pi}{4}, \frac{\pi}{3}, \frac{5\pi}{12}$. ($x$-scale: 1 sq = $\frac{\pi}{12}$ unit, y-scale: 5 sq = 1 unit) See Example 3.

15. $y = \tan x$, from $x = -\frac{5\pi}{12}$ to $x = \frac{5\pi}{12}$

16. $y = \frac{1}{2} \tan x$, from $x = -\frac{5\pi}{12}$ to $x = \frac{5\pi}{12}$

For Exercises 17-22, use intervals of .25 for x-values. (Write and check a calculator sequence.) See Example 4.

17. $y = 2 \cos x + \sin x$, from $x = 0$ to $x = 6.5$ (x-scale: 4 sq = 1 unit, y-scale: 5 sq = 1 unit)

18. $y = 2 \sin x - \cos x$, from $x = 0$ to $x = 6.5$ (x-scale: 4 sq = 1 unit, y-scale: 5 sq = 1 unit)

19. $y = \sin x + \tan x$, from $x = -1$ to $x = 1$ (x-scale: 4 sq = 1 unit, y-scale: 5 sq = 1 unit)

20. $y = \cos x - \tan x$, from $x = -1.25$ to $x = 1.25$ (x-scale: 4 sq = 1 unit, y-scale: 5 sq = 1 unit)

21. $y = x + \sin x$, from $x = 0$ to $x = 5$ (x-scale: 1 sq = .25 unit, y-scale: 5 sq = 1 unit)

22. $y = x - \cos x$, from $x = 0$ to $x = 5$ (x-scale: 1 sq = .25 unit, y-scale: 5 sq = 1 unit)

For Exercises 23-26, use intervals of .25 unit for x-values. (x-scale: 1 sq = .25 unit, y-scale: 5 sq = 1 unit) See Example 5.

23. $y = \text{Arc} \sin x$, from $x = -1$ to $x = 1$

24. $y = \text{Arc} \tan x$, from $x = -1.5$ to $x = 1.5$

25. $y = 2x + \text{Arc} \cos x$, from $x = -1$ to $x = 1$

26. $y = x + \text{Arc} \sin x$ from $x = -1$ to $x = 1$

From the graph of the function defined by each equation, specify the zeros of the function between $x = -\pi$ and $x = \pi$, inclusive. (x-scale: 1 sq = $\frac{\pi}{12}$ unit, y-scale: 5 sq = 1 unit) Use intervals of $\frac{\pi}{12}$ for x-values.

27. $y = \cos 2x$

28. $y = \sin 2x$

29. $y = \sin 3x$

30. $y = \cos 3x$

B-12 Decimal and Fraction Powers

OBJECTIVES

After completing this section, you should be able to

1. Change an expression in radical form to fraction exponent form.
2. Raise a positive number to a (positive or negative) fraction or decimal power.

In Section A-7 we used the power key $\boxed{y^x}$ to raise positive numbers to positive or negative integer powers. The $\boxed{y^x}$ key can also be used to raise numbers to powers written in decimal form.

EXAMPLE 1

To the nearest thousandth, $(1.004)^{.75} = 1.003$, as computed by one of the sequences

$$1.004 \; \boxed{y^x} \; .75 \; \boxed{=} \rightarrow 1.002999$$

$$1.004 \; \boxed{\text{ENT}} \; .75 \; \boxed{y^x} \rightarrow 1.002999$$

As stated in Section A-7, most calculators will not accept a negative number as a base to be raised to a power. Hence, we restrict our computations to *positive* bases only.

*n*th ROOT OF A NUMBER

An *nth root* of a number is one of its n equal factors. The second and third roots of a number are traditionally called the "square root" and "cube root," respectively.

EXAMPLE 2

a. $25 = 5 \times 5$. Hence, 5 is a square root of 25.

b. $8 = 2 \times 2 \times 2$. Hence, 2 is a cube root of 8.

c. $81 = 3 \times 3 \times 3 \times 3$. Hence, 3 is a fourth root of 81.

In Example 2a we state that 5 is a square root of 25. As you may recall, (-5)(-5) also equals 25, and so -5 is also a square root of 25. Thus, 25 has two square roots, +5 and -5. More generally, if n is an *even* natural number (2,4,6,...), then every positive number, r, has two nth roots— a positive nth root and a negative nth root. As another example, both +3 and -3 are fourth roots of 81. (This situation does not arise if n is an *odd* natural number.)

For any positive number, r, the symbols $\sqrt[n]{r}$ (*radical form*) and $r^{1/n}$ (*fraction exponent form*) are used to name the *positive* nth root of r.

EXAMPLE 3

a. $\sqrt{25} = 25^{1/2} = 5$

b. $\sqrt[3]{8} = 8^{1/3} = 2$

c. $\sqrt[4]{81} = 81^{1/4} = 3$

As in Example 3a, the square root of a number, r, is customarily written as $\sqrt{r}$ instead of $\sqrt[2]{r}$.

COMPUTING $r^{1/n}$ OR $r^{-1/n}$

The [y^x] key can be used to compute $r^{1/n}$, the nth root of a number. If the nth root is in radical form, we first change it to fraction exponent form. Then we use the decimal equivalent of the fraction exponent and compute as in Example 4 below.

In this section we have to find decimal equivalents of fractions, and we show the computations as part of our calculator sequences. However, for any calculations in which you can obtain such decimal equivalents mentally, you will be able to use shorter sequences. (Remember to use the [F] key if your calculator requires it.)

EXAMPLE 4

To the nearest thousandth, $\sqrt[6]{48.7} = 48.7^{1/6} = 1.911$, as computed by one of the sequences

48.7 [y^x] 6 [1/x] [=] → 1.910974

48.7 [ENT] 6 [1/x] [y^x] → 1.910974

EXAMPLE 5

To the nearest thousandth, $.046^{1/4} = .463$, as computed by one of the sequences

.046 [y^x] 4 [1/x] [=] → .4631157

.046 [ENT] 4 [1/x] [y^x] → .4631157

In Example 5, if you recognize that 1/4 = .25, you can use a slightly shorter sequence:

.046 [y^x] .25 [=] or .046 [ENT] .25 [y^x]

As in Section A-7, we use the sign change key [+/-] when computing with negative exponents.

EXAMPLE 6

To the nearest thousandth, $(48.7)^{-1/6}$ = .523, as computed by one of the sequences

48.7 [y^x] 6 [1/x] [+/-] [=] → .5232933

48.7 [ENT] 6 [1/x] [+/-] [y^x] → .5232933

If your calculator has a *root key* [$\sqrt[x]{y}$], or an *inverse key* [INV], you may prefer to compute $r^{1/n}$ or $r^{-1/n}$ as shown in Examples 7 and 8 below. If your calculator has neither of these keys, omit Examples 7 and 8.

EXAMPLE 7

To the nearest thousandth, $48.7^{1/6}$ = 1.911.

With the [$\sqrt[x]{y}$] key: 48.7 [$\sqrt[x]{y}$] 6 [=] → 1.910974

With the [INV] key: 48.7 [INV] [y^x] 6 [=] → 1.910974

EXAMPLE 8

To the nearest thousandth, $(48.7)^{-1/6}$ = .523

With the [$\sqrt[x]{y}$] key: 48.7 [$\sqrt[x]{y}$] 6 [+/-] [=] → .5232933

With the [INV] key: 48.7 [INV] [y^x] 6 [+/-] [=] → .5232933

COMPUTING $r^{m/n}$ OR $r^{-m/n}$

It is not convenient to use the reciprocal key [1/x] when a fraction exponent has a numerator different from 1 or -1. Instead, we find the decimal equivalent of the exponent by the methods discussed earlier for each type of calculator.

EXAMPLE 9

To the nearest thousandth, $126.94^{3/5}$ = 18.288. Some suggested sequences are:

3 [÷] 5 [=] [STO], 126.94 [y^x] [RCL] [=] → 18.2877

126.94 [y^x] [(] 3 [÷] 5 [)] [=] → 18.2877

126.94 [ENT], 3 [ENT] 5 [÷] [y^x] → 18.2877

You will find it instructive to consider how much shorter these sequences will be if you remember that 3/5 = .6.

EXERCISE SET B-12

Compute to three significant digits. See Example 1.

1. $15^{.46}$ 2. $27^{.59}$ 3. $(.345)^{2.6}$ 4. $(.875)^{3.5}$
5. $15^{-.46}$ 6. $27^{-.59}$ 7. $(.345)^{-2.6}$ 8. $(.875)^{-3.5}$

Express each *n*th root (a) in fraction exponent form and (b) as a whole number. See Example 3. Use your calculator *only* to check your answer.

9. $\sqrt{9}$ 10. $\sqrt{16}$ 11. $\sqrt{49}$ 12. $\sqrt{81}$
13. $\sqrt[3]{27}$ 14. $\sqrt[3]{64}$ 15. $\sqrt[3]{125}$ 16. $\sqrt[3]{216}$
17. $\sqrt[4]{1}$ 18. $\sqrt[4]{16}$ 19. $\sqrt[4]{625}$ 20. $\sqrt[5]{32}$

Compute to the nearest thousandth. See Examples 4, and 5 or 7.

21. $\sqrt[3]{12.8}$ 22. $\sqrt[4]{25.9}$ 23. $\sqrt[6]{32.5}$ 24. $\sqrt[5]{245}$
25. $\sqrt[5]{87.6}$ 26. $\sqrt[6]{1000}$ 27. $\sqrt[4]{95.4}$ 28. $\sqrt[3]{85.9}$
29. $100^{1/6}$ 30. $208^{1/4}$ 31. $(.48)^{1/3}$ 32. $(.059)^{1/2}$

Compute to the nearest thousandth. See Example 6 or 8.

33. $16^{-1/2}$ 34. $8^{-1/3}$ 35. $125^{-1/3}$ 36. $64^{-1/2}$
37. $167^{-1/6}$ 38. $245^{-1/5}$ 39. $1000^{-1/4}$ 40. $100^{-1/4}$
41. $(.059)^{-1/7}$ 42. $(.076)^{-1/8}$ 43. $(68.4)^{-1/5}$ 44. $(40.9)^{-1/7}$

Compute to the nearest thousandth. See Example 9.

45. $15^{2/3}$ 46. $45^{2/5}$ 47. $2000^{3/4}$ 48. $200^{4/5}$
49. $(27.8)^{5/8}$ 50. $(75.9)^{3/8}$ 51. $(4.052)^{5/6}$ 52. $(.0533)^{7/6}$
53. $15^{-2/3}$ 54. $45^{-2/5}$ 55. $2000^{-3/4}$ 56. $200^{-4/5}$
57. $(27.8)^{-5/8}$ 58. $(75.9)^{-3/8}$ 59. $(5.052)^{-5/6}$ 60. $(.0533)^{-7/6}$

B-13 Exponential Functions

OBJECTIVES

After completing this section, you should be able to

1. Draw graphs of exponential functions.
2. Do the computations needed to solve problems involving exponential functions.

If C and k are any two nonzero constants, then equations in the form

$$y = Cb^{kx} \tag{1}$$

where the base b is a positive number ($b \neq 1$), define *exponential* functions. For example, the equations

$$y = 5^{.65x} \quad \text{and} \quad y = 8^x$$

define exponential functions.

EXAMPLE 1

Graph the exponential function defined by

$$y = 1.8^x$$

from $x = -3$ to $x = 2$. Use intervals of .5 unit for x.

Solution

For convenience, enter the base 1.8 in the memory; use the $\boxed{y^x}$ key.

x	-3	-2.5	-2	-1.5	-1	-.5	0	.5	1	1.5	2
y	.17	.23	.31	.41	.56	.75	1	1.34	1.8	2.41	3.24

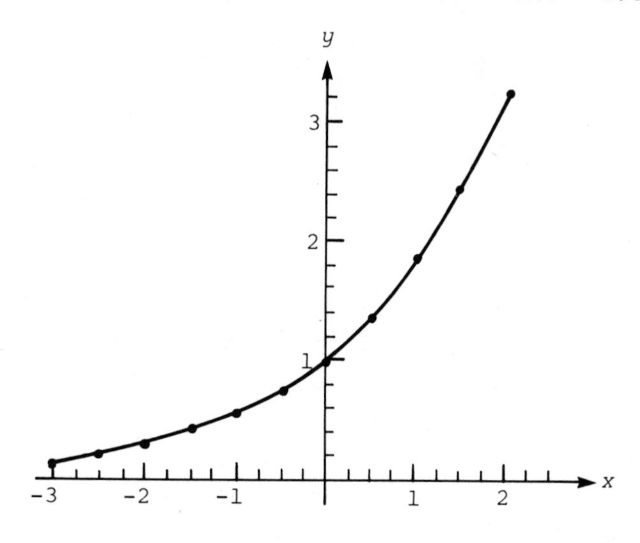

FIGURE B-13.1

THE [10^x] AND [e^x] KEYS

Two commonly used bases for exponential functions are 10 and e, where the letter e is used to name a (nonterminating) number approximately equal to 2.7182818. Many scientific calculators have separate [10^x] and [e^x] keys* that can be used to raise the numbers 10 and e, respectively, to various powers. (If your calculator has no such keys, continue to use the [y^x] key—enter 2.7182818 for e.) For calculators with an [F] key, it is understood that the [F] key is to be pressed before pressing the [10^x] or [e^x] keys.

EXAMPLE 2

a. $10^{3.4} = 2511.8864$, as computed by

3.4 [10^x] → 2511.8864

b. $10^{-3.4} = .0003981$, as computed by

3.4 [+/-] [10^x] → .0003981

c. $e^{1.5} = 4.481689$, as computed by

1.5 [e^x] → 4.481689

d. $e^{-1.5} = .22313016$, as computed by

1.5 [+/-] [e^x] → .22313016

EXPONENTIAL GROWTH OR DECAY

Exponential functions using base e are defined by equations in the form

$$y = Ce^{kx} \tag{2}$$

where C and k are constants as in Equation (1), and x may represent time. Such functions have many practical applications. If k is a *positive* number, then Equation (2) defines an *exponential growth function*, and we say that y-values increase exponentially as x-values increase.

EXAMPLE 3

If a laboratory dish contains 100 bacteria, the number y of bacteria in the dish after x hours is given by

$$y = 100e^{.13412x} \tag{3}$$

---

*As in the case of the [y^x] key, when using the [10^x] or [e^x] keys your answer may differ slightly from those in the book.

To the nearest whole number, how many bacteria will be in the dish after 2 days?

Solution

Because 2 days equals 48 hours, substitute 48 for x in Equation (3) and compute.

$$y = 100e^{(.13412)(48)} = 62,500.522$$

To the nearest whole number, there are 62,501 bacteria.

If the constant k in Equation (2) is a *negative* number, then the equation defines an *exponential decay function*, and we say that y-values decrease exponentially as x-values increase. A typical application of such functions is that of the decay of radioactive material. For example, after about 28 years, a 2-gram quantity of strontium-90 will decay (by disintegration) to a 1-gram quantity.

EXAMPLE 4

Starting with 12 grams of strontium-90, the number y of grams remaining after x years is given by

$$y = 12e^{-.024755x} \tag{4}$$

To the nearest tenth, find the number of grams remaining from a 12-gram quantity after 15 years.

Solution

Substitute 15 for x in Equation (4) and compute.

$$y = 12e^{-(.024755)(15)} = 8.2778366$$

To the nearest tenth, 8.3 grams remain after 15 years.

BASES OTHER THAN e

Exponential functions with bases other than e are also useful for certain applications. For example, *depreciation* (the loss in value of an object) can be computed by an exponential equation.

EXAMPLE 5

If an automobile depreciates by 20% of its original cost at the end of the first year and by 10% of its value each year after that, the value y of the automobile after x years is given by

$$y = .8V_0(.9)^{x-1} \tag{5}$$

where V_0 is the original cost of the automobile. To the nearest dollar, compute the value of a $7000 automobile after 5 years.

Solution

Substitute 7000 for V_0 and 5 for x in Equation (5).

$$y = .8 \times 7000 \times .9^4 = 3674.16$$

To the nearest dollar, the value is \$3674.

The word *appreciate* is used to mean that the value of an object increases.

EXAMPLE 6

It is anticipated that a certain diamond will appreciate by 3% of its original value V_0 after its purchase and by 4.5% of its value each year after the first. The value y of the diamond x years after the purchase is given by

$$y = 1.03V_0(1.045)^{x-1} \qquad (6)$$

If the diamond is bought for \$6850, find its anticipated value after 7 years (to the nearest dollar).

Solution

Substitute 6850 for V_0 and 7 for x in Equation (6).

$$y = 1.03(6850)(1.045)^6 = 9188.0954$$

To the nearest dollar, the value will be \$9188.

SEQUENCES FOR COMBINED OPERATIONS WITH EXPONENTIAL FUNCTIONS

The [e^x] and [10^x] keys have the same property as the trigonometric keys—they operate only on the number in the display (either a new entry or the result of a previous calculation). Consequently, we can plan and check calculator sequences that involve [e^x] and [10^x] in the same manner as we did for trigonometric functions in Section B-11.

EXAMPLE 7

Write and check a calculator sequence to compute the value of the expression

$$\frac{1}{2}(e^x + e^{-x})$$

Solution

Think of e^x as the number A, e^{-x} as the number B, and the given expression as $\frac{1}{2}(A + B)$ or, in on-line form, as

$$(A + B) \div 2$$

Some suggested sequences are:

B-TYPE or P-TYPE (with [e^x] key):

x [e^x] [+] x [+/−] [e^x] [÷] 2 [=]

B-TYPE or P-TYPE (without [e^x] key, use 2.7182818 for e):

e [y^x] x [=] [STO] , e [y^x] x [+/−] [=] [+] [RCL] [÷] 2 [=]

H-TYPE (with [e^x] key):

x [e^x] [+] x [+/−] [e^x] [=] [÷] 2 [=]

H-TYPE (without [e^x] key, use 2.7182818 for e):

e [STO] [y^x] x [+] [RCL] [y^x] x [+/−] [=] [÷] 2 [=]

[ENT] calculators:

x [e^x] , x [+/−] [e^x] [+] 2 [÷]

Check: Replace x by 2. Then,

$$(e^2 + e^{-2}) \div 2 = (7.3890561 + .13533528) \div 2$$
$$= 7.5243914 \div 2$$
$$= 3.7621957$$

Verify that a sequence appropriate for your calculator gives 3.7621957 as an answer when x is replaced by 2.

In Example 7 we showed sequences designed to be used with or without the [e^x] key. In the remaining example of this section we show only sequences that include the [e^x] key. It is understood that you will write sequences appropriate for your calculator if it has no [e^x] key.

Calculations that involve mixed exponential and trigonometric functions must be done in radian mode.

EXAMPLE 8

Write and check a sequence to compute values of

$$\frac{2}{3} e^x + \sin x$$

Compute values of the given expression for $x = .84$ and for $x = -.84$ (to the nearest hundredth).

Solution

Think of e^x as the number A, sin x as the number B, and the given expression as

$$\frac{2}{3}A + B$$

Some suggested sequences are:

2 [÷] 3 [×] x [e^x] [+] x [SIN] [=]

2 [ENT] 3 [÷] x [e^x] [×] x [SIN] [+]

Check: Replace x by 2. Then (radian mode)

$$\frac{2}{3}e^2 + \sin 2 = \frac{2}{3}(7.3890561) + .90929742$$
$$= 5.8353347$$

Verify that a sequence appropriate for your calculator gives 5.8353347 as an answer when x is replaced by 2. Then, use your sequence to verify that

$$\frac{2}{3}e^{.84} + \sin .84 = 2.29$$

and

$$\frac{2}{3}e^{-.84} + \sin(-.84) = -.46$$

EXERCISE SET B-13

If your calculator does not have an [e^x] key, use 2.7182818 for e. Compute each power. See Example 2.

1. $10^{2.3}$
2. $10^{1.9}$
3. $10^{-2.3}$
4. $10^{-1.9}$
5. $10^{.37}$
6. $10^{.62}$
7. $e^{3.9}$
8. $e^{4.2}$
9. $e^{-3.9}$
10. $e^{-4.2}$
11. $e^{.35}$
12. $e^{.75}$

Draw the graph of the exponential function defined by each equation. Use intervals of .5 unit for x. (x-scale: 4 sq = 1 unit, y-scale: 5 sq = 1 unit)

13. $y = 1.4^x$ from $x = -3$ to $x = 3$
14. $y = 1.2^x$ from $x = -3$ to $x = 3$
15. $y = 1.4^{-x}$ from $x = -3$ to $x = 2$
16. $y = 1.2^{-x}$ from $x = -3$ to $x = 2$
17. $y = e^x$ from $x = -3$ to $x = 1$
18. $y = e^{-x}$ from $x = -1$ to $x = 3$

For Exercises 19-34, see Examples 3 and 4.

If a laboratory dish contains 75 bacteria, the number y of bacteria in the dish after x hours is given by

$$y = 75e^{.13412x}$$

To the nearest whole number, find the number of bacteria in the dish after:

19. 12 hours
20. 18 hours
21. $1\frac{1}{2}$ days
22. 3 days

If P dollars is invested in a savings account for which interest is compounded "continuously" at 7% per year, the amount A to which P will increase in x years is given by

$$A = Pe^{.07x}$$

To the nearest cent, find the amount for each P and given time.

23. P = \$500, x = 1 yr
24. P = \$750, x = 1 yr
25. P = \$800, x = 2.5 yrs
26. P = \$900, x = 3.5 yrs

Assuming a world population of 3.9 billion and an exponential growth rate of 2.5%, in x years the population P (in billions) can be estimated by

$$P = 3.9e^{.025x}$$

To two significant digits, estimate the world population in:

27. 3 years
28. 5 years
29. 7.5 years
30. 10 years

Starting with 7 g of strontium-90, the number y of grams remaining after x years is given by

$$y = 7e^{-.024755x}$$

To the nearest tenth, find the number of grams remaining after

31. 5 years
32. 15 years
33. 25 years
34. 50 years

For Exercises 35-46, see Examples 5 and 6.

If a truck depreciates by 25% of its original value at the end of the first year and by 15% of its value each year after the first, the value y after x years is given by

$$y = .75V_0(.85)^{x-1}$$

where V_0 is the original cost of the truck. To the nearest dollar, compute the value of a truck after the given number of years if its original cost was \$8500.

35. 3 years
36. 5 years
37. 7 years
38. 10 years

If a home appreciates by 9% of its original value V_0 by the end of the first year after its purchase and by 7.5% of its value each year after the first, the value y of the home after x years is given by

$$y = 1.09V_0(1.075)^{x-1}$$

To the nearest dollar, find the value of a home purchased for \$33,500 after:

39. 5 years
40. 10 years
41. 15 years
42. 25 years

The value $[H^+]$, in moles per liter, of the concentration of hydrogen ions in an aqueous solution is given by

$$[H^+] = 10^{-pH}$$

where pH is the hydrogen potential of the solution. To two significant digits, find the hydrogen ion concentration $[H^+]$ for the solution with the given pH.

43. pH = 4.2
44. pH = 3.2
45. pH = 2.9
46. pH = 1.9

For each expression, write and check a calculator sequence. Use your calculator sequence for $x = -1.5, -1, -.5, 0, .5, 1, 1.5$. Round off the answers to the nearest hundredth. See Examples 7 and 8. (Sequences will not be shown in the answers.)

47. $\frac{3}{4}(e^x + e^{-x})$
48. $\frac{2}{3}(e^x - e^{-x})$
49. $\frac{3}{5}e^{-x} - \cos x$
50. $\frac{3}{5}e^x + \sin x$
51. $\frac{1}{2}(e^x - 2\tan x)$
52. $\frac{1}{2}(e^{-x} + 2\tan x)$

B-14 Logarithmic Functions

OBJECTIVES

After completing this section, you should be able to

1. Compute the common or natural logarithm of a number.
2. Compute the number, given its common or natural logarithm.
3. Graph logarithmic functions.
4. Do computations involving common or natural logarithms of numbers.

THE LOG AND LN KEYS

If x is any positive number, then either of the equations

$$y = \log x \quad \text{or} \quad y = \ln x$$

defines a *logarithmic function*. Each of the symbols "log x" and "ln x" can be read as "logarithm of x." (We consider the meaning of "logarithm" below.) Most scientific calculators have *logarithm keys*, LOG and LN, for computing logarithms of numbers. When a logarithm key is pressed, the resulting operation is applied only to the number in the display. Consequently, pressing the LOG or LN keys during a computation will not affect any previous calculations.

Either of the logarithm keys is used by entering the number first.* (If your calculator requires the use of an F key, the F key is pressed before the LOG or LN keys.)

EXAMPLE 1

a. log 18.63 = 1.27021 to five places, as computed by

18.63 LOG → 1.2702129

b. ln 18.63 = 2.92477 to five places, as computed by

18.63 LN → 2.9247732

GRAPHS OF LOGARITHMIC FUNCTIONS

Try to compute log 0, ln 0, log(-2), and ln(-2), and note that in each case the display shows an error signal. This results from the fact that logarithmic functions are defined for *positive* numbers only; that is, log x and ln x can be computed only when the number x is positive. For this reason, x-values in tables prepared for graphing logarithmic functions do not include negative numbers or zero.

---

*When using logarithm keys, your answers may differ slightly from those in the book.

Because y-values of logarithmic functions generally change slowly, when graphing such functions it is not convenient to choose x-values at equal intervals, as we did for graphs in previous sections.

EXAMPLE 2

Graph $y = \log x$. Use the x-values: .1, .3, 1, 2, 3, 5, 8, 10, 15, 25. (x-scale: 1 sq = 1 unit, y-scale: 5 sq = 1 unit)

Solution

Prepare a table of values. Round off the y-values to the nearest tenth.

x	.1	.3	1	2	3	5	8	10	15	25
y	-1	-.5	0	.3	.5	.7	.9	1.0	1.2	1.4

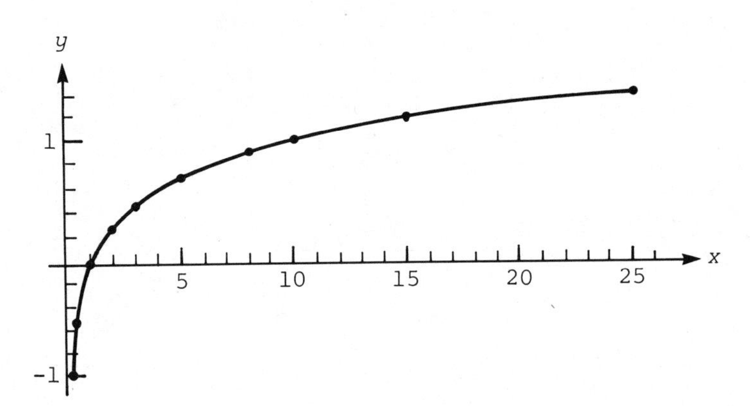

FIGURE B-14.1

LOGARITHMS TO THE BASE 10

If we compute $10^{1.6}$, we obtain 39.810717. That is,

$$39.810717 = 10^{1.6}$$

and we see that 39.810717 has been expressed as $10^{1.6}$, a power of 10. The exponent 1.6 on the base 10 is called the "logarithm of 39.810717 to the base 10," and we write

$$\log 39.810717 = 1.6$$

More generally, any positive number N can be expressed as a power of 10. If

$$N = 10^x \tag{1}$$

then x is the logarithm of N to the base 10 and we write

$$x = \log N \tag{2}$$

where it is understood that *log* refers to logarithms to the base 10. Logarithms to the base 10 are called *common logarithms*.

EXAMPLE 3

a. $10^{3.2} = 1584.8932$. Hence, $\log 1584.8932 = 3.2$.

b. $10^{-3.2} = .00063095$. Hence, $\log .00063095 = -3.2$.

Given a number N, the [LOG] key is used to find $\log N$. On the other hand, given the number $\log N$, we can find N by remembering that *log N* must be the exponent on 10. In fact, if from Equation (2) we substitute $\log N$ for x in Equation (1), we obtain

$$N = 10^{\log N} \tag{3}$$

Equation (3) shows that *the logarithm of the number N to the base 10 is the exponent on 10* such that the resulting power of 10 is equal to N. Equation (3) also provides a method of finding N when $\log N$ is given.

EXAMPLE 4

Given $\log N$, find N.

a. $\log N = 2.106419$ b. $\log N = -2.106419$

Solutions

In each case compute $10^{\log N}$.

a. $N = 10^{2.106419} = 127.76709$

b. $N = 10^{-2.106419} = .00782674$

Check: a. $\log 127.76709 = 2.106419$

b. $\log .00782674 = -2.106419$

If your calculator has an [INV] key, the following alternate sequence may be available for finding N when $\log N$ is given. (If your calculator has no such key, omit Example 5.)

EXAMPLE 5

If $\log N = 2.106419$, then $N = 127.76709$, as computed by

2.106419 [INV] [LOG] → 127.76709

LOGARITHMS TO THE BASE *e*

If we compute $e^{1.6}$, we obtain 4.9530324. That is,

$$4.9530324 = e^{1.6}$$

We say that "1.6 is the logarithm to the base e of 4.9530324," and write

$$1.6 = \ln 4.9530324$$

More generally, for any positive number N, if

$$N = e^x \tag{4}$$

then

$$x = \ln N \tag{5}$$

where it is understood that *ln* refers to logarithms to the base e. Logarithms to the base e are called *natural logarithms*.

EXAMPLE 6

a. $e^{3.2} = 24.53253$. Hence, $\ln 24.53253 = 3.2$.

b. $e^{-3.2} = .0407622$. Hence, $\ln .0407622 = -3.2$.

Reasoning as we did above for logarithms to the base 10, we can combine Equations (4) and (5) to obtain

$$N = e^{\ln N} \tag{6}$$

Equation (6) shows that *the logarithm to the base e of a number N is the exponent of e such that the resulting power of e is equal to N.* Equation (6) also provides a method for finding N when $\ln N$ is given.

EXAMPLE 7

Given $\ln N$, find N.

a. $\ln N = 2.106419$ b. $\ln N = -2.106419$

Solutions

In each case, compute $e^{\ln N}$.

a. $N = e^{2.106419} = 8.2187572$ b. $N = e^{-2.106419} = .1216729$

Check: a. $\ln 8.2187572 = 2.106419$ b. $\ln .1216729 = -2.106419$

For calculators with an [INV] key, see the next example.

EXAMPLE 8

If $\ln N = 2.106419$, then $N = 8.2187574$, as computed by

2.106419 [INV] [LN] → 8.2187572

APPLICATIONS

Following are two examples in which logarithms of numbers appear in the computations.

EXAMPLE 9

An amount R_0 grams of radium will decay to R grams in a period of t years. The number t is given by

$$t = \frac{\ln(R_0 \div R)}{.00041} \tag{7}$$

In how many years will 3 grams of radium decay to 2 grams (to the nearest whole number)?

Solution

Substitute 3 for R_0 and 2 for R in Equation (7).

$$t = \frac{\ln(3 \div 2)}{.00041} = 988.93929$$

To the nearest whole number, it will take 989 years.

EXAMPLE 10

If the interest on an amount of money is compounded daily (360 times per year) for t years, the yearly interest rate r at which the money will double can be found by solving the following equation for r:

$$\log(360 + r) = \frac{\log 2}{360\ t} + \log 360 \tag{8}$$

At what yearly interest rate will an amount of money double after 10 years?

Solution

Substitute 10 for t in Equation (8) and solve for r.

$$\log(360 + r) = \frac{\log 2}{3600} + \log 360$$

Compute the right side of the equation.

$$\log(360 + r) = 2.5563861 \tag{9}$$

Think of the number $(360 + r)$ as the number N. Then Equation (9) is in the form

$$\log N = 2.5563861$$

from which, by Equation (3),

$$N = 10^{2.5563861} = 360.0693$$

Now, replace N by $(360 + r)$ to obtain

$$360 + r = 360.0693$$

$$r = 360.0693 - 360 = .0693$$

Thus, the yearly interest rate is 6.93%.

EXERCISE SET B-14

(Note: Answers computed on a 10-digit calculator may differ slightly from those in the answer section of this book.)

Compute each logarithm to five decimal places. See Example 1.

1. log 304.54
2. log 672.89
3. log .05642
4. log .08957
5. ln 95.51
6. ln 67.43
7. ln .007853
8. ln .009616

Complete each statement. See Examples 3 and 6.

9. $10^{2.6} = 398.10717$. Hence, log 398.10717 = ________.
10. $10^{1.9} = 79.432823$. Hence, log 79.432823 = ________.
11. $10^{-2.6} = .00251188$. Hence, log .00251188 = ________.
12. $10^{-1.9} = .01258925$. Hence, log .01258925 = ________.
13. $e^{2.6} = 13.463738$. Hence, ln 13.463738 = ________.
14. $e^{1.9} = 6.6858944$. Hence, ln 6.6858944 = ________.
15. $e^{-2.6} = .07427357$. Hence, ln .07427357 = ________.
16. $e^{-1.9} = .14956862$. Hence, ln .14956862 = ________.

For each log N or ln N, find N (under floating decimal point operation). Check each answer. See Examples 4 and 7, or 5 and 8.

17. $\log N = 2.961435$
18. $\log N = 2.010517$
19. $\log N = -1.863716$
20. $\log N = -1.981342$
21. $\ln N = 1.863716$
22. $\ln N = 1.981342$
23. $\ln N = -1.863716$
24. $\ln N = -1.981342$

Solve each problem. See Example 9.

An amount R_0 grams of radium will decay to R grams in t years. The number t is given by

$$t = \frac{\ln(R_0 \div R)}{.00041}$$

To the nearest year, how many years will it take for each R_0 grams of radium to decay to R grams.

25. a. $R_0 = 4$, $R = 3$
    b. $R_0 = 3.5$, $R = 3$
26. a. $R_0 = 3.8$, $R = 2$
    b. $R_0 = 2.5$, $R = 2$

The age t (in years) of plant or animal remains which have retained P percent (in decimal form) of their radioactive carbon-14 is given by

$$t = \frac{\ln P}{-.00012}$$

To the nearest year, find the age of each item if it has retained the given percentage of its carbon-14.

27. a. bone, 60%

    b. wood, 35%

28. a. seal tusk, 75%

    b. mammal skeleton, 25%

If the interest on an amount of money is compounded 360 times* per year at a rate r (in decimal form), the number of years t needed for the money to double is given by

$$t = \frac{\log 2}{360 \log(1 + \frac{r}{360})}$$

To the nearest hundredth, in how many years will an amount of money double if compounded daily at each given interest rate?

29. a. 5%; b. $5\frac{1}{2}$%

30. a. 6%; b. $6\frac{1}{2}$%

To the nearest hundredth of a percent, find the yearly interest rate at which an amount of money will double in the given number of years. See Example 10.

31. a. 5 years; b. 8 years

32. a. 7 years; b. 15 years

For each expression, write and check a calculator sequence. Use your sequence for the given x-values. Round off the answers to the nearest hundredth.

33. $3(\log x) - 2 \cos x$, for $x = .5, 1, 1.5, 2, 2.5$
34. $2(\ln x) - 3 \sin x$, for $x = .5, 1, 1.5, 2, 2.5$
35. $2e^x - 2(\ln x)$, for $x = 2, 2.5, 3, 3.5, 4$
36. $2(10^x) - 15(\log x)$, for $x = .1, .2, .3, .4, .5$
37. $2.5x - 3.5(\ln x)$, for $x = .5, 1, 1.5, 2, 2.5$
38. $3.5x - 1.5(\log x)$, for $x = .5, 1, 1.5, 2, 2.5$
39. $10^x - 25(\log x)$, for $x = .5, 1, 1.5, 2, 2.5$
40. $e^x - 3(\ln x)$, for $x = .5, 1, 1.5, 2, 2.5$

For Exercises 41-44, graph the function defined by each equation, from $x = .5$ to $x = 15$. Use the axes provided and compute for $x = .5, 1, 2, 3, 4, 5, 8, 10, 15$. See Example 2. ($x$-scale: 2 sq = 1 unit, y-scale: 5 sq = 1 unit)

---

*The "business" year is commonly taken as 360 days.

41. $y = \ln x$

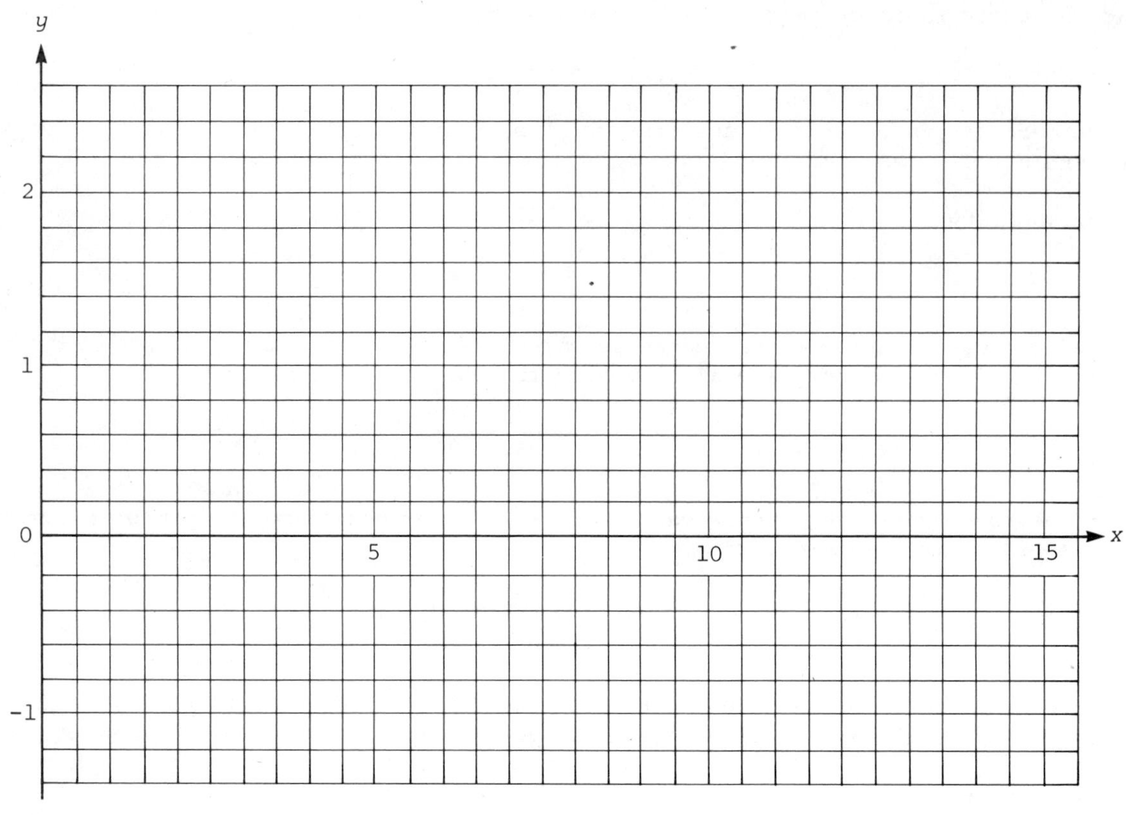

42. $y = .5(\ln x)$

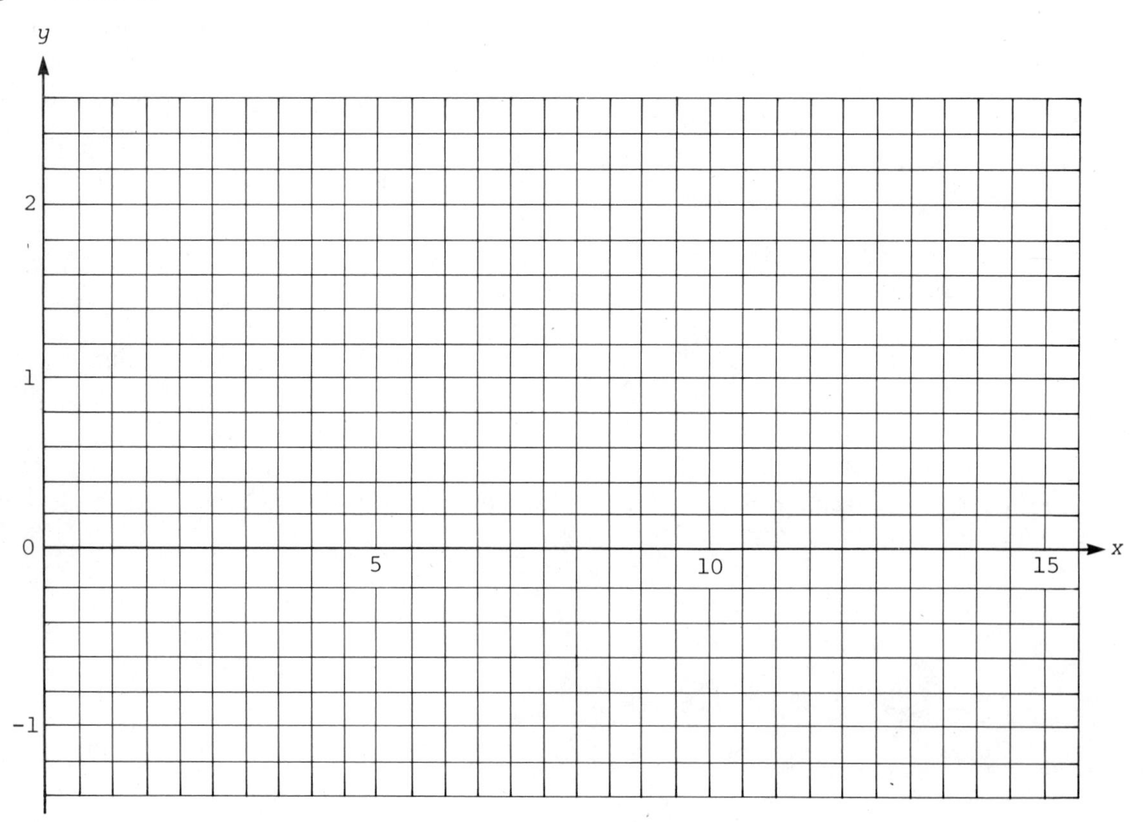

43. $y = 1.5(\log x)$

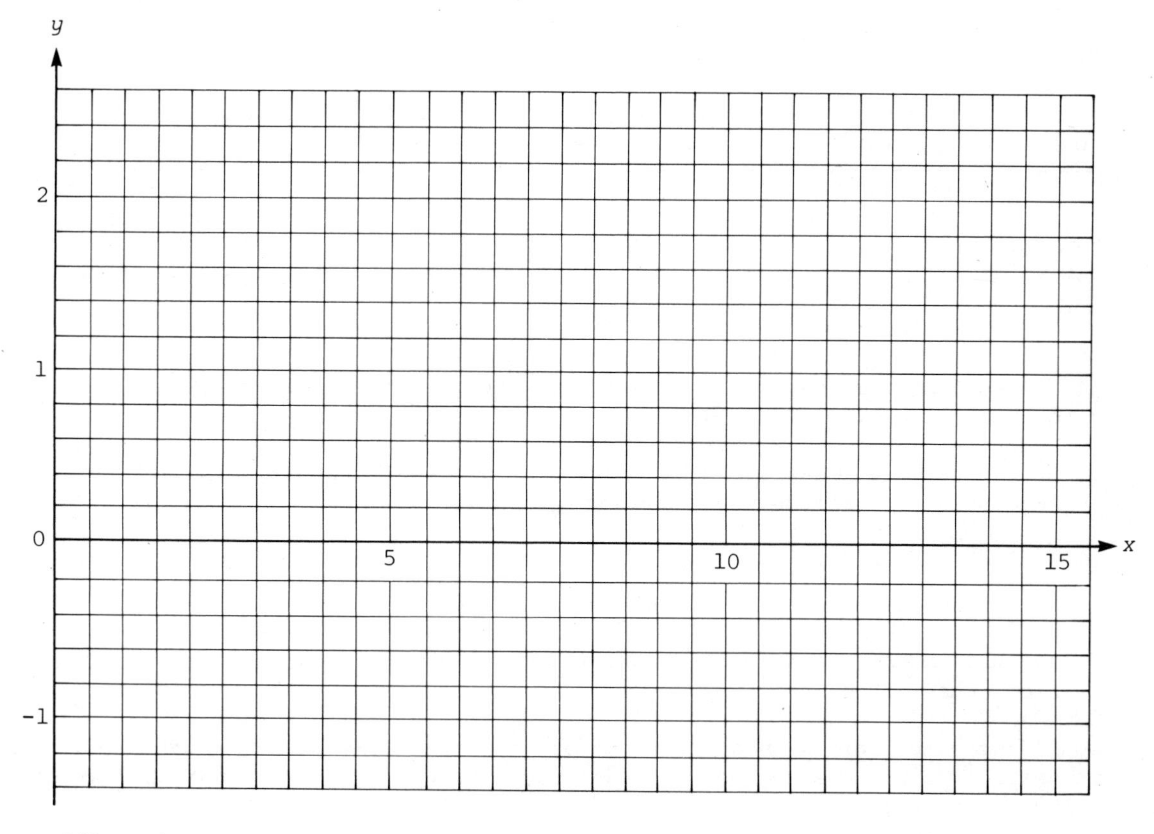

44. $y = 2(\log x)$

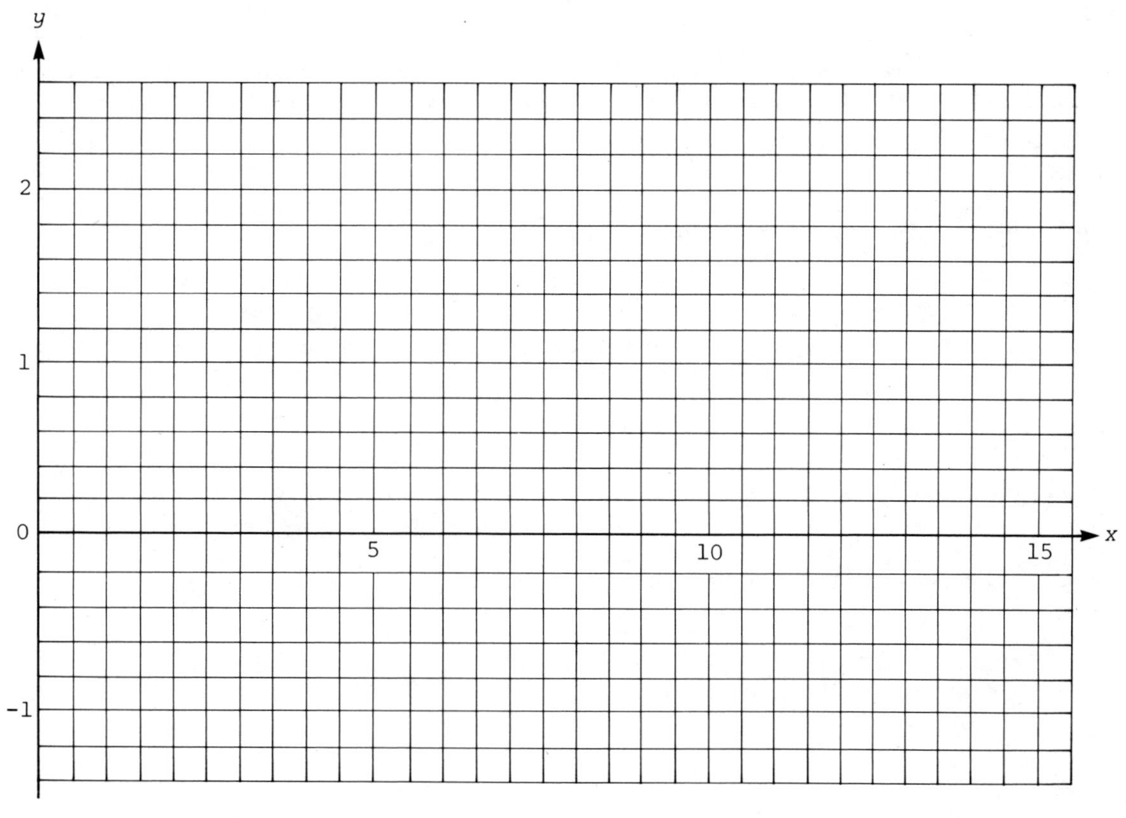

B-15 Solving Transcendental Equations

OBJECTIVE

After completing this section, you should be able to obtain solutions to transcendental equations to a specified number of decimal places.

Equations that include trigonometric, exponential, and/or logarithmic functions are referred to as *transcendental equations*. Given a transcendental equation in the form

$$A(x) = B(x)$$

where $A(x)$ and $B(x)$ name expressions involving the variable x, we shall use the following method to obtain solutions:

1. On the same set of axes, draw a graph of $y = A(x)$ and of $y = B(x)$. Estimate the x-value of any points where the two graphs intersect.
2. Rewrite the equation in the form

$$A(x) - B(x) = 0$$

   and use the *sign-change principle* (Section B-5) to obtain solutions, to a specified number of places.

In Step 2, the calculations needed for computing $A(x) - B(x)$ may be complicated. You will find it helpful to write and check a calculator sequence. (We will not show sequences in the following examples.)

EXAMPLE 1

The equation $2^x = 3x^2$ has a positive solution and a negative solution, both between $x = -2$ and $x = 2$. Find the two solutions, to the nearest hundredth.

Solution

On the same set of axes, draw the graphs of

$$y = 2^x \quad \text{and} \quad y = 3x^2$$

from $x = -2$ to $x = 2$, as shown. Estimate .7 and -.5 as the respective x-values of the two points where the graphs intersect. Rewrite the equation as

$$2^x - 3x^2 = 0 \tag{1}$$

Write and check a calculator sequence for the computations indicated by the left side of Equation (1). Apply the sign-change principle to obtain solutions.

a. To find the positive solution:

x	.7	.8
$2^x - 3x^2$	+	-

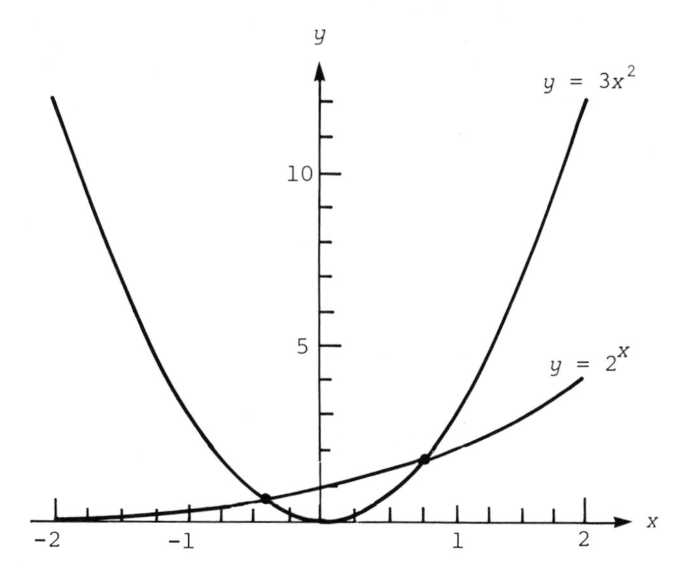

FIGURE B-15.1

The solution is between .7 and .8.

x	.70	.71	.72	.73	.74	.75
$2^x - 3x^2$	+	+	+	+	+	-

The solution is between .74 and .75. To determine whether the solution is closer to .74 or to .75, compute the table

x	.740	.745
$2^x - 3x^2$	+	+

Because there is no sign change between .740 and .745, the solution is greater than .745. Hence, the positive solution of the equation is .75, to the nearest hundredth.

b. To find the negative solution:

x	-.5	-.4
$2^x - 3x^2$	-	+

The solution is between -.5 and -.4.

x	-.50	-.49	-.48
$2^x - 3x^2$	-	-	+

The solution is between -.49 and -.48. To determine whether the solution is closer to -.49 or to -.48, compute the table.

x	-.490	-.485
$2^x - 3x^2$	-	+

Because there is a sign change between -.490 and -.485, the solution is closer to -.490. Hence, the negative solution is -.49, to the nearest hundredth.

EXAMPLE 2

The equation $3^{-x} = \ln x$ has exactly one positive solution. Find that solution to the nearest hundredth.

Solution

On the same set of axes, draw the graphs of

$$y = 3^{-x} \quad \text{and} \quad y = \ln x$$

as shown.

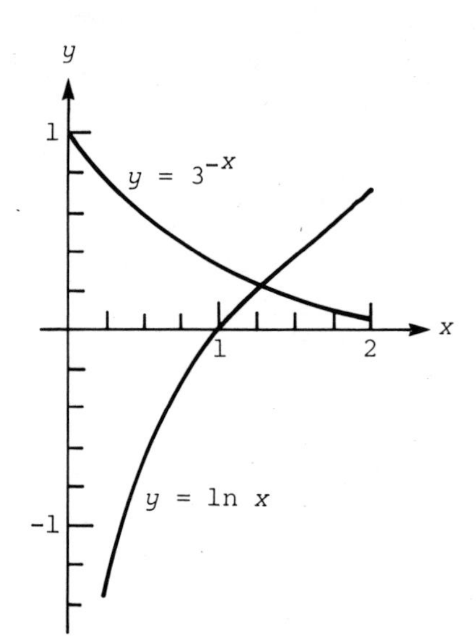

FIGURE B-15.2

Estimate 1.2 as the x-value of the point where the graphs intersect. Rewrite the equation as

$$3^{-x} - \ln x = 0$$

Write and check a calculator sequence for the computations indicated on the left side of the equation.

x	1.2	1.3
$3^{-x} - \ln x$	+	-

The solution is between 1.2 and 1.3.

x	1.20	1.21	1.22	1.23	1.24	1.25	1.26	1.27	1.28
$3^{-x} - \ln x$	+	+	+	+	+	+	+	+	-

The solution is between 1.27 and 1.28.

To determine whether the solution is closer to 1.27 or to 1.28, compute the table

x	1.270	1.275
$3^{-x} - \ln x$	+	+

Because there is no sign change between 1.270 and 1.275, the solution is greater than 1.275. Hence, the solution is 1.28, to the nearest hundredth.

EXERCISE SET B-15

The following equations are in the form $A(x) = B(x)$. For each equation:

a. Draw a graph of $y = A(x)$ and of $y = B(x)$ on the same axes. Unless specified otherwise, use *2 sq = 1 unit* as the scale on both axes.

b. To the nearest hundredth, find the indicated solution(s). Set to radian mode. See Examples 1 and 2.

1. $2^x = -x$ has one solution between $x = -2$ and $x = 2$. (x-scale: 2 sq = 1 unit, y-scale: 1 sq = 1 unit)
2. $.5^x = x$ has one solution between $x = -2$ and $x = 2$. (x-scale: 2 sq = 1 unit, y-scale: 1 sq = 1 unit)
3. $\frac{x}{2} = \sin x$ has one solution between $x = 0$ and $x = 3$.
4. $\frac{x}{3} = \cos x$ has one solution between $x = 0$ and $x = 3$.
5. $\frac{x}{4} = \ln x$ has one solution between $x = .5$ and $x = 4$.
6. $x = 7 \log x$ has one solution between $x = .5$ and $x = 4$.
7. $2e^x = \sin x$ has one solution between $x = -4$ and $x = 0$.
8. $e^x = \cos x$ has one solution between $x = -4$ and $x = 0$.
9. $x^2 = \frac{e^x}{2}$ has two solutions between $x = -2$ and $x = 2$. (x-scale: 2 sq = 1 unit, y-scale: 1 sq = 1 unit)
10. $e^x = 4 - x^2$ has two solutions between $x = -2$ and $x = 2$. (x-scale: 2 sq = 1 unit, y-scale: 1 sq = 1 unit)
11. $\cos 3x = \text{Arc tan } x$ has two solutions between $x = -1$ and $x = 2$.
12. $2 \text{ Arc tan } x = \frac{1}{3} e^x$ has two solutions between $x = -1$ and $x = 2$.

Each of the following equations has exactly one solution. To the nearest hundredth, find the solution of each equation.

13. $\ln x = \frac{\sqrt{x}}{2}$
14. $2 \log x = \sin x$

PART C
NON-
SCIENTIFIC
CALCULATORS
Applications

C-1 Formulas

OBJECTIVE

After completing this section, you should be able to do the computations indicated by given formulas.

Below is a list of the abbreviations for units of measurement used in the examples and exercises of this section.

in.:	inch	cm:	centimeter	sq:	square
ft:	foot	m:	meter	cu:	cubic
yd:	yard				

For formulas involving *square root*, you may have to refer to Appendix A. If your calculator has a *squaring key*, $\boxed{x^2}$, see Appendix B.

If A is the area of a rectangle of length ℓ and width w (Figure C-1.1), then the equation

$$A = \ell w \tag{1}$$

is a concise way of giving the rule, "The area of a rectangle is equal to the product of its length and its width."

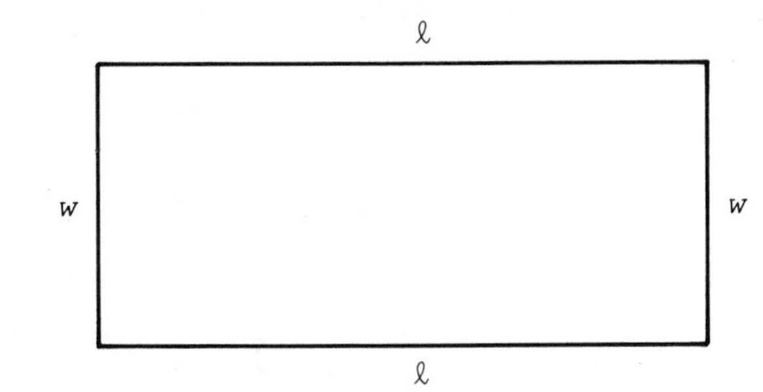

Figure C-1.1

Equations such as Equation (1) are often called *formulas;* it is understood that the letters that appear in formulas represent numbers. The procedure for using formulas, as illustrated in the examples below, can be followed whether or not the meaning of a formula is clear to you.

EXAMPLE 1

The area A of a trapezoid is given by

$$A = \frac{1}{2}h(b_1 + b_2)$$

To the nearest tenth, find the area of a trapezoid with h = 7.4 in., b_1 = 16.9 in., and b_2 = 12.5 in. (See Figure C-1.2.)

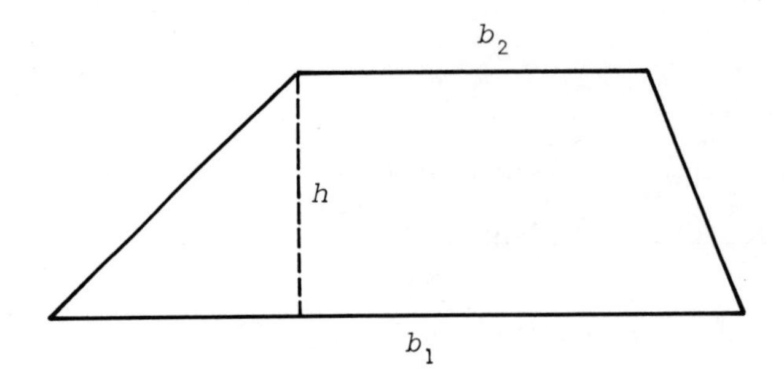

FIGURE C-1.2

Solution

Substitute 7.4 for h, 16.9 for b_1, 12.5 for b_2, and do the indicated computations.

$$A = \frac{1}{2} \times 7.4(16.9 + 12.5) = 108.78$$

To the nearest tenth, the area is 108.8 sq in.

EXAMPLE 2

The area A of a regular hexagon is given by

$$A = \frac{3s^2\sqrt{3}}{2}$$

To the nearest hundredth, find the area of the regular hexagon with s = 24.08 cm.

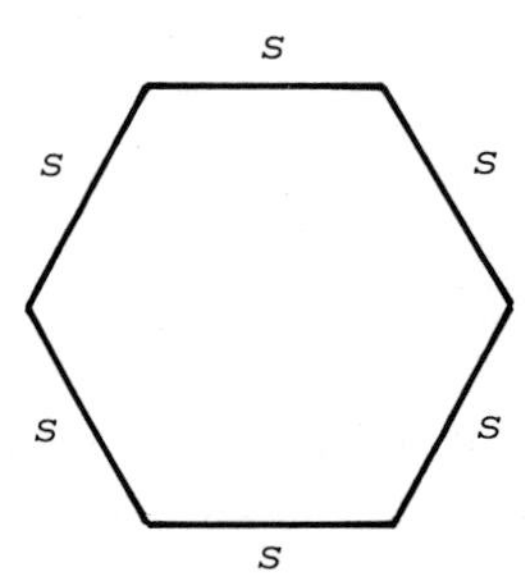

FIGURE C-1.3

Solution

Substitute 24.08 for s and do the computations.

$$A = \frac{3(24.08)^2\sqrt{3}}{2} = 1506.4851$$

To the nearest hundredth, the area is 1506.49 sq cm.

In the examples above we considered geometric figures in a plane (two-dimensional). Many formulas are applicable to geometric figures in space (three-dimensional).

EXAMPLE 3

The total surface area S of a right circular cylinder is given by

$$S = 2\pi rh + 2\pi r^2$$

To the nearest tenth, find the total surface area of a right circular cylinder with $r = 15.6$ ft and $h = 29.8$ ft. (Use 3.14159 for π.)

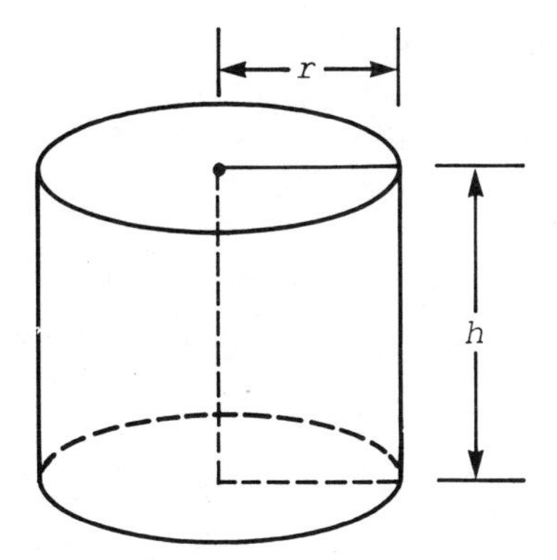

Figure C-1.4

Solution

Substitute 15.6 for r, 29.8 for h, 3.14159 for π, and do the computations.

$$S = 2(3.14159)(15.6)(29.8) + 2(3.14159)(15.6)^2$$

$$= 4449.9993$$

To the nearest tenth, the total surface area is 4450.0 sq ft.

EXAMPLE 4

The volume V of a hollow right circular cylinder is given by

$$V = \frac{\pi h}{4}(D^2 - d^2)$$

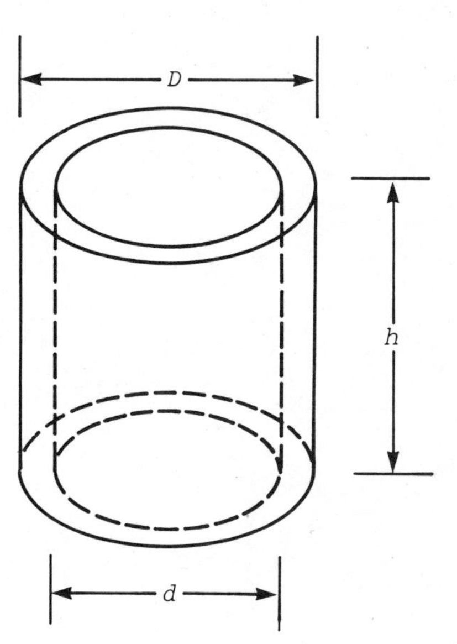

FIGURE C-1.5

Formulas

To the nearest whole number, find the volume of the hollow right circular cylinder with h = 12.05 m, D = 11.49 m, and d = 11.38 m.

Solution

Substitute 12.05 for h, 11.49 for D, 11.38 for d, 3.14159 for π, and do the computations.

$$V = \frac{3.14159 \times 12.05}{4}(11.49^2 - 11.38^2)$$

$$= 23.808685$$

To the nearest whole number, the volume is 24 cu m.

EXERCISE SET C-1

Use 3.14159 for π in formulas that include π.

In Exercises 1-24, find the area A of each figure, to the nearest tenth. See Examples 1 and 2.

The area of a trapezoid is given by $A = \frac{1}{2}h(b_1 + b_2)$.

1. h = 5.4 ft, b_1 = 12.2 ft, b_2 = 8.9 ft
2. h = 17.7 cm, b_1 = 9.8 cm, b_2 = 7.6 cm

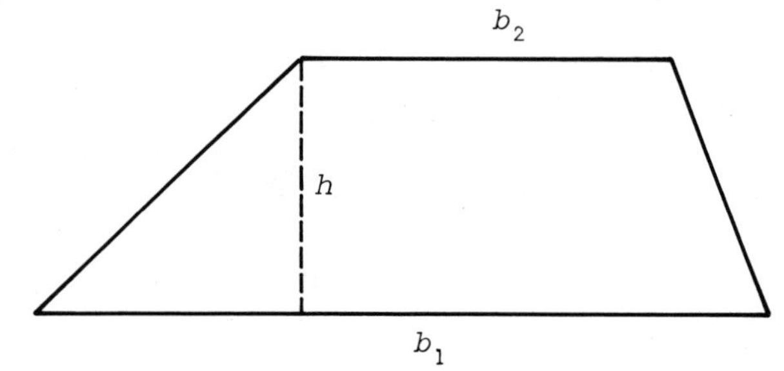

The area of a regular hexagon is given by $A = \frac{3s^2\sqrt{3}}{2}$.

3. s = 64.7 cm
4. s = 7.9 yd

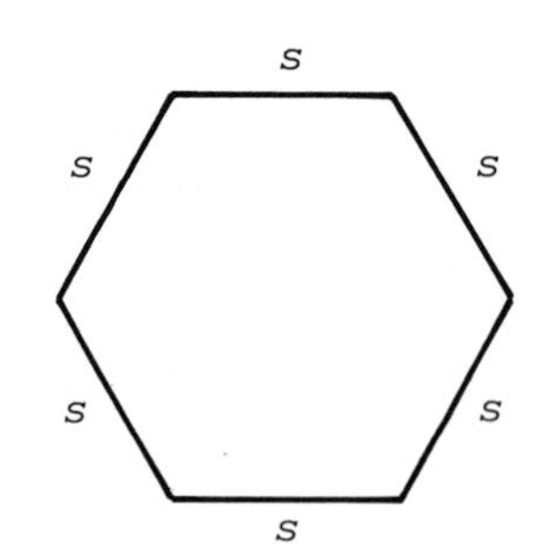

The area of an equilateral triangle is given by $A = \frac{s^2\sqrt{3}}{4}$.

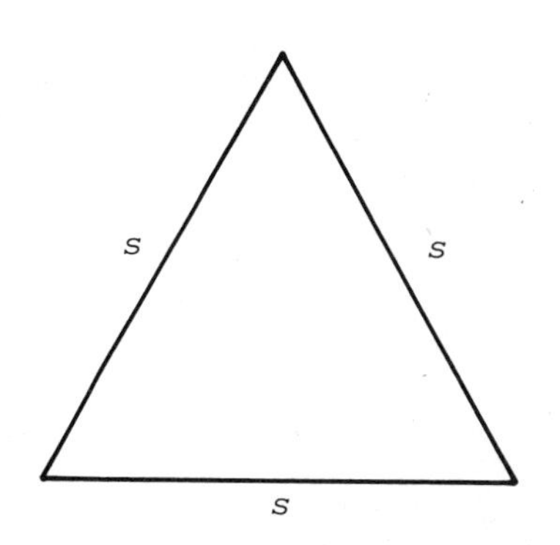

5. s = 25.7 in.
6. s = 34.7 mm
7. s = 108.9 cm
8. s = 216.4 yd

The area of a circle is given by $A = \pi r^2$ or $A = \frac{\pi d^2}{4}$.

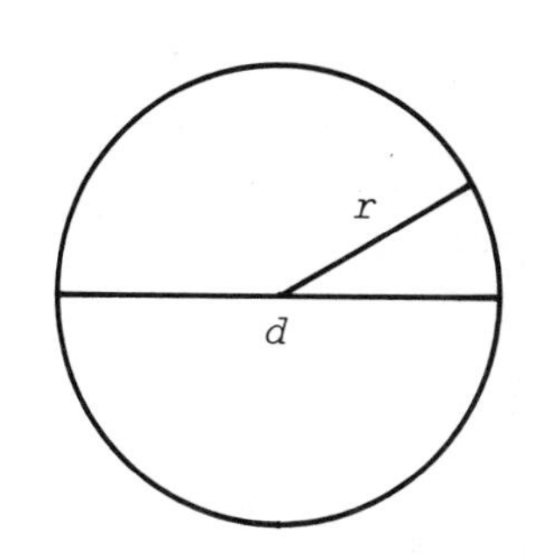

9. r = 89.4 ft
10. r = 76.8 m
11. d = 132.5 cm
12. d = 342.6 in.

The area of a sector of a circle is given by $A = \frac{\pi r^2\theta}{360}$.

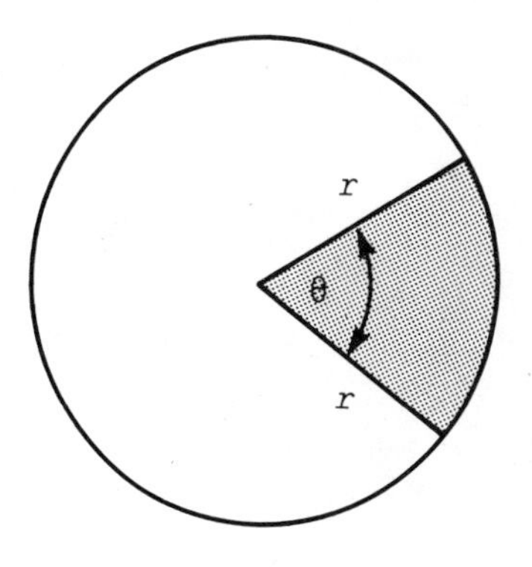

13. r = 19.8 ft, θ = 36.4°
14. r = 17.9 ft, θ = 16.4°
15. r = 75.7 mm, θ = 117.8°
16. r = 68.4 mm, θ = 125.3°

The area of the figure at the right is given by $A = \frac{b}{2}(2a + h)$.

17. a = 13.2 cm, b = 16.7 cm, h = 6.4 cm
18. a = 324.6 mm, b = 108.4 mm, h = 24.4 mm
19. a = 75.6 ft, b = 98.4 ft, h = 8.5 ft
20. a = 64.2 in., b = 58.8 in., h = 16.2 in.

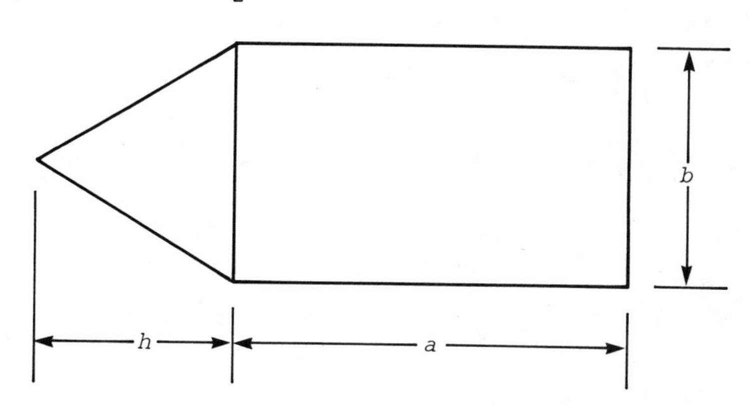

The area of a gothic arch is given by $A = \frac{\pi r^2\theta}{180} - \frac{r^2\sqrt{3}}{4}$.

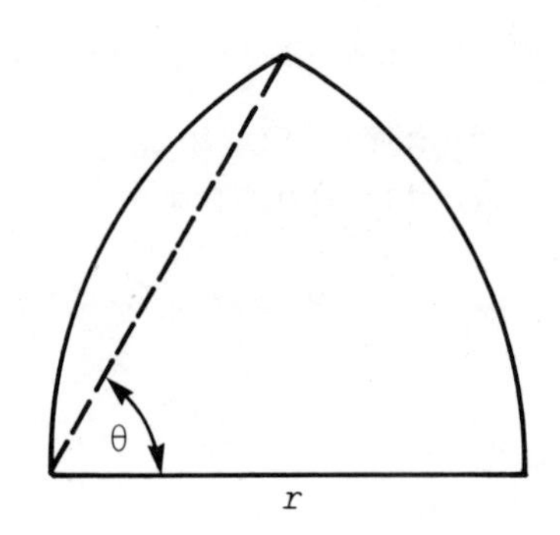

21. $r = 5.6$ cm, $\theta = 48.7°$

22. $r = 16.7$ mm, $\theta = 65.3°$

23. $r = 1.9$ m, $\theta = 38.1°$

24. $r = 2.6$ m, $\theta = 71.4°$

In Exercises 25-34, find the total surface area S of each figure, to the nearest tenth. See Example 3.

The total surface area of a right circular cylinder is given by $S = 2\pi rh + 2\pi r^2$.

25. $r = 12.2$ in., $h = 6.9$ in.

26. $r = 19.6$ ft, $h = 7.6$ ft

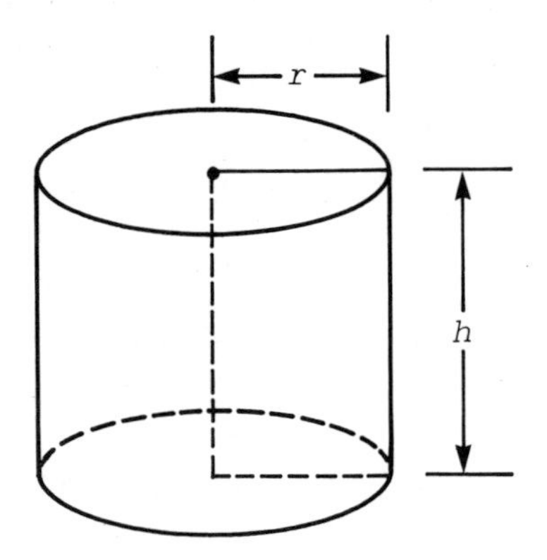

The surface area of a sphere is given by $S = 4\pi r^2$.

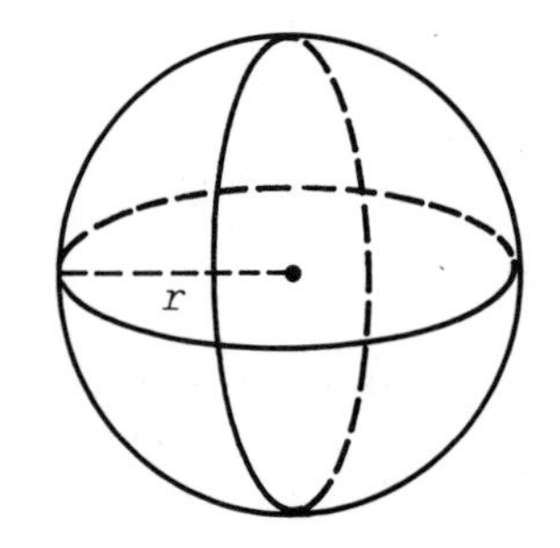

27. $r = 7.2$ cm

28. $r = 12.5$ mm

29. $r = 16.4$ ft

30. $r = 7.2$ yd

The total surface area of a hollow right circular cylinder is given by $A = \pi h(D + d) + \frac{\pi}{2}(D^2 - d^2)$.

31. $D = 12.2$ in., $d = 10.6$ in., $h = 15.7$ in.

32. $D = 8.9$ ft, $d = 7.8$ ft, $h = 12.7$ ft

33. $D = 68$ cm, $d = 67.6$ cm, $h = 42.4$ cm

34. $D = 75$ mm, $d = 74.4$ mm, $h = 12.5$ mm

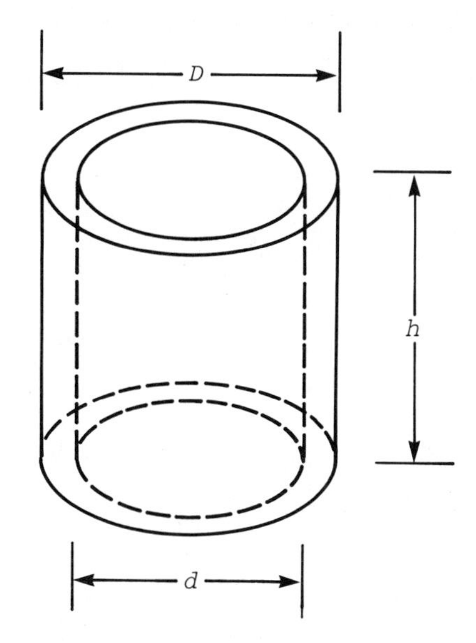

In Exercises 35-48, find the volume V of each figure, to the nearest whole number. See Example 4.

The volume of a hollow right circular cylinder is given by $V = \frac{\pi h}{4}(D^2 - d^2)$.

35. h = 6.15 cm, D = 8.57 cm, d = 8.46 cm

36. h = 17.24 ft, D = 9.15 ft, d = 8.97 ft

The volume of a right circular cone is given by $V = \frac{1}{3}\pi r^2 h$.

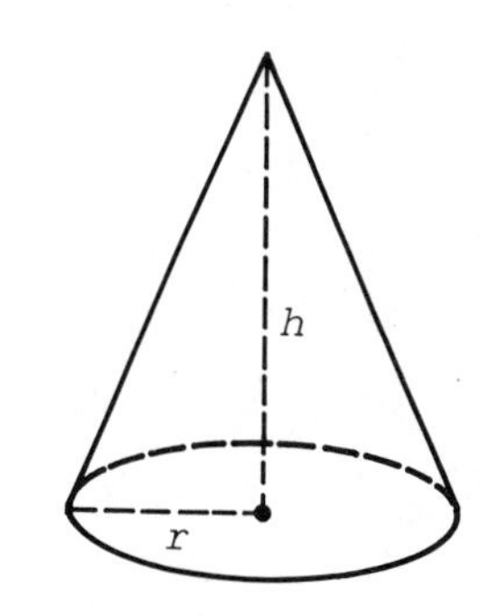

37. r = 19.45 m, h = 16.75 m

38. r = 75.62 mm, h = 43.17 mm

39. r = 40.96 ft, h = 27.55 ft

40. r = 70.76 in., h = 98.45 in.

The volume of a torus is given by $V = \frac{\pi^2 d^2 D^2}{4}$.

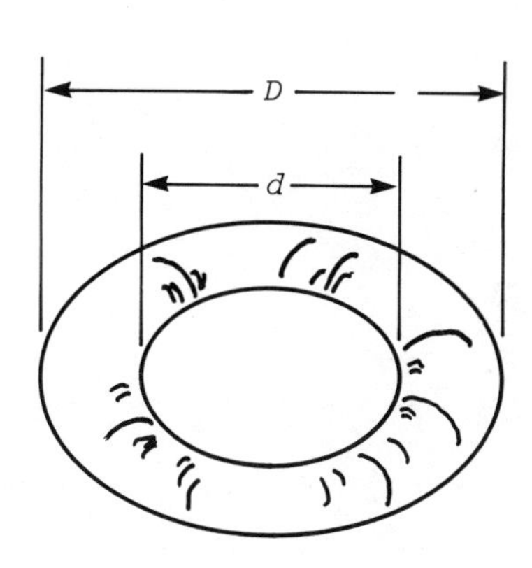

41. d = 4.61 cm, D = 5.73 cm

42. d = 8.96 cm, D = 10.54 cm

43. d = 6.62 in., D = 8.45 in.

44. d = 9.96 in., D = 12.75 in.

The volume of a hollow sphere is given by $V = \frac{4\pi}{3}(R^3 - r^3)$.

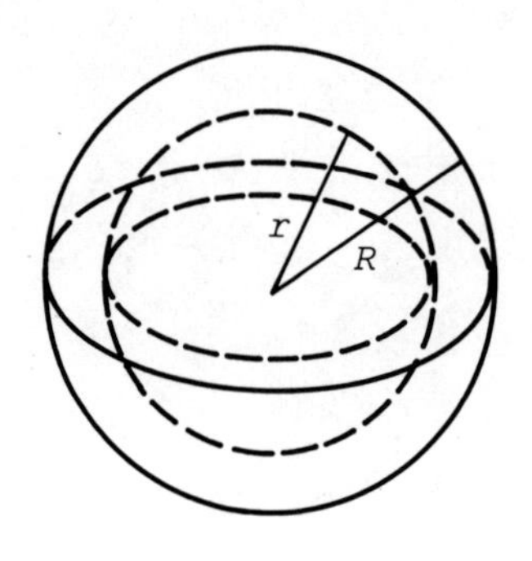

45. R = 73.69 m, r = 69.42 m

46. R = 35.91 cm, r = 33.89 cm

47. R = 15.75 yd, r = 13.50 yd

48. R = 18.63 ft, r = 16.92 ft

C-2 Three Types of Percent Problems

OBJECTIVES

After completing this section, you should be able to

1. Change a decimal to a percent or a percent to a decimal.
2. Change a fraction to a percent.
3. Recognize and solve three types of percent problems.

PERCENT EQUIVALENTS

The percent symbol, %, is used to mean *hundredths*. Thus, a decimal can be written as a percent, and a percent can be written as a decimal.

To change a decimal to a percent, move the decimal point two places to the right. Add or drop zeros as needed, and add the % symbol to follow the last digit.

EXAMPLE 1

a. .32 = 32%　　　　b. 2.05 = 205%

c. .124 = 12.4%　　　　d. 1 = 1.00 = 100%

To change a percent to a decimal, move the decimal point two places to the left. Add or drop zeros as needed, and drop the % symbol.

EXAMPLE 2

a. 45% = .45　　　　b. .02% = .0002

c. 123% = 1.23　　　　d. 200% = 2.00 = 2

Percents that involve fractions, such as 6 3/4% or 1/3%, can be changed to decimals by first changing the fraction to its decimal equivalent, as in Section A-6.

EXAMPLE 3

Change each percent to a decimal.

a. $16\frac{3}{4}\%$　　　　b. 3/4%　　　　c. 1/3%

Solutions

a. 3/4 = .75. Hence, 16 3/4% = 16.75% = .1675.

b. 3/4 = .75. Hence, 3/4% = .75% = .0075.

c. 1/3 = .33333333. Hence, 1/3% = .33333333% = .00333333

In Example 3c, the number .00333333 is a nonterminating decimal, and so it is an approximation to 1/3%. For most applications, such approximations are adequate.

To change a fraction to a percent, first change the fraction to its decimal equivalent. Then change the decimal to a percent.

EXAMPLE 4

a. $\frac{3}{5}$ = .6 = 60%

b. $\frac{13}{5}$ = 2.6 = 260%

c. $\frac{7}{8}$ = .875 = 87.5%

d. $\frac{1}{200}$ = .005 = .5%

e. $\frac{8}{11}$ = .72727273 = 72.73%, to the nearest hundredth of a percent

PERCENT: CASE I

The first type of percent problem is "*To find a percent of a number.*" First change the percent to a decimal, then multiply the result by the given number.

EXAMPLE 5

To the nearest hundredth, find

a. 47% of 349.12

b. $\frac{3}{4}$% of 8105.75

Solutions

a. 47% = .47: .47 × 349.12 = 164.0864, or 164.09

b. $\frac{3}{4}$% = .0075: .0075 × 8105.75 = 60.793125, or 60.79

THE PERCENT KEY

Many calculators have a *percent key* [%] that serves the purpose of moving the decimal point two places to the correct position during a computation. If your calculator has such a key, then you can find a percent of a number without having to change the percent to a decimal. (If your calculator has no such key, omit Example 6.)

EXAMPLE 6

47% of 349.12 can be computed as follows:

349.12 [×] 47 [%] → 164.0864

PERCENT: CASE II

The second type of percent problem can be described as "*To find what percent one number is of another.*"

EXAMPLE 7

16 is what percent of 98? Round off the answer to the nearest hundredth of a percent.

Solution

Let P represent the required percent. Then

$$16 = P \times 98$$

$$\frac{16}{98} = P$$

$$P = .1632653 = 16.32653\%$$

To the nearest hundredth of a percent, $P = 16.33\%$.

PERCENT: CASE III

The third type of percent problem can be stated as "*Given a percent of a number, find the number.*"

EXAMPLE 8

4.07% of what number is 27.3? Round off the answer to the nearest hundredth.

Solution

Let N represent the required number, and change 4.07% to .0407. Then

$$.0407 \times N = 27.3$$

$$N = \frac{27.3}{.0407}$$

$$N = 670.76167$$

To the nearest hundredth, $N = 670.76$.

EXERCISE SET C-2

Change each decimal to a percent. See Example 1.

1. .46
2. .95
3. .175
4. .637
5. .0625
6. .032
7. 4
8. 2

Change each percent to a decimal. If the decimal is nonterminating, round it off to three significant digits. See Examples 2 and 3.

9. 68%
10. 86%
11. .6%
12. .9%
13. 275%
14. 425%
15. 9.05%
16. 8.25%
17. $18\frac{3}{8}\%$
18. $28\frac{5}{8}\%$
19. $\frac{2}{3}\%$
20. $\frac{5}{6}\%$

Change each fraction to a percent. If the decimal equivalent is nonterminating, round off the percent to the nearest hundredth. See Example 4.

21. $\frac{3}{8}$
22. $\frac{5}{8}$
23. $\frac{51}{40}$
24. $\frac{47}{40}$
25. $\frac{3}{500}$
26. $\frac{7}{500}$
27. $\frac{7}{9}$
28. $\frac{5}{9}$

Find each of the following to the nearest hundredth. See Example 5 or 6.

29. 86% of 532
30. 34% of 98.5
31. $32\frac{1}{2}\%$ of 35.66
32. $16\frac{3}{4}\%$ of 450.65
33. $6\frac{2}{3}\%$ of 57.6
34. $15\frac{1}{3}\%$ of 2764.95
35. 215% of 68.9
36. 448% of 486.7
37. $\frac{1}{3}\%$ of 6742
38. $\frac{2}{3}\%$ of 9854

In each of the following, if the decimal equivalent has more than four significant digits, round off the percent to the nearest hundredth. See Example 7.

39. 16 is what percent of 25?
40. 63 is what percent of 200?
41. 33.5 is what percent of 72?
42. 21.7 is what percent of 43?
43. 306 is what percent of 83?
44. 786 is what percent of 98.4?
45. .025 is what percent of .009?
46. .012 is what percent of .007?

Find the required number to the nearest hundredth. See Example 8.

47. 32% of what number is 75?
48. 68% of what number is 53?
49. $12\frac{1}{2}\%$ of what number is 604?
50. $7\frac{3}{4}\%$ of what number is 104?
51. 23.4% of what number is 58.4?
52. 38.7% of what number is 815.1?
53. 215% of what number is 248.64?
54. 118% of what number is 185.95?

Solve each problem.

55. Four couples have dinner in a restaurant. The cost of eight dinners is \$60.80, to which $6\frac{1}{2}\%$ in sales tax must be added. (a) Find the total amount of the check. (b) If 15% of the check total is to be given as a tip, find the total cost of the eight dinners. (c) If the bill is to be shared equally, how much is the cost to each couple?

56. In computing the cost of taking a friend to lunch, a young woman notes that each lunch is \$3.95, to which 7% in sales tax must be added. (a) Find the total amount of the check. (b) If 15% of the check total is to be given as a tip, find the total cost of the two lunches.

57. The first Concorde flight from Paris to Rio de Janeiro took 3 hr and 38 min. A standard jet flight takes 6 hr and 20 min. To the nearest whole number, the Concorde time is what percent of the standard jet time?

58. An employee earning \$307 per week receives a 10% pay increase, unfortunately followed by a 10% pay decrease. How much is the employee now earning per week?

C-3 Applications of Percent

OBJECTIVE

After completing this section, you should be able to select the appropriate type of percent computation needed to solve a given problem involving an application of percent.

The three types of percent problems considered in Section C-2 can be used to help solve many different kinds of applied problems.

DISCOUNT AND PERCENT CHANGE

The price of an article is called the *list price*. When a retail dealer buys an article from a manufacturer, he or she usually pays the *net price*, which can be computed by subtracting a specified percent of the list price from the list price. The amount to be subtracted is called the *discount*; the percent used to compute the discount is called the *discount rate*. For a given article, the actual price paid by a customer to a retail dealer is called the *selling price*.

EXAMPLE 1

A typewriter listed at \$328.50 is sold to a dealer at a 48% discount. Find the net price of the typewriter.

$$\begin{aligned} 328.50 - (48\% \text{ of } 328.50) &= 328.50 - (.48 \times 328.50) \\ &= 328.50 - 157.68 \\ &= 170.82 \end{aligned}$$

The net price is \$170.82.

Sometimes a manufacturer offers more than one discount to a dealer. The following formula can be used to compute N, the net price after two discounts are computed:

$$N = L(1 - r_1)(1 - r_2) \qquad (1)$$

where L is the list price and r_1 and r_2 are the two discount rates in decimal form.

EXAMPLE 2

A manufacturer allows a 55.5% discount on all items sold to retail dealers and an additional 2% discount if the bill is paid within 30 days. Find the net price of a \$498.75 television set.

Solution

$L = 498.75$, $r_1 = .555$, $r_2 = .02$. Substitute into Formula (1):

$$N = 498.75(1 - .555)(1 - .02) = 217.50488$$

The net price is \$217.50, to the nearest cent.

Note that Formula (1) can also be used to solve problems with only *one* discount. As an example, for the typewriter of Example 1, we have L = \$328.50 and $r_1 = .48$. We can find the net price N as follows:

$$N = 328.50(1 - .48) = \$170.82$$

To compute a percent change (increase or decrease) from a given number N, first find the amount of the change (call it D) and then answer the question, "D is what percent of the *original number* N?"

EXAMPLE 3

If the cost of a gallon of gasoline increases from 59.9¢ per gallon to 71.9¢ per gallon, find the percent increase to the nearest tenth of a percent.

Solution

The amount of change, D, is given by

$$D = 71.9 - 59.9 = 12.0¢$$

Let P represent the percent change, and consider

12.0¢ is what percent of 59.9¢?

$$12.0 = P \times 59.9$$

$$\frac{12.0}{59.9} = P$$

$$P = .2003338 = 20.03338\%$$

To the nearest tenth of a percent, the percent increase is 20.0%.

THE ADD/SUBTRACT PERCENT SEQUENCES

Given a number N, certain types of problems are solved by adding to N a percent P of N, or by subtracting from N a percent P of N. Many calculators with a [%] key have special capabilities for doing such computations with a minimum number of key presses. The *add-on sequence* is

N [+] P [%] [=]

The *subtract-off sequence* is

N [-] P [%] [=]

If your calculator has a [%] key, you can test for these capabilities by pressing the sequence

50 [+] 10 [%] [=]

If your answer differs from 55, your calculator does *not* have them. Instead, such problems can be solved as follows.

1. Change the percent to a decimal.
2. Compute the appropriate percent of N and add it to, or subtract it from, N.

EXAMPLE 4

Find the total cost of a camera selling for $129.95 plus a 6% sales tax.

Solution

By the add-on sequence:

129.95 [+] 6 [%] [=] → 137.747

Without the add-on sequence:

$$129.95 + (.06 \times 129.95) = 137.747$$

By either method, the total cost is $137.75, to the nearest cent.

EXAMPLE 5

A typewriter priced at $328.50 is placed on sale at a 24% discount. Find the selling price.

Solution

By the subtract-off sequence:

328.50 [-] 24 [%] [=] → 249.66

Without the subtract-off sequence:

$$328.50 - (.24 \times 328.50) = 249.66$$

By either method, the selling price is $249.66.

The selling price of an article is frequently determined by "marking up" the net price. For example, a *markup* of 25% means that 25% of the net price is to be *added* to the net price to determine the selling price.

EXAMPLE 6

Find the selling price of a camera if the net price is $88.53 and the markup is 45%.

Solution

With the add-on sequence:

88.53 [+] 45 [%] [=] → 128.3685

Without the add-on sequence:

$$88.53 + (.45 \times 88.53) = 128.3685$$

By either method, the selling price is \$126.37, to the nearest cent.

DEPRECIATION, APPRECIATION

The word *depreciation* is used to mean that the value of an article decreases; the word *appreciation* is used to mean that the value of an article increases. For example, after one year the value of a car may depreciate by 25% of the original value. On the other hand, the value of a painting may appreciate by 25% of the original value.

EXAMPLE 7

The original value of an object is \$4823.12. What is the value of the object at the end of one year if it

(a) depreciates by 25%? (b) appreciates by 25%?

Solutions

In each case the *change* in value is

$$25\% \text{ of } 4823.12 = .25 \times 4823.12 = 1205.78$$

a. To find the depreciated value, *subtract the change:*

$$4823.12 - 1205.78 = 3617.34$$

The value depreciates to \$3617.34.

b. To find the appreciated value, *add the change:*

$$4823.12 + 1205.78 = 6028.90$$

The value appreciates to \$6028.90.

If the value V of an article depreciates or appreciates over a period of t years at a percent rate r (in decimal form), the following formulas can be used to compute the final value A.

$$\text{Depreciation:} \quad A = V(1 - r)^t \tag{2}$$

$$\text{Appreciation:} \quad A = V(1 + r)^t \tag{3}$$

EXAMPLE 8

If a \$6243.80 automobile depreciates by 15% of its value each year, find the value of the car at the end of 5 years.

Solution

$V = 6243.80$, $r = .15$, $t = 5$. Substitute into Formula (2):

$$A = 6243.80(1 - .15)^5 = 2770.4065$$

The value is \$2770.41, to the nearest cent.

EXAMPLE 9

An ancient Chinese vase sold originally for \$3550. If the value appreciates by 7% of its value each year, find the value of the vase at the end of 8 years.

Solution

$V = 3550$, $r = .12$, $t = 8$. Substitute into Formula (3).

$$A = 3550(1 + .07)^8 = 6099.5603$$

The value is \$6099.56, to the nearest cent.

EXERCISE SET C-3

For the given list prices and discount rates, find the (total) net price of each purchase, to the nearest cent. See Example 1.

1. Slacks: \$37.50, 35%
2. Sport jacket: \$55.95, 28%
3. 4 shirts: \$7.99 each, 25%
4. 4 ties: \$4.98 each, 35%
5. 1 suit: \$175, 45%; and 2 shirts: \$11.69 each, 26%
6. 1 suit: \$169.95, 42%; and 2 shirts: \$12.99 each, 33%

A wholesaler of appliances gives a discount (which varies from item to item) to retail dealers and an additional 3.5% discount if the bill is paid on time. To the nearest cent, find the net price of each order with the given list prices and discount rates, if each order is paid for on time, thus earning the second 3.5% discount. See Example 2.

7. Toaster oven: \$42.95, 42.3%
8. Blender: \$28.76, 40%
9. Washing machine: \$315.85, 47.5%
10. Dishwasher: \$372.98, 38%
11. Stereo system: \$672.15, 35.6%
12. Stereo system: \$715.72, 53.4%
13. Blender: \$32.18, toaster: \$17.25, and electric griddle: \$34.95, 26.5%
14. Slow cooker: \$22.37, clothes dryer: \$279.67, electric fry pan: \$32.76, 33.3%

For each of the changes described below, find the percent change to the nearest tenth of a percent. See Example 3.

15. The price of coffee changed from \$3.98 per pound to \$4.48 per pound.
16. The price of eggs changed from 65 cents a dozen to 72 cents a dozen.
17. The price of shoes on sale was marked down from \$26.95 to \$19.99.
18. During a close-out, loudspeakers were marked down from \$210.95 a pair to \$135.90.
19. Records were reduced from \$6.98 to \$4.32.

20. Last year a certain car cost \$5200. This year it costs \$5350.

21. Last year property taxes on a certain house were \$998.75. This year they are \$1200.22.

22. Enrollment in a mathematics class went from 38 at the beginning of a semester to 25 at the end of the semester.

23. Enrollment at Mt. Everest Community College last year was 2248. This year it is 2497.

24. Rainfall in 1875 was 17.68 inches. In 1876 it was 6.52 inches.

To the nearest cent, find the total cost of each item. See Example 4.

25. A used car listed at \$2148.75, plus a 6% sales tax.

26. A stereo set listed at \$1245.96, plus a 5% sales tax.

27. A pair of ski boots listed at \$68.99, plus a $5\frac{1}{2}$% sales tax.

28. A concert ticket for \$9.50, plus a $6\frac{1}{2}$% tax.

29. A restaurant meal for \$10.95, plus a 15% tip.

30. A restaurant meal for \$8.95, plus a 15% tip.

31. A hotel charge for \$68.70, plus a 12% tip for services.

32. A hotel charge for \$48.90, plus a 15% tip for services.

Find the selling price, to the nearest cent of each item with list price and discount rate as given. See Example 5.

33. Chair: \$88.95, 33%

34. Mattress: \$110.35, 28%

35. Carpet: \$215.69, 18%

36. Lamp: \$76.75, 35%

37. Calculator: \$46.95, 15%

38. Slide projector: \$114.95, 38%

Find the selling price, to the nearest cent, of each item with net price and percent mark-up as given. See Example 6.

39. Television set: \$359.50, 28%

40. Microwave oven: \$299.75, 32%

41. Loudspeaker: \$189.95, 21%

42. Record player: \$110.45, 18%

43. Lamp: \$68.15, 33%

44. Coffee table: \$116.25, 45%

To the nearest dollar, find the value of each item at the end of one year if it (a) depreciates and (b) appreciates by the given percent from the given original value. See Example 7.

45. Automobile: \$4250, 15%

46. Camper: \$6575, 17%

47. Jade carving: \$758.95, 12%

48. Painting: \$1250.65, 21%

49. Home: \$45,950; 9%

50. Home: \$62,500; 11%

To the nearest dollar, find the value of each item at the end of the specified number of years if it (a) depreciates yearly or (b) appreciates yearly by the given percent from the given original value. See Examples 8 and 9.

51. Boat: $18,950; 14%; 4 years
52. Boat: $12,675; 12%; 3 years
53. Home: $72,000; 9.2%; 5 years
54. Home: $85,500; 8.5%; 5 years
55. Sculpture: $250, 14.5%, 10 years
56. Sculpture: $175, 12.8%, 8 years

C-4 Simple and Compound Interest

OBJECTIVES

After completing this section, you should be able to

1. Do computations involving the simple interest formula.
2. Do computations involving the compound interest formula.
3. Use factoring to raise a number to a power greater than 7.

In this section we use the following words and symbols:

P *Principal:* money being borrowed, loaned, deposited, or invested.

I *Interest:* money paid for the use of principal.

r *Interest rate:* the percent per year used to compute this interest.

t *Time:* the time period over which interest is computed.

A *Amount:* the sum of the principal and the interest.

SIMPLE INTEREST

If the principal does not change during the time of a loan, the interest to be paid is called *simple interest* and can be computed by the *simple interest formula*.

$$I = P \times r \times t \tag{1}$$

For this formula, the interest rate is first changed to decimal form; the time must be expressed as a fraction of a year or a number of years. It is business practice to use 360 as the number of days in a year; we shall follow this practice.

EXAMPLE 1

To the nearest cent, compute the simple interest and the amount on \$826.53 at a $7\frac{1}{2}\%$ yearly interest rate for

a. 30 days b. 30 months c. 30 years

Solutions

In each case, change $7\frac{1}{2}\%$ to .075 and use Formula (1).

a. Change 30 days to $\frac{30}{360}$ year. Then $t = \frac{30}{360}$ and

$$I = 826.53 \times .075 \times \frac{30}{360} = 5.1658125, \text{ or } 5.17$$

$$A = 826.53 + 5.17 = 831.70$$

The interest is \$5.17; the amount is \$831.70.

b. Change 30 months to $\frac{30}{12}$ years. Then $t = \frac{30}{12}$ and

$$I = 826.53 \times .075 \times \frac{30}{12} = 154.97437, \text{ or } 154.97$$

$$A = 826.53 + 154.97 = 981.50$$

The interest is $154.97; the amount is $981.50.

c. The time t is 30 years. Then

$$I = 826.53 \times .075 \times 30 = 1859.6925, \text{ or } 1859.69$$

$$A = 826.53 + 1859.69 = 2686.22$$

The interest is $1859.69; the amount is $2686.22.

EXAMPLE 2

If $11.50 is the simple interest on a loan (principal) of $725 for 60 days, find the yearly interest rate (to the nearest hundredth of a percent).

Solution

$P = 725$, $I = 11.50$, $t = \frac{60}{360}$. Substitute into Formula (1):

$$11.50 = 725 \times r \times \frac{60}{360} = 725 \times \frac{60}{360} \times r$$

$$11.50 = 120.83333 \times r$$

$$r = .09517241$$

To the nearest hundredth of a percent, $r = 9.52\%$.

COMPOUND INTEREST

When money is deposited into a savings account, in most savings institutions the interest is computed at the end of specified time periods and *added* to the principal before the next interest computation is done. This procedure is referred to as *compounding* the interest; the resulting interest is called *compound interest*. For example, suppose that $5000 is deposited in a savings account for 3 days at an 8% yearly interest rate, compounded daily. Using the simple interest formula, we can compute the compound interest, on a day-to-day basis, as follows. The time t equals $\frac{1}{360}$ year, 8% equals .08. At the end of the first day,

$$I = 5000 \times .08 \times \frac{1}{360} = 1.1111111, \text{ or } \$1.11$$

The principal now changes to $5000 + $1.11, or $5001.11. At the end of the second day,

$$I = 5001.11 \times .08 \times \frac{1}{360} = 1.1113572, \text{ or } \$1.11$$

The principal now changes to $5001.11 + $1.11, or $5002.22. At the end of the third day,

$$I = 5002.22 \times .08 \times \frac{1}{360} = 1.1116044, \text{ or } \$1.11$$

and the principal now changes to \$5003.33. The compound interest is

$$\$5003.33 - \$5000 = \$3.33$$

Even with a calculator, the above day-to-day procedure is not practical for long periods of time. However, this procedure can be used to develop the following *daily compound interest formula:*

$$A = P\left(1 + \frac{r}{360}\right)^{d} \qquad (2)$$

where d is the total number of days, and A, P, and r are as listed at the start of this section. (In the following examples, we use K-MULT, as in Section A-7, to raise numbers to powers.)

EXAMPLE 3

To the nearest cent, find the amount and the compound interest on \$5000 at 8% for 3 days.

Solution

$P = 5000$, $r = .08$, and $d = 3$. Substitute into Formula (2).

$$A = 5000\left(1 + \frac{.08}{360}\right)^{3}$$

Follow the order of operations rules. First, compute the expression in parentheses, then raise the result to the third power and multiply by 5000.

.08 [÷] 360 [+] 1 [=] [×] [=] [=] [×] 5000 [=] → 5003.33

The amount is \$5003.33. The compound interest is

$$\$5003.33 - \$5000 = \$3.33$$

EXPONENTS GREATER THAN 7

In Example 3, to compute compound interest for three days we had to raise a number to the third power. Using K-MULT, we had to press the [=] key only twice. To compute compound interest for a greater number of days, say for 90 days, we would have to press the [=] key 89 times—not an efficient procedure. Fortunately, in many cases we can combine K-MULT with factoring and a special form of exponential notation to reduce the number of times that we need to press the [=] key.

Recall from Section A-7 that the product of two or more identical factors can be expressed in exponential notation. For example,

$$2 \cdot 2 \cdot 2 \cdot 2 \cdot 2 \cdot 2 = 2^{6}$$

Now, observe that

$$2 \cdot 2 \cdot 2 \cdot 2 \cdot 2 \cdot 2 = (2 \cdot 2) \cdot (2 \cdot 2) \cdot (2 \cdot 2)$$

$$= 2^2 \cdot 2^2 \cdot 2^2 = (2^2)^3$$

The last expression, which may also be written as $2^{2 \cdot 3}$, can be viewed as meaning, "First square 2, then raise the result to the power 3." Using K-MULT for each of the two factors, this can be done by the sequence

$$\underbrace{2\ \boxed{\times}\ \boxed{=}}_{\text{2nd power}}\ \underbrace{\boxed{\times}\ \boxed{=}\ \boxed{=}}_{\text{3rd power}}$$

This procedure can be used for exponents that can be factored into two or more factors. However, answers to computations that involve raising numbers to powers *may differ* slightly among different calculators. Hence, your answers to the following examples and to some of the exercises in the exercise set may differ from those in the book.

EXAMPLE 4

Compute: $(1.007)^{30}$

Solution

First, completely factor the exponent: $30 = 2 \cdot 3 \cdot 5$. Hence,

$$(1.007)^{30} = (1.007)^{2 \cdot 3 \cdot 5}$$

Next, apply K-MULT for each of the factors, remembering to press the $\boxed{\times}$ key at the start of each such sequence, as follows.

$$1.007\ \underbrace{\boxed{\times}\ \boxed{=}}_{\text{2nd power}}\ \underbrace{\boxed{\times}\ \boxed{=}\ \boxed{=}}_{\text{3rd power}}\ \underbrace{\boxed{\times}\ \boxed{=}\ \boxed{=}\ \boxed{=}\ \boxed{=}}_{\text{5th power}} \rightarrow 1.2327751$$

Thus, $(1.007)^{30} = 1.2327751$.

EXAMPLE 5

To the nearest cent, find the amount and the compound interest on \$27,403 at $8\frac{3}{4}\%$ for 30 days.

Solution

$P = 27{,}403$; $r = .0875$; and $d = 30 = 2 \cdot 3 \cdot 5$. Substitute into Formula (2).

$$A = 27{,}403\left(1 + \frac{.0875}{360}\right)^{2 \cdot 3 \cdot 5}$$

Compute by the sequence

$$.0875\ \boxed{\div}\ 360\ \boxed{+}\ 1\ \boxed{=}\ \boxed{\times}\ \boxed{=}\ \boxed{\times}\ \boxed{=}\ \boxed{=}\ \boxed{\times}\ \boxed{=}\ \boxed{=}\ \boxed{=}\ \boxed{=}\ \boxed{\times}\ 27403\ \boxed{=} \rightarrow 27{,}603.428$$

The amount is \$27,603.43; the compound interest is \$200.43.

On a nonscientific calculator, the procedure above is the preferred method for exponents greater than 7. Of course, if an exponent is a large *prime* number, this procedure is not appropriate—a scientific calculator could be used instead.

Problems such as, "If a bank pays interest compounded daily, how much must be deposited today in order to have a specified amount of money in the account at the end of a given number of days?" can be solved by a variation of Formula (2).

$$P = \frac{A}{\left(1 + \frac{r}{360}\right)^d} \qquad (3)$$

where P is the amount of money to be deposited today, and A is the amount required to be in the account at the end of d days.

EXAMPLE 6

To the nearest dollar, how much must be deposited in a savings account if the interest is compounded daily at $9\frac{1}{2}$% and the account is to contain \$9400 at the end of 180 days?

Solution

$A = 9400$, $r = .095$, and $d = 180 = 2 \cdot 2 \cdot 3 \cdot 3 \cdot 5$. Substitute into Formula (3).

$$P = \frac{9400}{\left(1 + \frac{.095}{360}\right)^{2 \cdot 2 \cdot 3 \cdot 3 \cdot 5}} = 8963.9744$$

To the nearest dollar, \$8964 should be deposited.

EXERCISE SET C-4

(Note: In this set of exercises your answers may differ slightly from the answers in the book.)

For the given principal, rate, and time, compute (a) the simple interest and (b) the amount. Answers to the nearest cent. See Example 1.

1. \$7450, 6%, 3 years
2. \$9375, 8%, 4 years
3. \$654.65, 5%, 2 years
4. \$567.43, 7%, 1.5 years
5. \$480, 8.5%, 16 months
6. \$855, 9.5%, 18 months
7. \$1200, $10\frac{1}{4}$%, 2 years 9 months
8. \$2550, $9\frac{3}{4}$%, 3 years 3 months
9. \$9500, 7.5%, 200 days
10. \$710.50, 8.4%, 173 days
11. \$635.45, 9.05%, 165 days
12. \$333.57, 12.08%, 307 days

For the given interest, principal, and time, compute the yearly interest rate to the nearest hundredth of a percent. See Example 2.

13. I = \$12.50, P = \$875, 90 days
14. I = \$15.75, P = \$915, 60 days

15. I = \$30.95, P = \$1000, 120 days

16. I = \$42.45, P = \$1200, 150 days

17. I = \$57.60, P = \$2500, 6 months

18. I = \$65.23, P = \$2100, 9 months

19. I = \$101.17, P = \$2800, 10 months

20. I = \$91.02, P = \$1900, 8 months

21. I = \$152.90, P = \$1650, 2 years 2 months

22. I = \$986.95, P = \$5400, 3 years 4 months

23. I = \$184.88, P = \$2400, 2 years

24. I = \$410.05, P = \$2750, 3 years

Use K-MULT to compute each power. Round off to five decimal places. See Example 4.

25. $(1.05)^{10}$

26. $(1.02)^{12}$

27. $(1.04)^{15}$

28. $(1.025)^{20}$

29. $(1.006)^{24}$

30. $(1.009)^{28}$

31. $(1.001)^{16}$

32. $(1.005)^{18}$

33. $(1.104)^{14}$

34. $(1.103)^{25}$

35. $(1.02)^{20}$

36. $(1.05)^{24}$

For the given principal, rate, and time, compute (a) the amount and (b) the compound interest. Answers to the nearest dollar. See Examples 3 and 5.

37. \$12,500; 10%; 10 days

38. \$25,450; 12%; 9 days

39. \$65,000; 11.4%; 14 days

40. \$75,500; 10.25%; 12 days

41. \$19,700; 12.3%; 16 days

42. \$18,750; 11.75%; 18 days

43. \$15,675; 9.05%; 30 days

44. \$14,922; 10.06%; 27 days

45. \$9580, $6\frac{1}{4}$%, 50 days

46. \$8760, $5\frac{3}{4}$%, 45 days

47. \$6500, $8\frac{3}{4}$%, 75 days

48. \$11,000; $7\frac{1}{4}$%, 60 days

Find the amount of money to the nearest dollar that would have to be deposited in an account today in order to have the given amount in the account at the end of the time specified, if the account pays interest compounded daily at the rate given. See Example 6.

49. A = \$10,000; r = 8%; 50 days

50. A = \$9500, r = 9%, 60 days

51. A = \$6000, r = 10.5%, 45 days

52. A = \$7500, r = 12.4%, 90 days

53. A = \$6300, r = $8\frac{1}{4}$%, 120 days

54. A = \$4200, r = $9\frac{3}{4}$%, 100 days

55. A = \$5100, r = $7\frac{3}{8}$%, 150 days

56. A = \$3950, r = $8\frac{5}{8}$%, 180 days

57. Bank A pays 5% interest compounded daily; Bank B pays $5\frac{1}{4}$% interest compounded daily. To the nearest dollar, how much more interest will \$10,000 earn in one year (360 days) if it is deposited in Bank B rather than in Bank A?

58. Do Exercise 57 if the time is 2 years (720 days).

C-5 Proportions

OBJECTIVES

After completing this section, you should be able to

1. Solve a given proportion for an unknown number.
2. Set up and solve a proportion in order to solve a problem.

An equation in the form

$$\frac{x}{B} = \frac{C}{D} \tag{1}$$

which states an equality between two fractions is called a *proportion*. In Proportion (1), letters B, C, and D represent *known numbers*, the letter x represents an *unknown number*. Note that x appears as the numerator on the left side of the equation. This is the only form of a proportion that we shall need. (It can be shown that any proportion can be changed to this form.)

Proportion (1) can readily be solved for the unknown number x by multiplying each side of the equation by B, the denominator below x, to obtain

$$x = \frac{C \cdot B}{D}$$

EXAMPLE 1

Solve for x to the nearest hundredth.

$$\frac{x}{134.65} = \frac{18.9}{24.3}$$

Solution

The denominator below x is 134.65. Multiply each side of the equation by 134.65 to obtain

$$x = \frac{18.9 \times 134.65}{24.3} = 104.72778$$

To the nearest hundredth, $x = 104.73$.

APPLYING PROPORTIONS

Many different kinds of problems can be solved by setting up and solving a proportion.

EXAMPLE 2

If an automobile uses 18 gallons of gasoline to travel 386 miles, how many gallons (to the nearest tenth) are needed to travel 755 miles?

Solution

Let G represent the required number of gallons, and set up a proportion as follows. Label a gallons column (*gal*) and a miles column (*mi*) as in (a). Because G gallons is paired with 755 miles, enter G as the numerator in the *gal* column and 755 as the numerator in the *mi* column, as in (b). Because 18 gallons is paired with 386 miles, enter 18 as the denominator in the *gal* column, and 386 as the denominator in the *mi* column, as in (c). Solve the resulting proportion.

(a)	(b)	(c)
gal *mi*	*gal* *mi*	*gal* *mi*
$\frac{\quad}{\quad} = \frac{\quad}{\quad}$	$\frac{G}{\quad} = \frac{755}{\quad}$	$\frac{G}{18} = \frac{755}{386}$

$$G = \frac{755 \times 18}{386} = 35.207253$$

To the nearest tenth, 35.2 gallons are needed.

CONVERTING UNITS OF MEASUREMENT

The following *conversion proportion*,

$$\frac{\text{U.S. units}}{1} = \frac{\text{Metric units}}{\text{Conversion number}}$$

together with Tables I, II, and III of *conversion numbers*, can be used to change units of measurement from the United States to the metric system, or from the metric to the United States system. The conversion tables list U.S. units on the left of the equal sign and related metric units on the right.

TABLES OF CONVERSION NUMBERS

I LENGTH

1 inch = 2.54 centimeters	1 yard = .9144 meter
1 foot = .3048 meter	1 mile = 1.6093 kilometers

II LIQUID CAPACITY	III WEIGHT
1 pint = .4732 liter	1 ounce = 28.3495 grams
1 quart = .9464 liter	1 pound = 453.592 grams
1 gallon = 3.7854 liters	1 pound = .4536 kilogram

EXAMPLE 3

To the nearest thousandth, 14 liters = ? quarts.

Solution

Let Q be the number of quarts. From Table II, the quarts-liters conversion number is .9464. Set up and solve a conversion proportion.

quarts		*liters*

$$\frac{Q}{1} = \frac{14}{.9464} \qquad Q = 14 \div .9464 = 14.792899$$

To the nearest thousandth, 14 liters = 14.793 quarts.

Sometimes it is more convenient to enter the metric units on the left side and the U.S. units on the right side of the proportion.

EXAMPLE 4

To the nearest thousandth, 14 yards = ? meters.

Solution

Let M be the number of meters. From Table I, the yards-meters conversion number is .9144. Set up and solve a conversion proportion.

meters		*yards*

$$\frac{M}{.9144} = \frac{14}{1} \qquad M = 14 \times .9144 = 12.8016$$

To the nearest thousandth, 14 yards = 12.802 meters.

EXERCISE SET C-5

Solve for x to the nearest hundredth. See Example 1.

1. $\frac{x}{634.2} = \frac{4.006}{29.13}$
2. $\frac{x}{1.0004} = \frac{5.36}{.086}$
3. $\frac{x}{55} = \frac{297}{3409}$
4. $\frac{x}{.094} = \frac{986}{2143}$
5. $\frac{x}{2.015} = \frac{6.137}{.00536}$
6. $\frac{x}{.0151} = \frac{67.47}{1.513}$
7. $\frac{x}{3.44 \times 10^{11}} = \frac{1.809 \times 10^{-2}}{5.13 \times 10^{6}}$
8. $\frac{x}{2.59 \times 10^{10}} = \frac{4.637 \times 10^{-3}}{8.24 \times 10^{5}}$
9. $\frac{x}{1{,}283{,}300{,}000} = \frac{.000000017}{.0033673}$
10. $\frac{x}{7{,}945{,}000{,}000} = \frac{.0000000024}{.0006834}$

In Exercises 11-22, use a proportion to solve each problem. Answer to the nearest tenth or, if the answer involves money, to the nearest cent. See Example 2.

11. If a car uses 12 gallons of gasoline to travel 219 miles, how many gallons are needed to travel 2973 miles?

12. If a car uses 27.3 gallons of gasoline to travel 424 miles, how many gallons are needed to travel 655 miles?

13. If the car of Exercise 11 has a tank that holds 23 gallons, how far can it go on a tankful of gasoline?

14. If the car of Exercise 12 has a tank that holds 18 gallons, how far can it go on a tankful of gasoline?

15. If 6.4 pounds of detergent sell for $8.80, find the cost of 13.75 pounds of detergent.

16. If 24.8 feet of wire sell for $1.76, find the cost of 87.2 feet of the wire.

17. If 45 floor tiles cost $16.65, find the cost of 580 floor tiles.

18. If 85 feet of fencing costs $582.25, find the cost of 231.25 feet of fencing.

19. If 6 ounces of "diet" root beer contain 1.5 calories, how many calories are contained in a quart (32 ounces)?

20. If the property tax on a $32,500 home is $935, what is the property tax on a $39,850 home in the same neighborhood (at the same rate)?

21. If the property tax on a $47,400 home is $1420.22, what is the property tax on a $52,650 home in the same neighborhood (at the same rate)?

22. If 500 one-dollar bills weigh 1.17 pounds, find the weight of $1,850,000 in dollar bills.

Compute each conversion to the nearest thousandth. Refer to Tables I, II, and III, page 202. See Examples 3 and 4.

23. 17.3 inches = ? centimeters
24. 9.82 feet = ? meters
25. 46.04 yards = ? meters
26. 423 miles = ? kilometers
27. 168.4 centimeters = ? inches
28. 1835 kilometers = ? miles
29. 1000 meters = ? yards
30. 336 feet = ? meters
31. 32.1 pints = ? liters
32. 32.1 liters = ? pints
33. 98 ounces = ? grams
34. 98 grams = ? ounces
35. 53.2 pounds = ? kilograms
36. 53.2 kilograms = ? pounds
37. .163 kilogram = ? pounds
38. .163 pound = ? kilograms
39. 12.6 liters = ? gallons
40. 12.6 gallons = ? liters
41. 1.08 quarts = ? liters
42. 1.08 liters = ? quarts
43. 21.63 liters = ? pints
44. 21.63 pints = ? liters

For Exercises 45-48, use the fact that 1 hectare is equal to 2.471 acres.

45. 36.5 hectares = ? acres
46. 19.7 hectares = ? acres
47. 56.9 acres = ? hectares
48. 49.1 acres = ? hectares

For Exercises 49-52, use the fact that the Japanese unit of weight, the *kwan*, is equal to 8.267 pounds.

49. 109.6 pounds = ? kwan
50. 215.7 pounds = ? kwan
51. 74.3 kwan = ? pounds
52. 64.5 kwan = ? pounds

Solve each problem (to the nearest cent).

53. If gasoline sells for 66.9 cents per gallon, what is the price per liter? (Hint: First convert gallons to liters.)

54. If paint sells for $3.25 per gallon, what is the price per liter?

55. If a quart of milk sells for 37 cents, what is the price per liter?

56. If 520 grams of breakfast cereal sells for 69 cents, what is the price per pound?

57. If a liter of gasoline sells for 21 cents, what is the price per gallon?

58. If a liter of milk sells for 34 cents, what is the price per quart?

59. If .76 kilogram of cheese sells for $1.05, what is the price per pound?

60. If 38.7 grams of caviar sells for $6.75, what is the price per ounce?

C-6 The Pythagorean Rule

OBJECTIVES

After completing this section, you should be able to

1. Do the computations required by the Pythagorean rule.
2. Use the Pythagorean rule to solve applied problems.

Figure C-6.1 shows right triangle *ABC*. Side *AB*, opposite the right angle (90°), is called the *hypotenuse*; it is the longest side of the triangle. In the examples and exercises of this section we shall use the letter c to represent the length of the hypotenuse, and the letters a and b to represent the respective lengths of the other two sides.

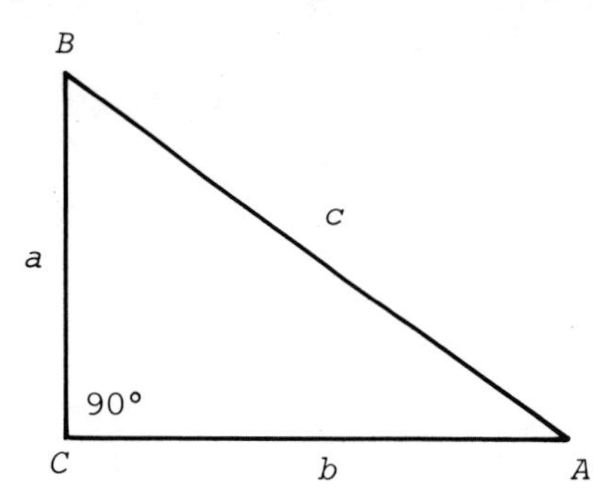

FIGURE C-6.1

A relationship between the lengths of the sides of a right triangle, called the Pythagorean rule (or theorem), has been known for at least 2000 years.

$$c^2 = a^2 + b^2 \tag{1}$$

The following three formulas are derived from Equation (1):

$$c = \sqrt{a^2 + b^2}, \qquad a = \sqrt{c^2 - b^2}, \qquad \text{and} \qquad b = \sqrt{c^2 - a^2}$$

They enable us to compute the length of one of the sides of a right triangle if we know the lengths of the other two sides. Note that each formula requires the computation of a square root. (You may have to refer to Appendix A.)

EXAMPLE 1

In a right triangle, if $a = 8.6$ cm and $b = 11.2$ cm, find the length c of the hypotenuse, to the nearest tenth.

Solution

Choose the formula that enables you to solve for c:

$$c = \sqrt{a^2 + b^2} = \sqrt{8.6^2 + 11.2^2}^{\,*}$$

*If your calculator has an $\boxed{x^2}$ key, see Appendix B.

Use K-MULT and record intermediate results, as follows:

8.6 [×] [=] → 73.96

Record the intermediate result 73.96. Then, square 11.2, add the intermediate result 73.96, and take the square root of the result.

11.2 [×] [=] [+] 73.96 [=] [√] → 14.120906

To the nearest tenth, $c = 14.1$ cm.

APPLICATIONS

The Pythagorean rule can be applied to solve problems that involve right triangles.

EXAMPLE 2

A ladder 27.4 ft long rests against a wall. The foot of the ladder is 6.5 ft from the base of the wall. At what distance from the ground does the top of the ladder touch the wall? (Answer to the nearest tenth.)

Solution

Let a (or b) represent the required length. Draw and label a figure, as shown. Choose the formula that enables you to solve for a:

$$a = \sqrt{c^2 - b^2} = \sqrt{27.4^2 - 6.5^2} = 26.617851$$

The ladder touches the wall (approximately) 26.6 ft from the ground.

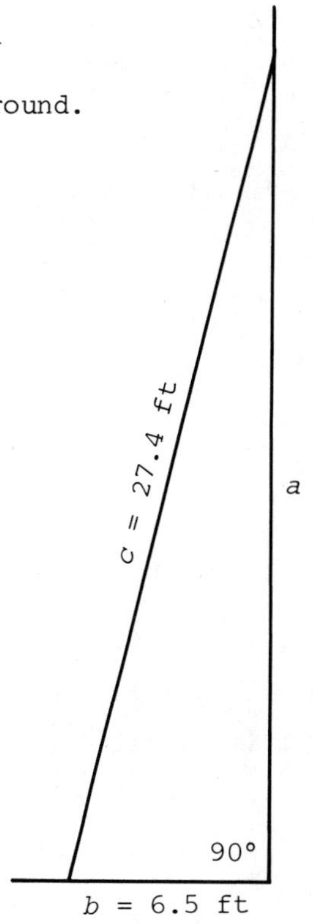

FIGURE C-6.2

EXAMPLE 3

A steel frame in the form of a rectangle is 3.9 m long and 1.4 m wide. A steel brace is to be welded to the frame, as indicated in the figure. To the nearest tenth, how long is the brace?

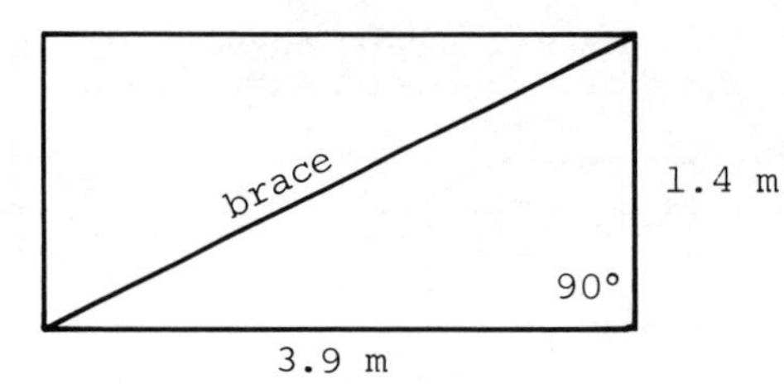

FIGURE C-6.3

Solution

The brace forms the hypotenuse of a right triangle. Choose the formula that enables you to solve for the hypotenuse, c.

$$c = \sqrt{a^2 + b^2} = \sqrt{1.4^2 + 3.9^2} = 4.1436698$$

To the nearest tenth, the brace is 4.1 m long.

EXERCISE SET C-6

The notation used in this set of exercises is shown in triangle ABC.

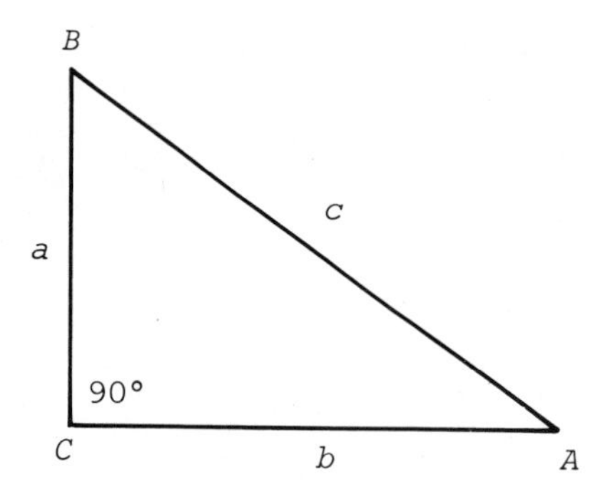

Find the specified side of each right triangle to the nearest tenth. See Example 1.

1. Find c if a = 6.7 cm and b = 8.9 cm.
2. Find c if a = 12.6 mm and b = 15.4 mm.
3. Find c if a = 15.8 in. and b = 15.8 in.
4. Find c if a = 25.4 ft and b = 25.4 ft.
5. Find c if a = 1.9 m and b = .8 m.
6. Find c if a = 2.4 m and b = .6 m.

7. Find b if $a = 3.5$ yd and $c = 8.4$ yd.
8. Find b if $a = 4.2$ mi and $c = 6.8$ mi.
9. Find b if $a = 17$ cm and $c = 32$ cm.
10. Find b if $a = 35$ mm and $c = 87$ mm.
11. Find b if $a = 245.6$ ft and $c = 300.9$ ft.
12. Find b if $a = 186.7$ yd and $c = 489.5$ yd.
13. Find a if $b = 247.3$ cm and $c = 358.2$ cm.
14. Find a if $b = 175.9$ mm and $c = 216.4$ cm.
15. Find a if $b = 98.4$ ft and $c = 127$ ft.
16. Find a if $b = 149.1$ in. and $c = 162.5$ in.
17. Find a if $b = 806$ m and $c = 909$ m.
18. Find a if $b = 777$ m and $c = 1126$ m.

Solve. Find each answer to the nearest tenth. See Examples 2 and 3.

19. A guy wire 18.6 ft long is to be attached to the top of a 12.5-ft television antenna mast. How far from the base of the mast will the guy wire reach?

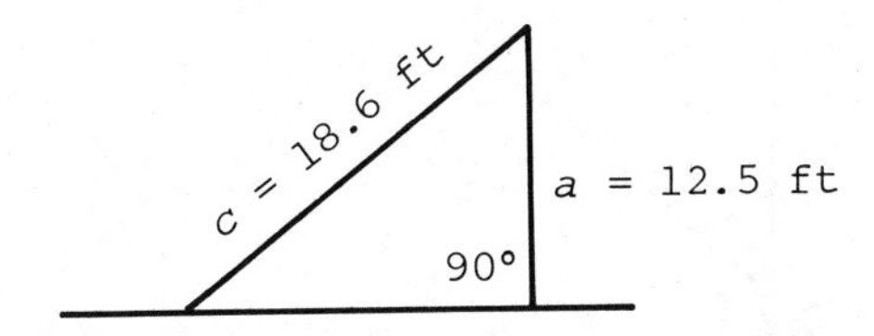

20. Solve Exercise 19 if the guy wire is 21.3 ft long and the mast is 15.5 ft high.

21. A gate in the shape of a rectangle is 1.4 m wide and 2.6 m long. How long is a diagonal brace?

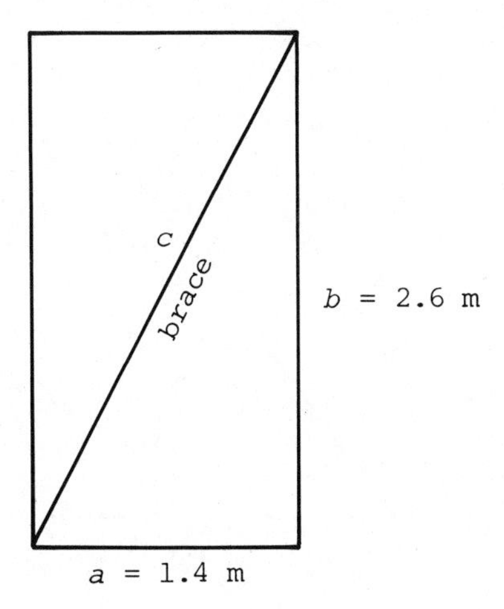

22. Solve Exercise 21 if the gate is 1.9 m long and 1.3 m wide.

23. Starting at point A, a man rows across a river 454 ft wide. The current carries him downstream to point C, 42.6 ft from point B. How far did he travel?

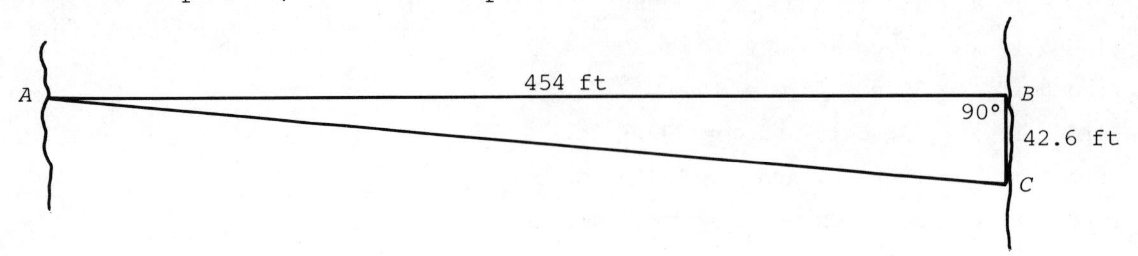

24. Solve Exercise 23 if the river is 356 ft wide and the current carries the man 62.5 ft downstream.

25. A ship travels due north for 28.6 mi and then travels due east for 31.9 mi. How far is it from its starting point A?

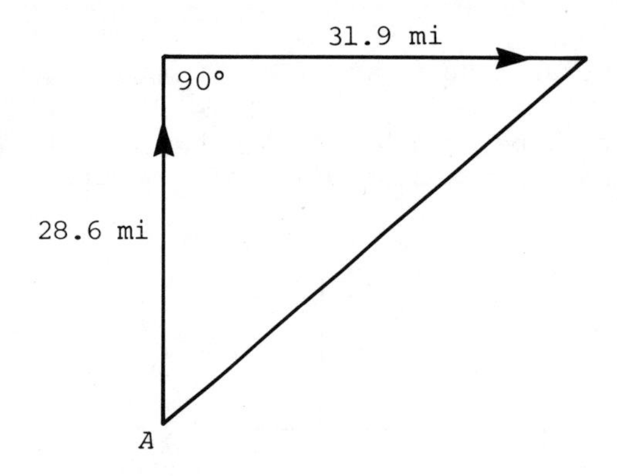

26. Solve Exercise 25 if the ship first travels due south for 53.5 mi and then due west for 43.2 mi.

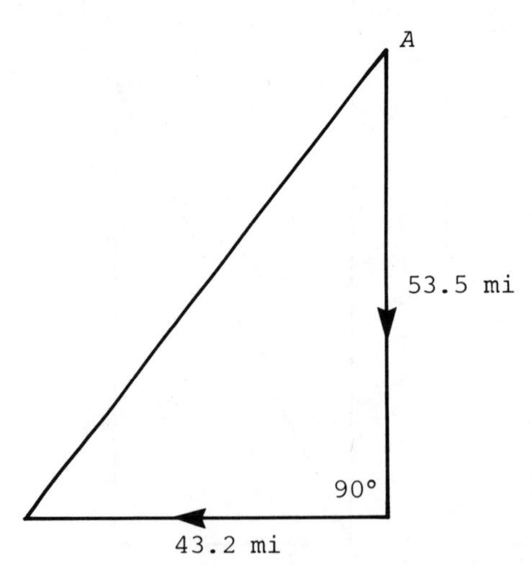

27. A ship S is due west of a lighthouse L. It travels 43.5 km due south and then finds that it is 86.7 km from the lighthouse. How far was it originally from the lighthouse?

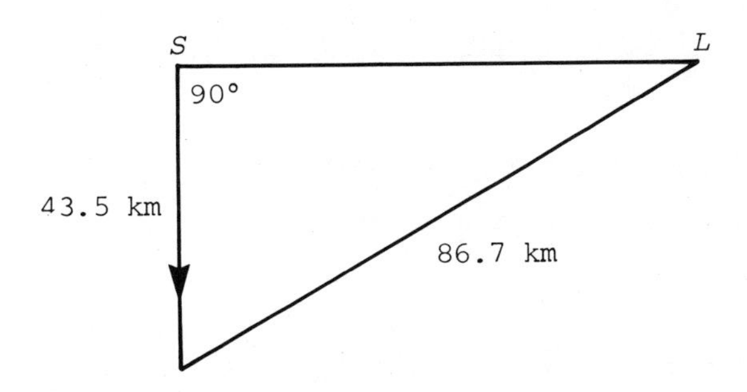

28. Solve Exercise 27 if the ship travels due south 32.9 km and then finds that it is 77.4 km from the lighthouse.

29. A rope 62.4 ft long when dropped from a window of a tall building and stretched taut reaches a point on the ground 24.7 ft from the foot of the building. How high is the window?

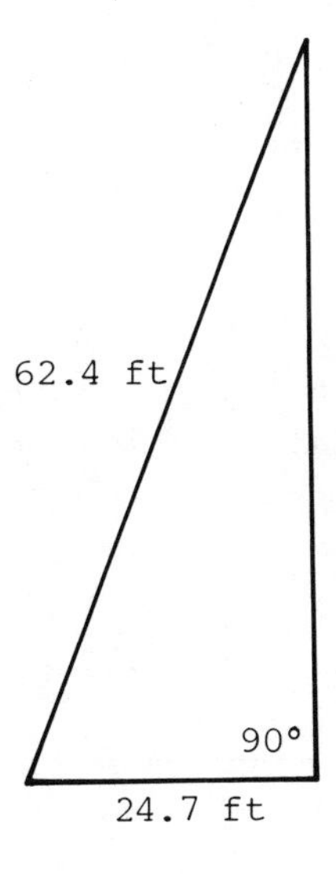

30. Solve Exercise 29 if the rope is 75.3 ft long and it reaches a point on the ground 22.6 ft from the foot of the building.

31. In the figure find the distance from point A to point D. Hint: First find the square of the distance from A to C.

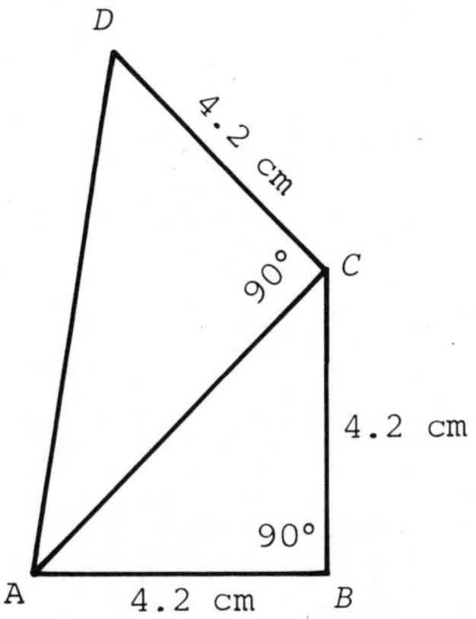

32. Solve Exercise 31 if the distances AB, BC, and CD are each 6.7 cm.

C-7 Average, Standard Deviation

OBJECTIVES

After completing this section, you should be able to

1. Compute the average of a set of numbers.
2. Compute an average by the weighted average method.
3. Compute the standard deviation of a set of numbers.

The *average* (also called the *mean*) of a set of n numbers (the given *data*) can be found by the rule

$$\frac{\text{sum of } n \text{ numbers}}{n}$$

If we use m to represent the average, and $x_1, x_2, \ldots, x_n$ to represent the n numbers, respectively, then a formula for computing the average is

$$m = \frac{x_1 + x_2 + \cdots + x_n}{n} \tag{1}$$

EXAMPLE 1

Find the average of 27.61, 44.02, 41.86, 37.14, 18.01, 26.99, 31.51. Round off the answer to the same number of decimal places as the given data.

Solution

There are seven numbers. Thus, $n = 7$.

$$m = \frac{27.61 + 44.02 + 41.86 + 37.14 + 18.01 + 26.99 + 31.51}{7}$$

$$= 32.448571$$

To the nearest hundredth, the average is 32.45.

THE WEIGHTED AVERAGE METHOD

Given the set of eighteen numbers

3, 3, 3, 3, 5, 5, 5, 8, 8, 8, 8, 11, 11, 11, 11, 11, 11, 12

we could use Formula (1) to compute the average. An alternate method is to observe that there are *four* 3's, *three* 5's, *four* 8's, *six* 11's, and *one* 12. The italic words indicate the *frequency* of each of the numbers—how many times each number appears. Note that the sum of the frequencies

$$4 + 3 + 4 + 6 + 1 = 18$$

is the number n of numbers. Now, because $3 + 3 + 3 + 3 = 4 \times 3$, $5 + 5 + 5 = 3 \times 5$, $8 + 8 + 8 + 8 = 4 \times 8$, $11 + 11 + 11 + 11 + 11 + 11 = 6 \times 11$, and $12 = 1 \times 12$, we can find the sum of the numbers by adding the products

$$(4 \times 3) + (3 \times 5) + (4 \times 8) + (6 \times 11) + (1 \times 12) = 137$$

Because a sum of products is not a chain calculation on most calculators, we will record intermediate results (or use the memory). We can now compute the average:

$$m = \frac{137}{18} = 7.611111$$

which result can be rounded off as needed. We will refer to this method of finding an average as the *weighted average method* and arrange the work as in the next example.

EXAMPLE 2

Given the following listings of numbers and their respective frequencies, the weighted average method can be used to compute the average as follows.

Number		Frequency		Product
31.4	×	5	=	157.0
32.7	×	6	=	196.2
33.0	×	8	=	264.0
33.9	×	11	=	372.9
34.2	×	9	=	307.8
35.3	×	4	=	141.2
		$n = 43$		1439.1

$$m = \frac{1439.1}{43} = 33.467441$$

To the nearest tenth, the average is 33.5.

The weighted average method is particularly useful when a set of numbers includes repetitions and n is large. Such sets of numbers are sometimes given in number-frequency tables, as in Example 2. Such sets may also be given in the form of a listing. In such cases we first organize the data into a number-frequency table, and then compute the average.

EXAMPLE 3

Construct a number-frequency table for the data 8.6, 7.9, 8.2, 8.5, 8.2, 8.2, 7.9, 8.6, 8.5, 8.5, 8.5, 8.6, 8.5, 8.6, 8.6, 8.6, 7.9, 7.9, 8.2, 8.2, 8.2, 8.6.

Solution

First, list all the *different* numbers that appear, from the least to the greatest:

7.9, 8.2, 8.5, 8.6

Next, find the frequency of each different number by counting:

Number		Frequency
7.9	||||	4
8.2	~~||||~~ |	6
8.5	~~||||~~	5
8.6	~~||||~~ ||	7

EXAMPLE 4

Use the weighted average method to find the average (to the nearest tenth) of the numbers in Example 3.

Solution

Number		Frequency		Product
7.9	×	4	=	31.6
8.2	×	6	=	49.2
8.5	×	5	=	42.5
8.6	×	7	=	60.2
		$n = 22$		183.5

$$m = \frac{183.5}{22} = 8.340909$$

To the nearest tenth, the average is 8.3.

STANDARD DEVIATION

Consider the following two sets of numbers, and the averages (m):

a. 3, 4, 5, 6, 7; $m = \dfrac{3 + 4 + 5 + 6 + 7}{5} = 5$

b. 1, 2, 3, 9, 10; $m = \dfrac{1 + 2 + 3 + 9 + 10}{5} = 5$

and note that each set has the same average, 5. A graph of set a is shown in Figure C-7.1(a), a graph of set b is shown in Figure C-7.1(b). Note that the points in Figure C-7.1(a) are clustered "close" to the average, 5, whereas the points in Figure C-7.1(b) are spread rather "far" from the average, 5.

FIGURE C-7.1 a b

Statisticians use the following formula to obtain a measure of how "close" a set of n numbers is clustered about the average of those numbers.

$$s = \sqrt{\frac{(x_1 - m)^2 + (x_2 - m)^2 + \cdots + (x_n - m)^2}{n - 1}} \qquad (2)$$

The result s is called the *standard deviation* of the numbers. The less the standard deviation, the "closer" the numbers are clustered about the average. In fact, to the nearest tenth the standard deviations for sets a and b are

$$s_a = 1.6 \quad \text{and} \quad s_b = 4.2$$

In the following example, we use x_i to represent each of the numbers $x_1, x_2, \ldots, x_n$, in turn.

EXAMPLE 5

To the nearest tenth, compute the standard deviation of

12.3, 18.5, 17.2, 14.7

Solution

First compute the average, m.

$$m = \frac{12.3 + 18.5 + 17.2 + 14.7}{4} = 15.675^*$$

Next, compute the results shown in the table under $(x_i - 15.675)^2$.

x_i	$(x_i - 15.675)^2$
12.3	11.390625
18.5	7.980625
17.2	2.325625
14.7	.950625

Now, note that $n - 1 = 4 - 1 = 3$, and substitute into Formula (2).

$$s = \sqrt{\frac{11.390625 + 7.980625 + 2.325625 + .950625}{3}}$$

$$= \sqrt{7.5491666} = 2.7475746$$

To the nearest tenth, the standard deviation is 2.7.

EXERCISE SET C-7

In Exercises 1-16, round off answers to the same number of decimal places as in the given data.

Find the average of each set of numbers. See Example 1.

1. 27.61, 44.02, 41.86, 37.14, 18.01, 26.99, 31.51
2. 55.03, 86.75, 94.19, 86.15, 74.95, 81.43, 88.90
3. 98, 76, 71, 83, 87, 65, 82, 59, 61, 48, 93, 100
4. 74, 88, 96, 90, 78, 82, 82, 93, 91, 85, 80, 91
5. 43.012, 42.987, 41.765, 44.005, 44.573, 43.145, 41.960, 42.763, 41.652, 44.711, 43.775, 44.008
6. 152.33, 156.99, 154.90, 159.89, 157.76, 160.27, 156.26, 158.69, 157.48, 160.06, 157.76, 162.86

---

*Store m in the memory, if available.

7. The test scores of a certain student are: 72, 85, 50, 47, 82, and 63. Find the average test score.

8. A golfer obtained the following scores on his last six games: 89, 92, 85, 100, 94, and 97. What is his average score?

Complete the following number-frequency tables, and find the average of the numbers. See Example 2.

9.

Number		Frequency		Product
15.8	×	18	=	
14.6	×	14	=	
15.3	×	14	=	
13.6	×	16	=	
12.3	×	12	=	
11.9	×	13	=	______
		TOTAL	=	

n = ________ m = ________

10.

Number		Frequency		Product
68.5	×	13	=	
70.7	×	12	=	
75.6	×	15	=	
69.7	×	15	=	
70.9	×	14	=	
75.2	×	14	=	______
		TOTAL	=	

n = ________ m = ________

11.

Number		Frequency		Product
4.03	×	12	=	
4.42	×	13	=	
4.57	×	10	=	
4.62	×	18	=	
4.59	×	24	=	
4.10	×	15	=	
4.81	×	11	=	______
		TOTAL	=	

n = ________ m = ________

12.

Number		Frequency		Product
1.08	×	19	=	
1.15	×	11	=	
1.10	×	14	=	
.98	×	14	=	
1.18	×	22	=	
1.11	×	23	=	
1.20	×	12	=	______
		TOTAL	=	

n = ________ m = ________

In Exercises 13-16, construct a number-frequency table for the given data, and use the weighted-average method to find the average. See Examples 3 and 4.

13. 42.3, 42.5, 43.4, 42.9, 42.9, 42.9, 43.4, 43.5, 43.5, 43.5, 42.5, 42.3, 42.3, 42.3, 42.9, 42.7, 42.7, 42.7, 42.7, 43.5, 43.5, 42.3, 42.3, 42.5, 43.4, 42.9

14. 71.8, 71.4, 71.3, 71.8, 71.5, 71.8, 72.0, 72.1, 72.1, 71.8, 71.4, 71.3, 71.8, 71.5, 71.8, 72.1, 71.4, 71.6, 72.1, 71.1, 71.8, 71.4, 71.8, 72.1, 71.4, 72.0

15. 88.5, 88.3, 87.7, 88.5, 87.7, 88.1, 88.0, 88.5, 88.8, 88.0, 88.8, 88.5, 88.8, 88.0, 88.5, 88.1, 88.0, 88.3, 88.3, 88.1, 88.5, 88.3, 87.7, 88.0, 88.5, 87.7, 88.8

16. 98.4, 98.1, 98.7, 98.3, 98.4, 97.9, 98.1, 98.3, 98.1, 98.4, 97.8, 98.0, 97.9, 98.0, 97.8, 98.4, 98.4, 98.1, 98.7, 97.9, 97.9, 98.3, 98.0, 97.9, 98.1, 98.1, 97.8, 98.0, 98.4

17. The ages of 36 presidents of the United States, at the time of first inauguration, are tabulated below. The *frequency* indicates how many of the presidents were at each given age. Find the average age of the 36 presidents at the time of inauguration, to the nearest year.

Age	Frequency	Age	Frequency	Age	Frequency
42	1	51	4	60	1
43	1	52	1	61	2
46	1	54	4	62	1
47	1	55	3	64	1
48	1	56	3	65	1
49	2	57	4	68	1
50	2	58	1		

18. The scores of a professional golfer for one season are tabulated below. Find the average score for the season, to the nearest whole number.

Score	Frequency	Score	Frequency
72	1	80	10
74	2	81	7
75	1	82	4
77	4	83	4
78	7	85	2
79	5	87	1

19. Hourly wages and the number of employees at each rate at a certain factory are listed below. Find the average hourly rate, to the nearest cent.

Level	Hourly rate	Number of employees
Laborer	$3.50	20
Semi-skilled	$4.00	7
Journeyman	$4.25	5
Leadman	$5.15	3
Foreman	$6.10	1

20. A company has 100 employees: 10 are paid $3.75 per hour; 8 at $4.05 per hour; 5 at $4.20 per hour; 3 at $4.75 per hour; 2 at $6.30 per hour; 1 at $7.20 per hour; the remainder at $3.10 per hour. Find the average hourly rate, to the nearest cent.

21. A car is driven 35 miles per hour for .8 hour, 40 miles per hour for 1.7 hours, 45 miles per hour for 3.2 hours, 50 miles per hour for 5.3 hours, and 55 miles per hour for 6.4 hours. Find the average speed, to the nearest tenth.

22. A car is driven 30 miles per hour for .5 hour, 35 miles per hour for .75 hour, 40 miles per hour for 1.4 hours, 45 miles per hour for 2.9 hours, 50 miles per hour for 4.2 hours, and 55 miles per hour for 5.5 hours. Find the average speed, to the nearest tenth.

In Exercises 23-28, round off answers to the same number of decimal places as in the given data.

Compute the standard deviation for each set of numbers. See Example 5.

23. 16.4, 18.5, 19.6, 21.2, 17.2

24. 43.5, 38.6, 37.1, 40.0, 42.8

25. 89.9, 95.2, 87.8, 91.0, 90.8, 89.8

26. 65.3, 68.2, 65.0, 67.3, 65.2, 68.1, 65.1

27. 1.051, 1.090, 1.002, 1.043, 1.050, 1.052, 1.097, 1.101, 1.094

28. .35, .40, .41, .35, .45, .43, .35, .35, .38

29. A traffic count at a certain intersection produced the following data, using an hour-by-hour count over a 10-hour period:

    210, 156, 93, 45, 16, 73, 595, 1152, 1054, 675

    Find the average and the standard deviation, to the nearest tenth.

30. Ten college seniors had the following grade point averages at the end of the spring semester:

    2.20, 3.60, 2.40, 3.60, 2.55, 2.87, 1.95, 2.40, 3.04, and 2.32

    Find the average and the standard deviation, to the nearest hundredth.

APPENDICES

Appendix A Square Root

If a number is written as the product of two identical factors, either of the factors is called the *square root* of the number. The symbol $\sqrt{N}$ (read "the square root of N") is used to name the positive square root of a number.

EXAMPLE 1

a. $\sqrt{25} = 5$ because $5 \cdot 5 = 25$

b. $\sqrt{81} = 9$ because $9 \cdot 9 = 81$

If your calculator has a *square root key* [√], continue reading this section through Example 2. There is no need for you to read further than that. If your calculator has no such key, omit the material from here to the end of Example 2, and then continue from there.

In the next example, follow the sequence that is suitable for your calculator.

EXAMPLE 2

$\sqrt{304.86} = 17.460241$, as computed by

304.86 [√] → 17.460241

or by

304.86 [F] [√] → 17.460241

The square root key operates only on the number in the display. Hence, if the number N under the radical results from one or more operations, all the operations under the radical must be completed before pressing the [√] key.

EXAMPLE 3

$\sqrt{144 + 98} = 15.56$ to two decimal places, as computed by

144 [+] 98 [=] [√] → 15.556349

or by

144 [ENT] 98 [+] [√] → 15.556349

If your calculator does not have a [√] key, the following *quotient-average* method can be used to compute the square root of a number to a specified number of decimal places.

EXAMPLE 4

Compute $\sqrt{304.86}$ to two decimal places.

Solution

Begin by guessing a possible square root (it need not be very "close"), say 20. Then proceed as indicated.

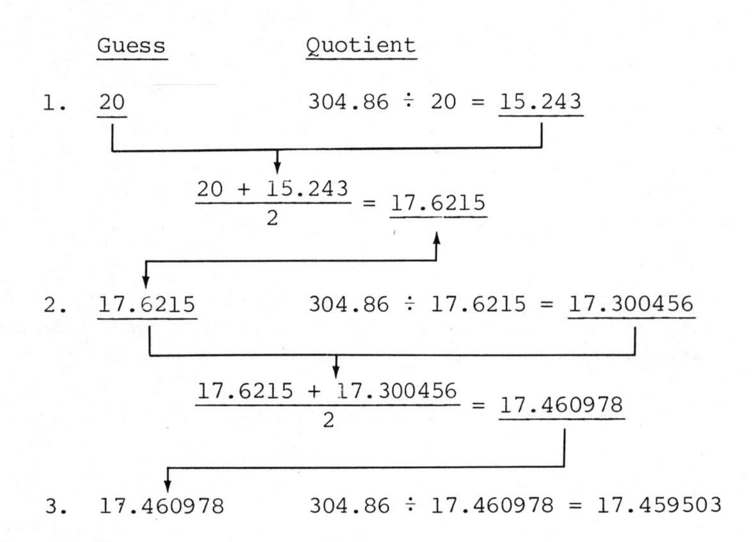

Guess
Quotient
1. 20
304.86 ÷ 20 = 15.243
(20 + 15.243)/2 = 17.6215
2. 17.6215
304.86 ÷ 17.6215 = 17.300456
(17.6215 + 17.300456)/2 = 17.460978
3. 17.460978
304.86 ÷ 17.460978 = 17.459503

In Step 3, note that if both the guess and the quotient are rounded off to two places (as asked for), the results are the same. At this point the procedure ends and, to two places,

$$\sqrt{304.86} = 17.46$$

EXERCISE SET APPENDIX A

Compute to two decimal places. See Example 2 or 4.

1. $\sqrt{756}$	2. $\sqrt{542}$	3. $\sqrt{87.4}$	4. $\sqrt{69.5}$
5. $\sqrt{6675}$	6. $\sqrt{7542}$	7. $\sqrt{.765}$	8. $\sqrt{.432}$
9. $\sqrt{.0506}$	10. $\sqrt{.0957}$	11. $\sqrt{6,845,000}$	12. $\sqrt{7,578,000}$

Compute to two decimal places. See Example 3.

13. $\sqrt{49 + 36}$
14. $\sqrt{49 - 36}$
15. $\sqrt{11.56 - .64}$
16. $\sqrt{11.56 + .64}$
17. $\sqrt{9 + 16 - 2(3)(4)(.87)}$
18. $\sqrt{1.44 + 11.56 - 2(1.2)(3.4)(.7)}$

Answers

1. 27.50	*2. 23.28*	*3. 9.35*	*4. 8.34*
5. 81.70	*6. 86.84*	*7. .87*	*8. .66*
9. .22	*10. .31*	*11. 2616.30*	*12. 2752.82*
13. 9.22	*14. 3.61*	*15. 3.30*	*16. 3.49*
17. 2.03	*18. 2.70*		

Appendix B The x^2 Key

The *squaring key*, $\boxed{x^2}$, is used to raise a number to the second power. For a given number *N*, the sequence *N* $\boxed{x^2}$ squares the number *N*. Thus, 8^2 can be computed by

$$8 \ \boxed{x^2} \rightarrow 64$$

Furthermore, the $\boxed{x^2}$ key will square only the number in the display and will not affect earlier entries or calculations. For example, in the sequence

$$2 \ \boxed{+} \ 8 \ \boxed{x^2}$$

the $\boxed{x^2}$ key squares only the number 8 and has no effect upon the previously entered 2 $\boxed{+}$

The $\boxed{x^2}$ key is particularly useful for computations that involve sums and differences of squares.

EXAMPLE 1

a. $14.9^2 + 6.7^2 = 266.9$, as computed by

$$14.9 \ \boxed{x^2} \boxed{+} \ 6.7 \ \boxed{x^2} \boxed{=} \rightarrow 266.9$$

b. $14.9^2 - 6.7^2 = 177.12$, as computed by

$$14.9 \ \boxed{x^2} \boxed{-} \ 6.7 \ \boxed{x^2} \boxed{=} \rightarrow 177.12$$

EXAMPLE 2

$\sqrt{8.6^2 + 11.2^2} = 14.120906$, as computed by

$$8.6 \ \boxed{x^2} \boxed{+} \ 11.2 \ \boxed{x^2} \boxed{=} \boxed{\sqrt{\ }} \rightarrow 14.120906$$

EXERCISE SET APPENDIX B

Compute to two decimal places.

1. $12.6^2 + 7.9^2$
2. $16.7^2 + 15.2^2$
3. $27.7^2 + 35.5^2$
4. $45.3^2 + 33.3^2$
5. $67.95^2 - 25.27^2$
6. $87.95^2 - 62.25^2$
7. $125^2 - 78^2$
8. $232^2 - 187^2$
9. $\sqrt{9.7^2 + 8.5^2}$
10. $\sqrt{7.7^2 + 5.5^2}$
11. $\sqrt{242.7^2 - 116.6^2}$
12. $\sqrt{354.9^2 - 278.6^2}$

Answers

1. 221.17 *2. 509.93* *3. 2027.54* *4. 3160.98*
5. 3978.63 *6. 3860.14* *7. 9541.00* *8. 18,855.00*
9. 12.90 *10. 9.46* *11. 212.86* *12. 219.85*

Appendix C Addition of Signed Numbers

Numbers preceded by a minus sign, such as -5 and -2, are called *negative* numbers. If a (nonzero) number is not preceded by a minus sign, it is a *positive* number. Positive numbers, such as 5 or 2, may sometimes be preceded by a plus sign, +5 or +2. We refer to the *value* of a signed number without its sign as its *numerical value*.

EXAMPLE 1

a. The numerical value of +5 is 5.

b. The numerical value of -5 is 5.

EXAMPLE 2

Which number in each pair has the *lesser* numerical value?

a. -6, +2　　　　b. -3, +5

Solutions

a. The numerical value of -6 is 6; the numerical value of +2 is 2. Because 2 is less than 6, +2 has the lesser numerical value.

b. The numerical value of -3 is 3; the numerical value of +5 is 5. Because 3 is less than 5, -3 has the lesser numerical value.

To add two signed numbers

1. *If the numbers have the same sign, add the numerical values and place that same sign in front of the sum.*
2. *If the numbers have different signs, subtract the lesser numerical value from the greater numerical value and place the sign of the number with the greater numerical value in front of the difference.*

EXAMPLE 3

Find each sum (no calculator needed).

a. +6 + (+3)　　　　b. -6 + (-3)　　　　c. +6 + (-3)　　　　d. -6 + (+3)

Solutions

a. The numbers have the same sign (both +). Add the numerical values, 6 + 3, to obtain 9, and place that same (+) sign in front of the sum.

$$+6 + (+3) = +9$$

b. The numbers have the same sign (both -). Add the numerical values, 6 + 3, to obtain 9, and place that same (-) sign in front of the sum.

$$-6 + (-3) = -9$$

c. The numbers have different signs, and the numerical value of -3 is less than the numerical value of +6. Subtract numerical values, 6 - 3, to obtain the difference, 3. Because +6 has the greater numerical value, place a + sign in front of the difference.

$$+6 + (-3) = +3$$

d. The numbers have different signs and the numerical value of +3 is less than the numerical value of -6. Subtract numerical values, 6 - 3, to obtain the difference, 3. Because -6 has the greater numerical value, place a - sign in front of the difference.

$$-6 + (+3) = -3$$

For clarity in the examples above, we put + signs before positive numbers with + signs. In actual practice this is not usually done. For example, the results of Example 3 would most often be shown as

a. $6 + 3 = 9$ b. $-6 + (-3) = -9$

c. $6 + (-3) = 3$ d. $-6 + 3 = -3$

The rules for adding two signed numbers can be applied to finding the sum of more than two signed numbers.

EXAMPLE 4

Find the sum: 4 + (-3) + (-2) + 6 + (-7).

Solution

$$\underbrace{4 + (-3)} + (-2) + 6 + (-7)$$
$$\underbrace{1 + (-2)} + 6 + (-7)$$
$$\underbrace{-1 + 6} + (-7)$$
$$5 + (-7) = -2$$

EXERCISE SET APPENDIX C

Determine which number in each pair has the lesser numerical value. See Examples 1 and 2.

1. -5, 7	2. -4, 8	3. -7, 5	4. -8, 4
5. -10, 9	6. -7, 6	7. 10, -9	8. 7, -6

Find each sum (no calculator needed). See Examples 3 and 4.

9. +7 + (+4)	10. +5 + (+9)	11. +2 + (+6)	12. +3 + (+4)

13. $-2 + (-3)$
14. $-3 + (-5)$
15. $-4 + (-6)$
16. $-5 + (-7)$
17. $+7 + (-3)$
18. $+8 + (-4)$
19. $+5 + (-2)$
20. $+4 + (-2)$
21. $-7 + (+3)$
22. $-8 + (+4)$
23. $-5 + (+2)$
24. $-4 + (+2)$
25. $7 + (-2) + (-3) + 4$
26. $8 + (-3) + (-4) + 5$
27. $-3 + 7 + (-2) + 4$
28. $-7 + 8 + (-3) + 6$
29. $-3 + 6 + (-7) + (-8) + 9$
30. $-5 + 9 + (-2) + (-7) + 4$

Answers

1. -5	*2. -4*	*3. 5*	*4. 4*	*5. 9*
6. 6	*7. -9*	*8. -6*	*9. +11*	*10. +14*
11. +8	*12. +7*	*13. -5*	*14. -8*	*15. -10*
16. -12	*17. +4*	*18. +4*	*19. +3*	*20. +2*
21. -4	*22. -4*	*23. -3*	*24. -2*	*25. 6*
26. 6	*27. 6*	*28. 4*	*29. -3*	*30. -1*

Appendix D Restricted Trigonometric x-Values

In this appendix we use A to represent the measure of an angle in degrees or radians. The symbol $<$ is read "is less than," the symbol $>$ is read "is greater than."

DEGREE MEASURE

Some scientific calculators compute trigonometric y-values only for angle measures from -180° to 180°, inclusive. For such calculators, use the following rule to compute y-values for angle measures outside these limits.

$\underline{A < -180°}$ or $\underline{A > 180°}$

1. For *sine* or *cosine*: add (or subtract) 360° to A until the result is between -180° and 180°. Find the sine or cosine of the result.

2. For *tangent*: add (or subtract) 180° to A until the result is between -180° and 180°. Find the tangent of the result.

EXAMPLE 1

Set to degree mode.

a. $\sin 750° = \sin(750 - 360 - 360)° = \sin 30° = .5$

b. $\cos(-340°) = \cos(-340 + 360)° = \cos 20° = .93969262$

c. $\tan 340° = \tan(340 - 180)° = \tan 160° = -.36397023$

RADIAN MEASURE

Calculators that are restricted to angle measures from -180° to 180° will only compute trigonometric y-values for radian angle measures from $-\pi$ to π, inclusive. To compute y-values for angle measures outside these limits, use the following rule.

$\underline{A < -\pi}$ or $\underline{A > \pi}$

1. For *sine* and *cosine*: add (or subtract) 2π to A until the result is between -3.1415927, $(-\pi)$, and 3.1415927, (π). Find the sine or cosine of the result.

2. For *tangent*: add (or subtract) π to A until the result is between -3.1415927 and 3.1415927. Find the tangent of the result.

EXAMPLE 2

Set to radian mode.

a. $\sin(-3.19) = \sin(-3.19 + 2\pi) = \sin 3.0931852 = .04838844$

b. $\cos 6.25 = \cos(6.25 - 2\pi) = \cos(-.033185) = .99944942$

c. $\tan 6.5 = \tan(6.5 - \pi - \pi) = \tan .21681 = .2202772$

EXERCISE SET APPENDIX D

To five decimal places, find each y-value. See Example 1.

1. sin 670°
2. tan 590°
3. cos 410°
4. cos(-830°)
5. tan 700°
6. sin 810°

To five decimal places, find each y-value. See Example 2.

7. sin(-4.35)
8. cos(-8.97)
9. tan 3.23
10. tan 6.34
11. cos 7
12. sin 8

Answers

1. -.76604 2. 1.19175 3. .64279 4. -.34202 5. -.36397 6. 1.00000 7. .93505 8. -.89836 9. .08864 10. .05688 11. .75390 12. .98936

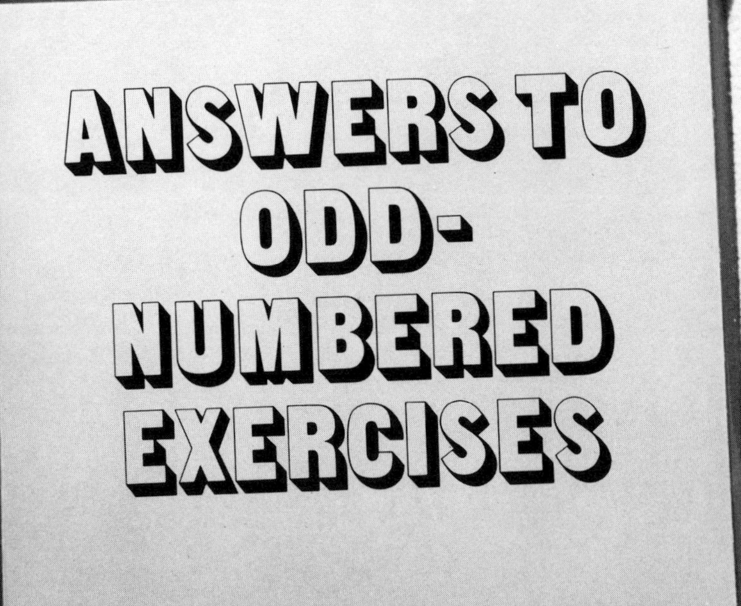
ANSWERS TO
ODD-
NUMBERED
EXERCISES

Answers to Odd-Numbered Exercises

SECTION A

EXERCISE SET A-1

1. 150.4 3. 148.44 5. 2036.991 7. 251.3 9. 230.62 11. 363,636

13. 91.4 15. 305.95 17. 244.2 19. 709.66

21. (a) A: $8790.69; B: $345.83; C: $4841.75; D: ($904.07)
(b) Jan.: $6064.61; Feb.: $3408.85; Mar.: $3600.74
(c) $13,074.20

23. $287.35 25. ($34.73) 27. 22,875 29. .4032938 31. 24.044025 33. 62

35. 2810 37. 7.8 39. 16 41. 140.36 43. 14.22 45. .0135 × 4.76 ÷ .27; .2335 47. 175 × 586 ÷ 700; 146.5 49. $171.00 51. $13.75 53. $.045

55. $.084 57. 271.25 miles

EXERCISE SET A-2

1. (a) 6374.1592
(b) 6374.1592
(c) 6374.1592
(d) 6374.1592
(e) 6374.1592
(f) 6374.1592
(g) 6374.1592

3. (a) 20,468.13509
(b) 20,468.13509
(c) 20,468.13509
(d) 20,468.13509
(e) 20,468.13509
(f) 20,468.13509
(g) 20,468.13509

5. (a) 1,034,592.00563
(b) 1,034,592.00563
(c) 1,034,592.00563
(d) 1,034,592.00563
(e) 1,034,592.00563
(f) 1,034,592.00563
(g) 1,034,592.00563

7. (a) 647.8
(b) 647.77
(c) 647.774
(d) 648
(e) 600

9. (a) 786.7
(b) 786.68
(c) 786.683
(d) 787
(e) 800

11. (a) 2486.9
(b) 2486.88
(c) 2486.883
(d) 2487
(e) 2500

13. (a) 6874.0
(b) 6874.01
(c) 6874.012
(d) 6874
(e) 6900

15. (a) 6015.6
(b) 6015.64
(c) 6015.635
(d) 6016
(e) 6000

17. (a) 1585.0
(b) 1584.96
(c) 1584.960
(d) 1585
(e) 1600

19. (a) 5.7
(b) 5.68
(c) 5.676

21. (a) 19.5
(b) 19.46
(c) 19.461

23. (a) 108.1
(b) 108.07
(c) 108.068

25. (a) 94.1
(b) 94.05
(c) 94.051

27. (a) 555.6
(b) 555.556

29. (a) 451.5
(b) 451.454

31. (a) $78.58
(b) $79

33. (a) $140.50
(b) $140

35. (a) $50
(b) $0

37. (a) $7.50
(b) $8

EXERCISE SET A-3

1. approximate 3. exact 5. exact 7. approximate 9. approximate 11. four

13. one 15. four 17. five 19. four 21. five 23. four 25. four

27. three 29. five 31. one 33. two 35. one 37. (a) 62; (b) 62.4; (c) 62.35 39. (a) 19; (b) 18.5; (c) 18.51 41. (a) 8.3; (b) 8.34; (c) 8.340

43. (a) .015; (b) .0148; (c) .01477 45. (a) 50,000; (b) 50,000; (c) 50,040
47. (a) 130; (b) 135; (c) 134.9 49. (a) 1.3; (b) 1.26 51. (a) 32; (b) 32.4
53. (a) 9.2; (b) 9.16

EXERCISE SET A-4

1. 24.7 3. 10,001 5. .005 7. .07 9. 1.9 11. 404 13. 23.737
15. 748 17. 13.922 19. 132 21. 295.3 23. 14,400 25. 83.5 27. 3.0
29. 2 31. 177,900 33. 800.0 35. (a) 113; (b) 112.9 37. (a) 201.5;
(b) 201.54 39. (a) 40.7; (b) 40.682 41. (a) 230; (b) 231 43. (a) 3100;
(b) 3120 45. (a) 6.7; (b) 6.7

EXERCISE SET A-5

1. 13 3. neither 5. 41 7. 29 9. 2 11. 5 13. 2 and 5 15. 3
17. none 19. 3 21. 23 23. 31 25. 43 27. 29 29. 2 × 2 × 7 × 13
31. 2 × 5 × 5 × 13 33. 3 × 3 × 13 × 37 35. prime 37. 3 × 5 × 7 × 17
39. 2 × 2 × 2 × 3 × 5 × 5 × 5 41. prime 43. 3 × 11 × 13 45. 5 × 19 × 23
47. 3 × 3 × 7 × 29 49. 5 × 7 × 7 × 19 51. 3 × 3 × 7 × 7 × 47 53. 5 × 7 × 97
55. 3 × 5 × 191 57. 3 × 3 × 3 × 5 × 5 × 179

EXERCISE SET A-6

1. terminating 3. terminating 5. nonterminating 7. terminating
9. terminating 11. nonterminating
13. (a) .91666667; (b) .9; (c) .92; (d) .917
15. (a) .5625; (b) .6; (c) .56; (d) .563
17. (a) .09765625; (b) .1; (c) .10; (d) .098
19. (a) .3260274; (b) .3; (c) .33; (d) .326
21. (a) 5.71428571; (b) 5.7; (c) 5.71; (d) 5.714
23. (a) 14.671875; (b) 14.7; (c) 14.67; (d) 14.672
25. (a) .08375; (b) .1; (c) .08; (d) .084
27. (a) .408333333; (b) .4; (c) .41; (d) .408
29. (a) 1/16; (b) .0625; (c) .06; (d) .063
31. (a) 1/15; (b) .06666666; (c) .07; (d) .067
33. (a) 1/.09; (b) 11.111111; (c) 11.11; (d) 11.111
35. (a) 1/.75; (b) 1.3333333; (c) 1.33; (d) 1.333
37. (a) 5/32; (b) .15625; (c) .16; (d) .156
39. (a) 11/9; (b) 1.2222222; (c) 1.22; (d) 1.222
41. (a) 7/40; (b) .175; (c) .18; (d) .175
43. (a) 360/2937; (b) .12257406; (c) .12; (d) .123

EXERCISE SET A-7

1. 2^3 3. 4^4 5. 10^1 7. 6^6 9. $3 \times 3 \times 3 \times 3 \times 3 \times 3$ 11. $10 \times 10 \times 10 \times 10$
13. 5 15. 1 17. 1/10 or $1/10^1$ 19. $1/7^3$ 21. $1/4^2$ 23. $1/3^5$ 25. 10^2
27. 2^3 29. 40.8; 182.4; 307.2 31. 6.44; 18.86; 42.78 33. 23.2; 27.2; 30
35. .285; .315; .495 37. 1296 39. 729 41. 4096 43. -226.981
45. .2219006 47. .0282576 49. .1428571 51. .05668934 53. .3644315
55. .01155582 57. 10^5 59. 10^{-1} 61. 10^{-4} 63. 1 65. 10^{-9} 67. 10^5

EXERCISE SET A-8

1. 723 3. .985 5. 2250 7. 35.4 9. .0354 11. .0756 13. 3.4768×10^3
15. 6.44×10^1 17. 1.234×10^2 19. 5.61×10^{-3} 21. 4.56×10^{-1}
23. 6×10^{-4} 25. 5.98×10^2 27. 2.5×10^{-3} 29. 593 31. .0723 33. 1670
35. .006874 37. 84,220 39. .00060073 41. four 43. one 45. none
47. one 49. [6.875 03] 51. [5.437 -03] 53. [4.743 06]
55. [7.3333 -01] 57. [6. 02] 59. [1.9 -05]
61. $(4.876 \times 8.5) \times 10^1 = 414.46$
63. $(2.5 \times 9.29) \times 10^3 = 23{,}225$
65. $\dfrac{9.83 \times 3.42}{5.55} \times 10^4 = 60{,}574.054$
67. $\dfrac{2.46 \times 2.45}{1.85} \times 10^{-3} = .0032578378$
69. $(4.725 \times 8.72) \times 10^{11} = 4{,}120{,}200{,}000{,}000$
71. $(3.68 \times 5.555) \times 10^{11} = 2{,}044{,}240{,}000{,}000$
73. $\dfrac{6.842}{2.5} \times 10^9 = 2{,}736{,}800{,}000$
75. $(4.5 \times 3.8) \times 10^{-7} = .00000171$
77. $\dfrac{4.3 \times 3.6 \times 2}{9 \times 5.4} \times 10^{-10} = .000000000063703704$

EXERCISE SET A-9

1. Add 3. Subtract 5. Divide 7. Multiply 9. Subtract 11. Multiply
13. 12 ÷ (8 - 4) 15. 32 ÷ (12 + 4) 17. (8 - 2) ÷ (12 + 3)
19. (12 - 2) ÷ (19 - 14) 21. [8 × (6 + 3)] ÷ 12 23. [(18 - 3) × 12] ÷ 20
25. [6 × (15 + 12)] ÷ (12 - 3) 27. [30 ÷ (12 + 4)] ÷ (16 - 4) 29. 64 31. 16
33. 216 35. 24 37. 9 39. 1 41. 12 43. 6 45. 9 47. 5 49. 18
51. 19 53. 15 55. 15 57. 15 59. 23 61. 7 63. 6 65. 5
67. 4 69. 5 71. 8 73. 2 75. 2

EXERCISE SET A-10

1. 1744 3. 342 5. 3805 7. 9 9. 12

EXERCISE SET A-11

1. 59 3. .40 5. 28 7. 11 9. 14 11. .53 13. 33 15. 3.9
17. 4305 19. 35.33 21. 10.21 23. 1067 25. 789.0 27. -1.314
29. 17.42 31. 132.3 33. 37,400 35. 3.07 37. 1.35 39. 90.7 41. 40.7
43. 218 45. 75.8 47. .652 49. 2.77 51. 12.346 53. 48.1325
55. 12.693 57. 67.0521 59. 68.97 61. 64.2408 63. 3.94 65. 235.8
67. 51

SECTION B

EXERCISE SET B-1

1. 1.46 3. 21.13 5. 4.61 7. 15.77

9.

x	1.30	1.32	1.34	1.36
y	1.16	1.18	1.20	1.22

11.

x	.56	.60	.64	.68
y	-2.65	-2.34	-2.06	-1.80

13.

x	.25	.50	.75	1.25
y	-13.62	-7.94	-6.31	-4.58

15.

x	.25	.75	1.5	2.5
y	-25.30	-.83	10.91	49.12

17.

x	-.50	-.25	.25	.50
y	1.78	33.32	74.79	22.33

EXERCISE SET B-2

1. (4.2,21.0), (12.5,62.5), (22,110.0), (38.6,193.0)
3. (.6,-.3), (2.4,4.2), (6.9,15.5), (11.5,27.0)
5. (1.5,10.4), (14.2,13.6), (24.3,16.1), (35.7,18.9)
7. (4.7,-2.9), (10.4,-1.4), (21.7,.6), (38.4,2.8)
9. (.8,.8), (2.3,11.5), (5.9,55.4), (9.3,120.7)

11.

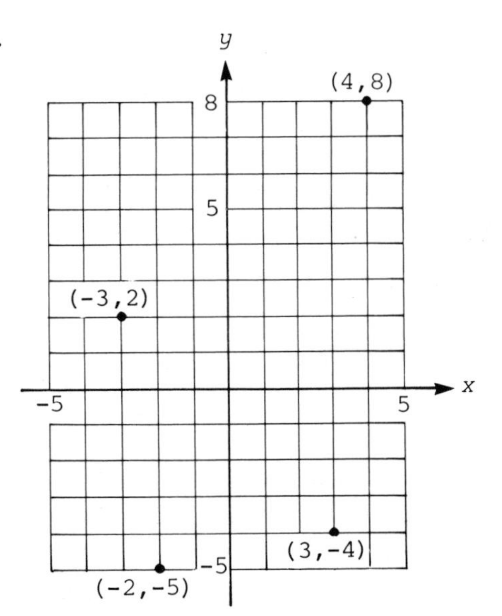

13.

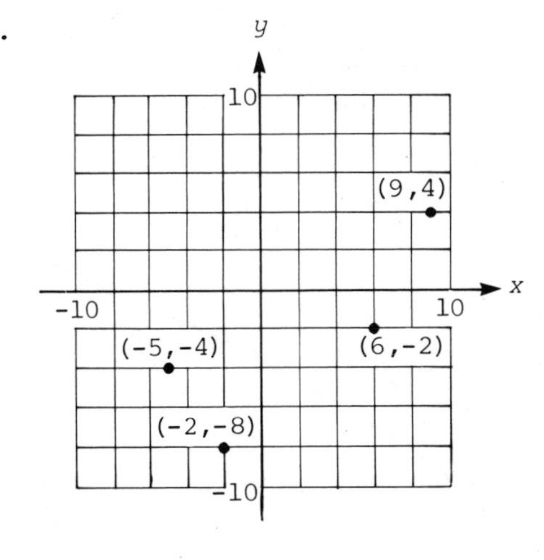

15.

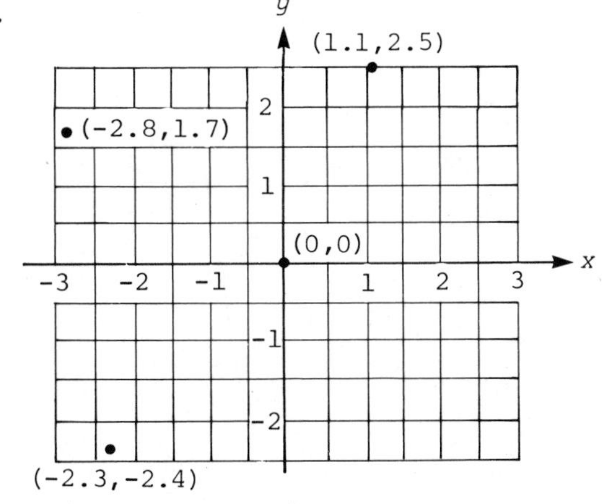

17.

x	0	5	10	15	20	25	30
y	-20	-10	0	10	20	30	40

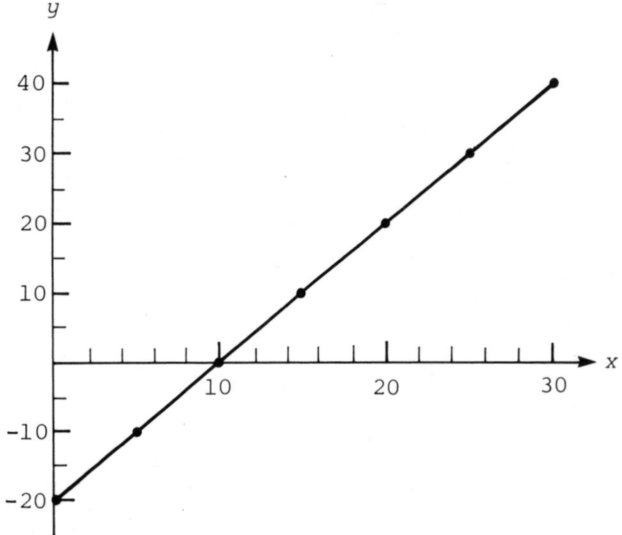

19.

x	0	5	10	15	20	25	30
y	8	10	12	14	16	18	20

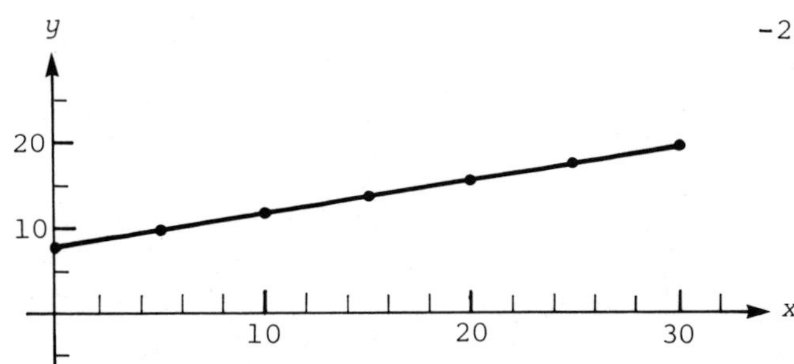

21.

x	0	5	10	15	20	25	30
y	0	8.9	12.6	15.5	17.9	20.0	21.9

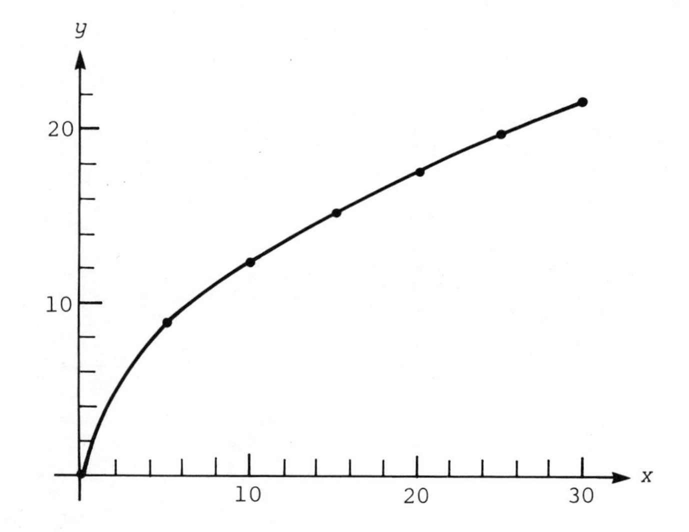

23.

x	0	2	4	6	8	10
y	-10	-20	-22	-16	-2	20

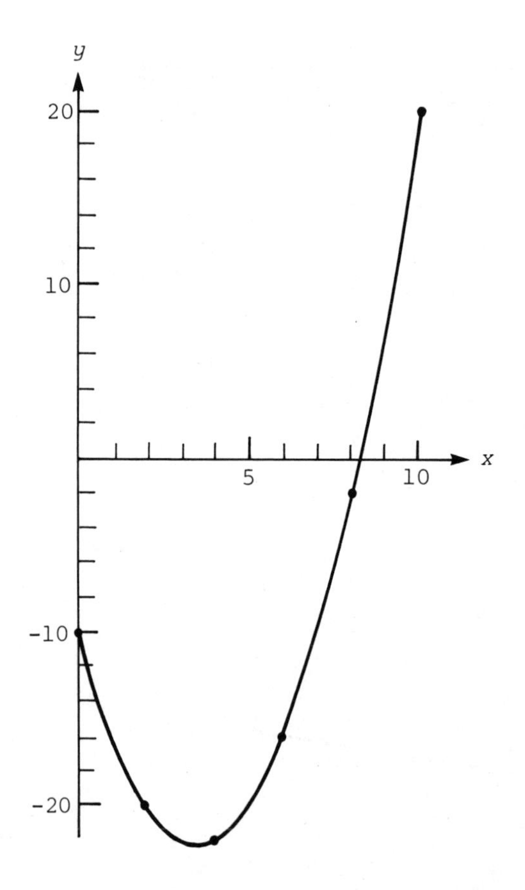

EXERCISE SET B-3

1. 3, 5, -2 3. 2, -3, 1 5. 1, 2, 1, -1 7. 2, -1, 1, 2 9. 1, 0, 2.1, 3.2, -1
11. 1, 0, 0, -3.3, -2.4 13. -2.1, 0, 0, -1.9, 4.5 15. 1, 13 17. -23, -11
19. -15.21, 26.03, -11.98, 21.58 21. 2.26, 3.94, 5.26, .94 23. -.08, -2.24
25. 62.38, 57.22 27. .76, 1.86, .55, 2.09

EXERCISE SET B-4

(Note: Your estimated zeros may differ slightly from those listed here.)

1.

x	-.5	-.25	0	.25	.5	.75	1	1.25	1.5	1.75	2	2.25
y	5.6	4.9	4.0	3.0	1.9	.86	0	-.6	-.9	-.7	0	1.3

Zeros: 1.0, 2.0

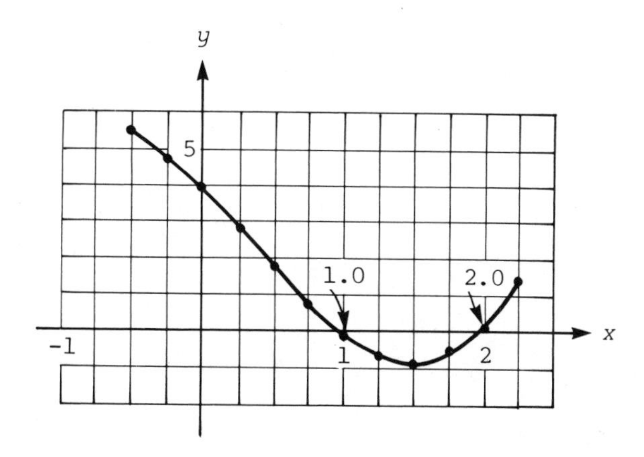

3. Zeros: -3.0, -2.0, .5

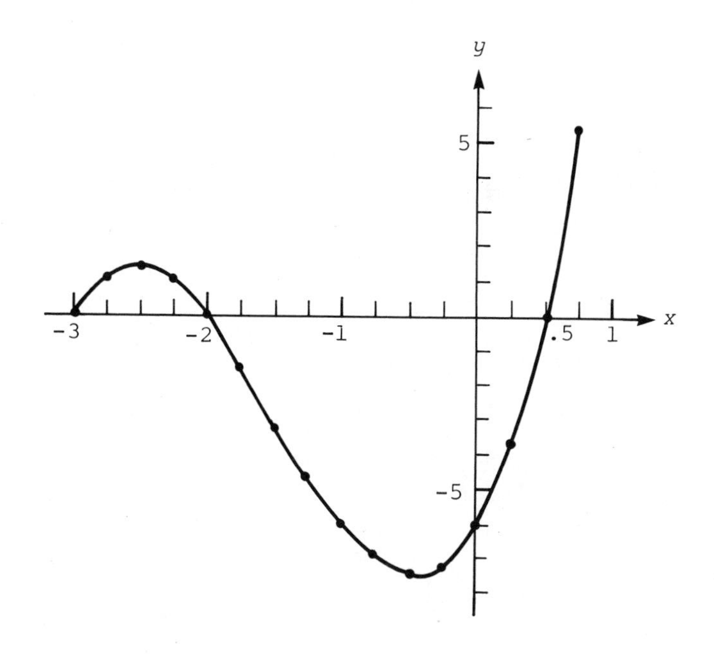

5. Zeros: -1.0, -.3, .5, 1.0

7. Zeros: -1.0, -.5, .5, 1.0

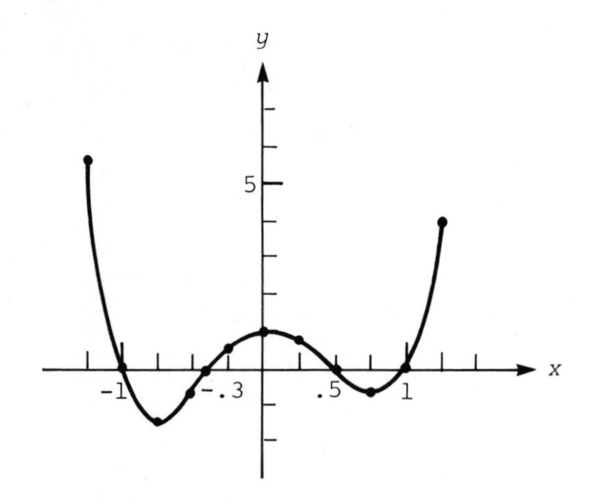

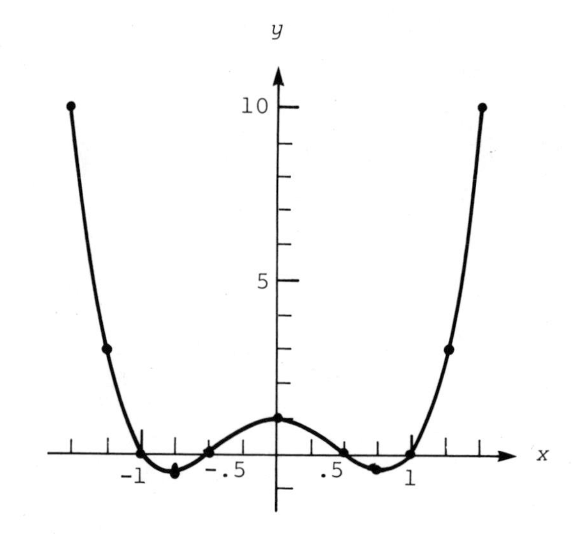

9. (-3,9); (3,9)

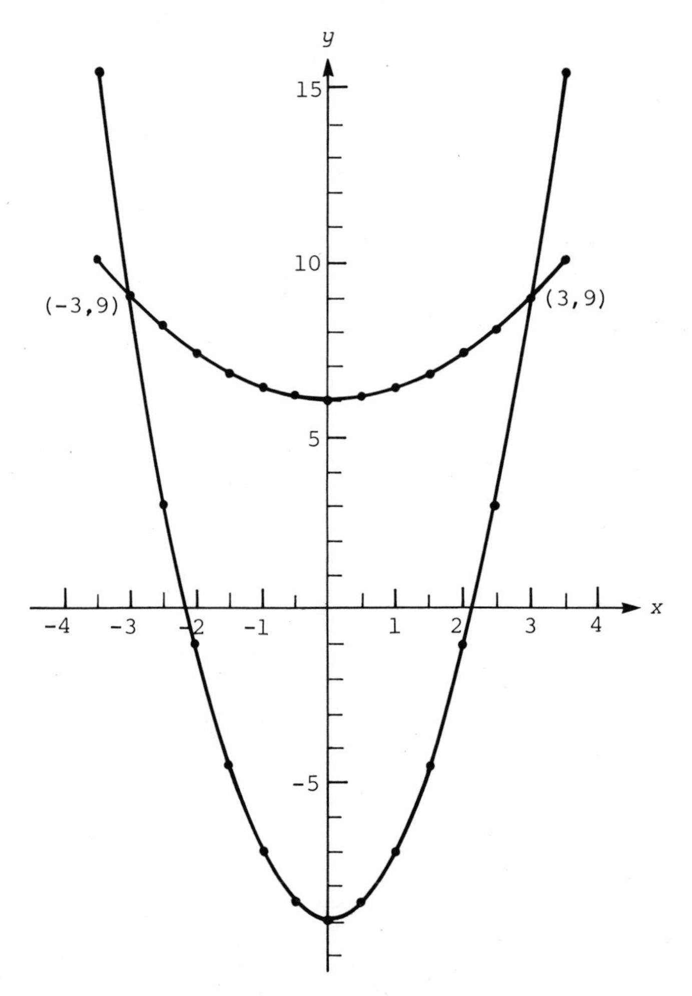

11. (-1,0); (2,9)

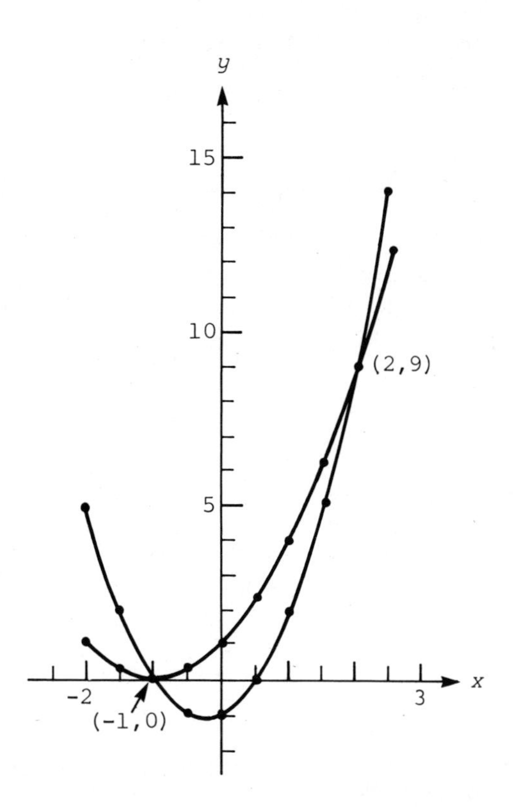

EXERCISE SET B-5

1. 8.24 3. 4.65 5. 1.40 7. -7.16 9. 2.06 11. -3.59

13. (a)

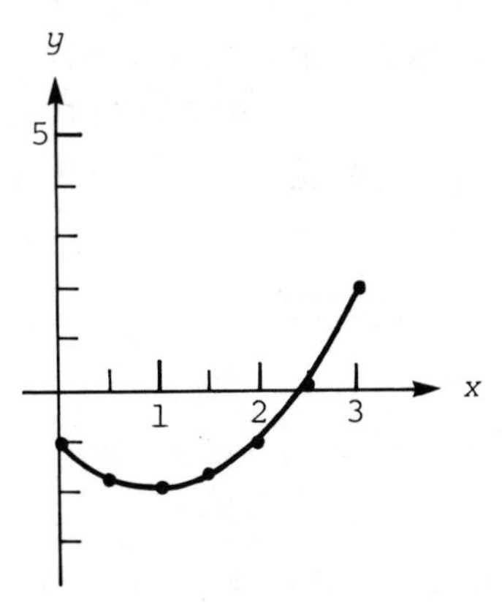

(b) 2.41

15. (a)

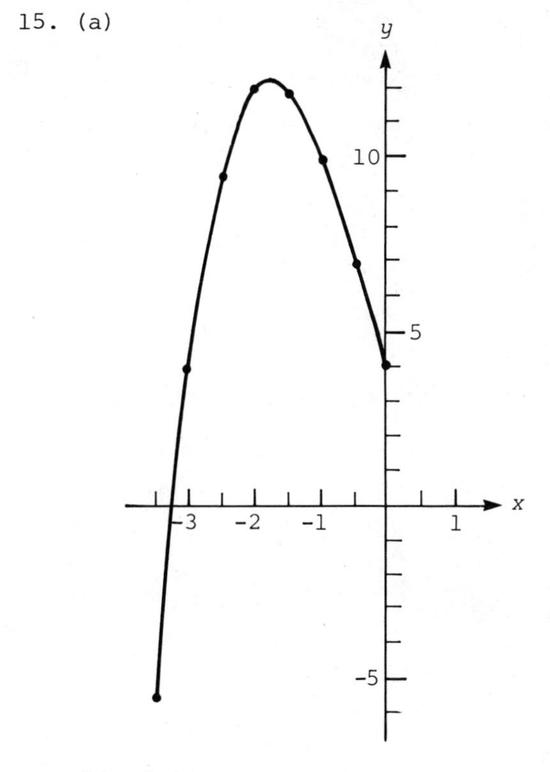

(b) -3.24

17. (a)

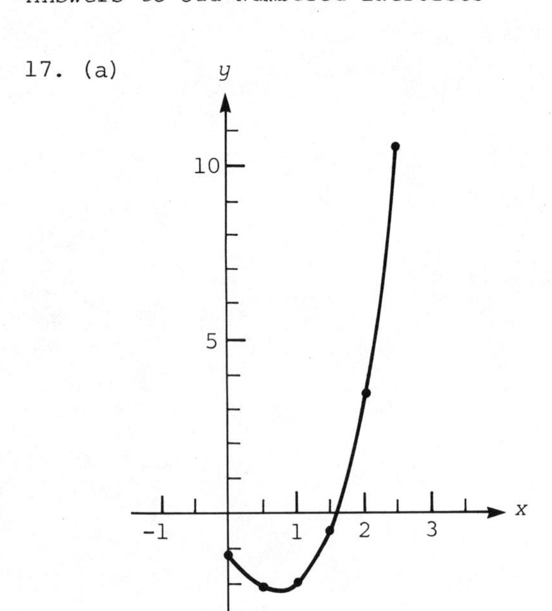

(b) 1.58

19. (a)

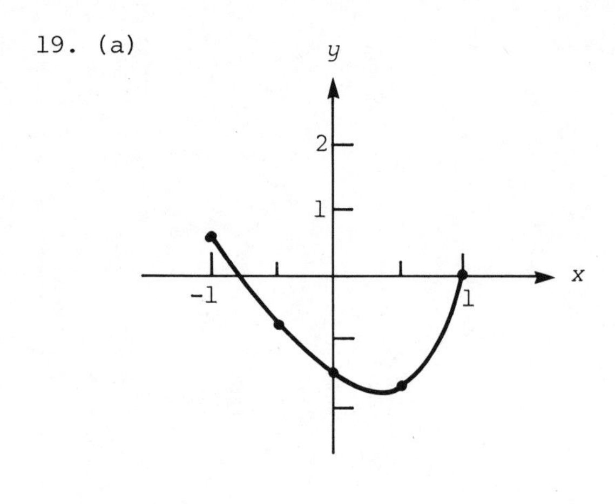

(b) -.79

EXERCISE SET B-6

1. .32° 3. .68° 5. 56.28° 7. 158.88° 9. -245.52° 11. -63.08°
13. 36' 15. 8°32' 17. 38°9' 19. 172°28' 21. -356°5' 23. -42°54'
25. 1.047 27. 2.356 29. 1.833 31. -3.665 33. 1.05 35. .92 37. 4.12
39. -1.19 41. .311 43. 4.218 45. -.153 47. -5.370 49. 91.7°
51. 28.6° 53. 137.5° 55. -217.7° 57. -361.0° 59. 2.9° 61. 225°
63. 75° 65. 140° 67. -216° 69. 3.0 in. 71. 1.6 cm 73. 1.5 km
75. 1.5 ft

EXERCISE SET B-7

1. .95106 3. .84805 5. 19.08114 7. -.32557 9. 1.60033 11. -.67086
13. -.37289 15. .48818 17. .72911 19. .54936 21. .87989 23. -.13639
25. .86603 27. -1.00000 29. .86603 31. -.86603 33. 1.03528 35. .39593
37. -1.30541 39. 1.03209 41. .41012 43. 1.15284 45. (a) 20.22°; (b) .35
47. (a) 80.00°; (b) 1.40 49. (a) 57.16°; (b) 1.00 51. (a) -11.40°; (b) -.20
53. (a) -77.23°; (b) -1.35 55. (a) 106.24°; (b) 1.85

EXERCISE SET B-8

1. 22.7 3. 92.5 5. 60.6 7. 79.9 9. -151 11. -19.3 13. 1.67
15. .124 17. 62.9 19. 24.4 21. (a) 38.7°; (b) .7 23. (a) 60.7°; (b) 1.1

25. (a) 44.4°; (b) .8 27. (a) 111.7°; (b) 1.9 29. 4.7 31. 1.7 33. 6.1
35. 41,894,000 mi 37. 43,350,000 mi

EXERCISE SET B-9

1. 16.6° 3. 47.7° 5. 21.5° 7. two 9. three 11. two 13. four
15. (a) 14.6 ft; (b) 15.8 ft 17. (a) 35.7 cm; (b) 39.6 cm 19. nearest whole number
21. nearest hundredth 23. nearest thousandth 25. (a) 15°; (b) 75° 27. (a) 36°;
(b) 54° 29. (a) 27.3°; (b) 62.7° 31. 22 ft 33. 24.93 m 35. .75 in.
37. 7.7 ft 39. 119 ft 41. 472 yd 43. 553 mi 45. 5.7°, 258 yd

EXERCISE SET B-10

1. 82.44° 3. 27.28° 5. 88.03° 7. .64 9. .93 11. (a) 14.62 ft;
(b) 83.95° 13. (a) 35.91 cm; (b) 44.23° 15. (a) 2.43 m; (b) 52.83°
17. (a) 26.73°; (b) 118.72° 19. (a) 32.5°; (b) 40.7° 21. (a) 31°; (b) 117°
23. 4.4 in. 25. 5.20 cm 27. 29.564 in. 29. (a) 33.6°; (b) 95.7°; (c) 50.7°
31. (a) 4°00'; (b) 31°36'; (c) 144°23'

EXERCISE SET B-11

1. -1.56, .30 3. -1.28, -1.65 5. -1.11, -4.84 7. .71, -.71 9. 2.71, 6.10
11.

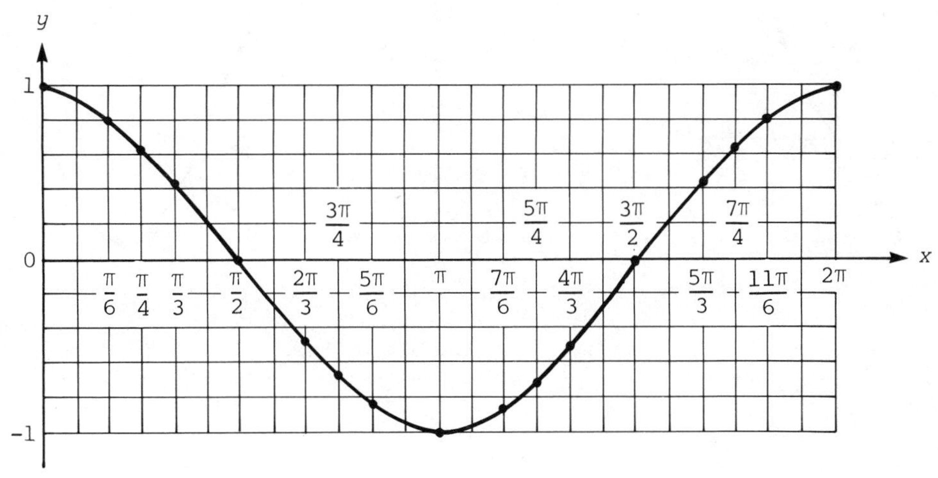

13.

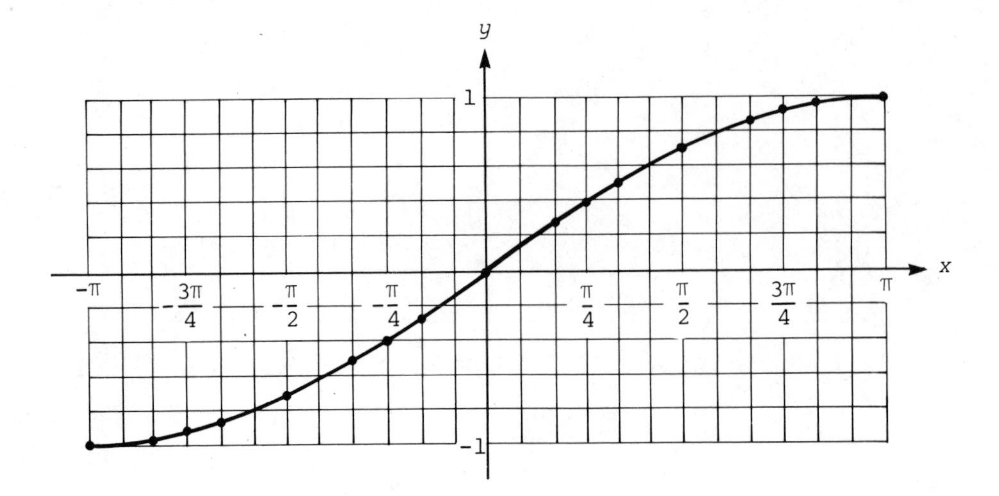

15.

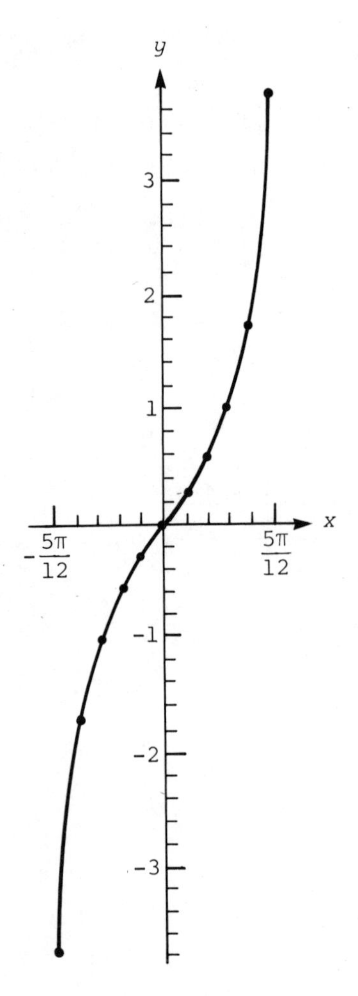

17.

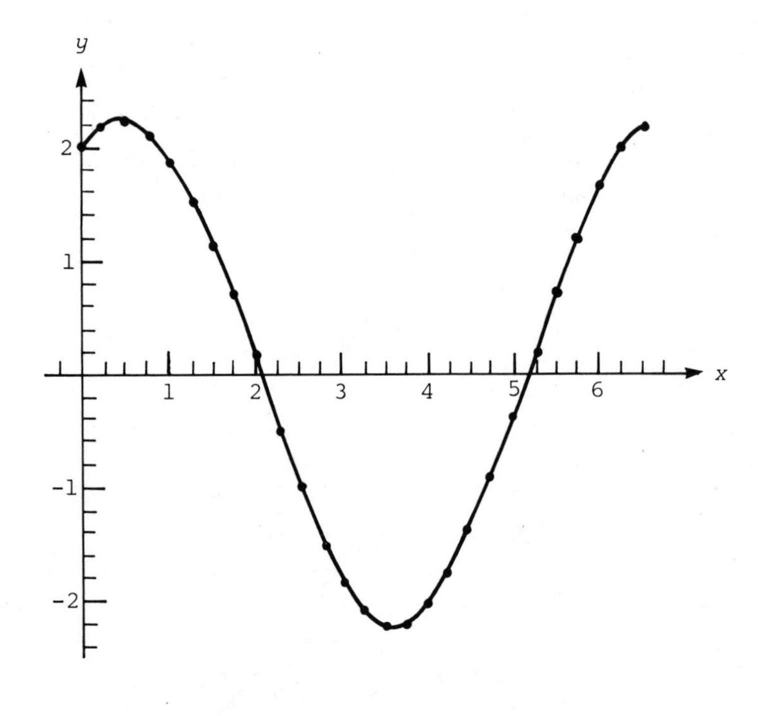

19.

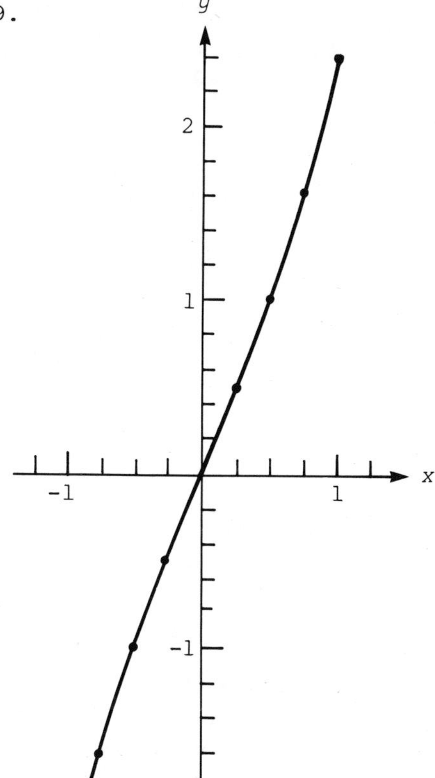

21.

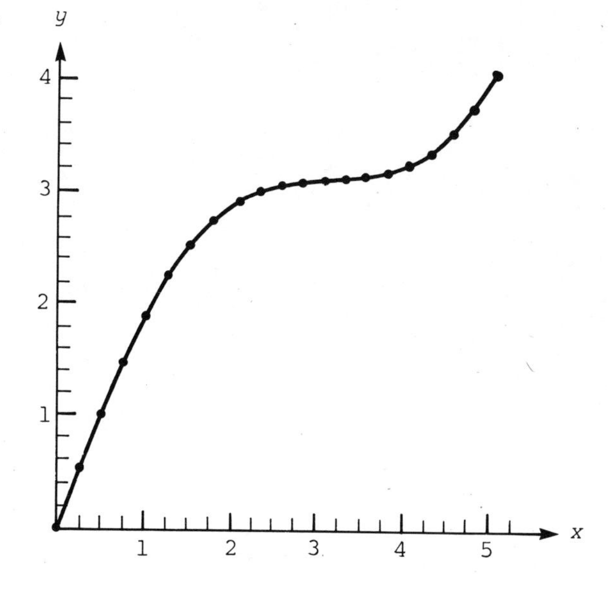

23.

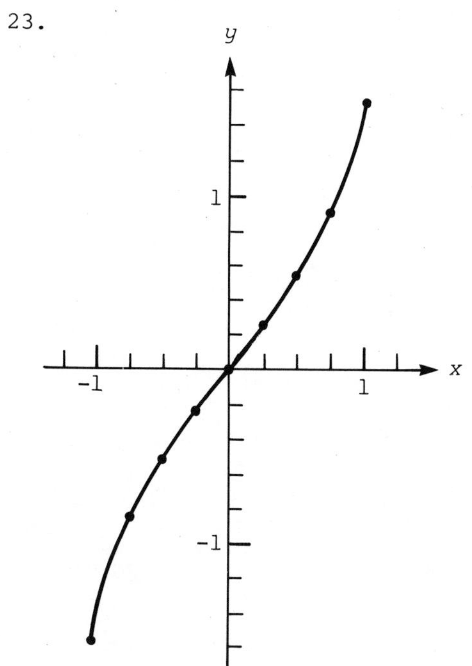

25.

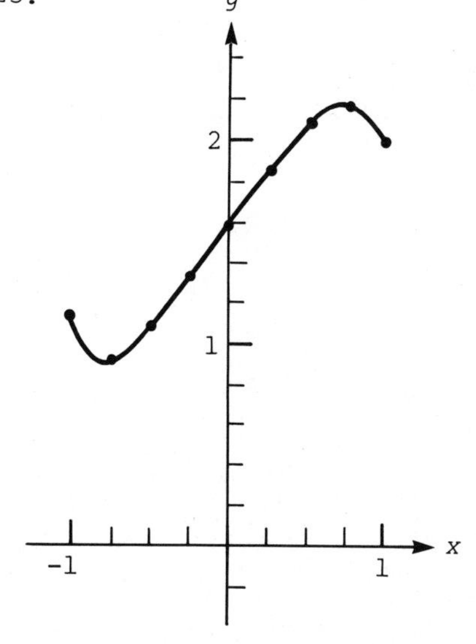

27.

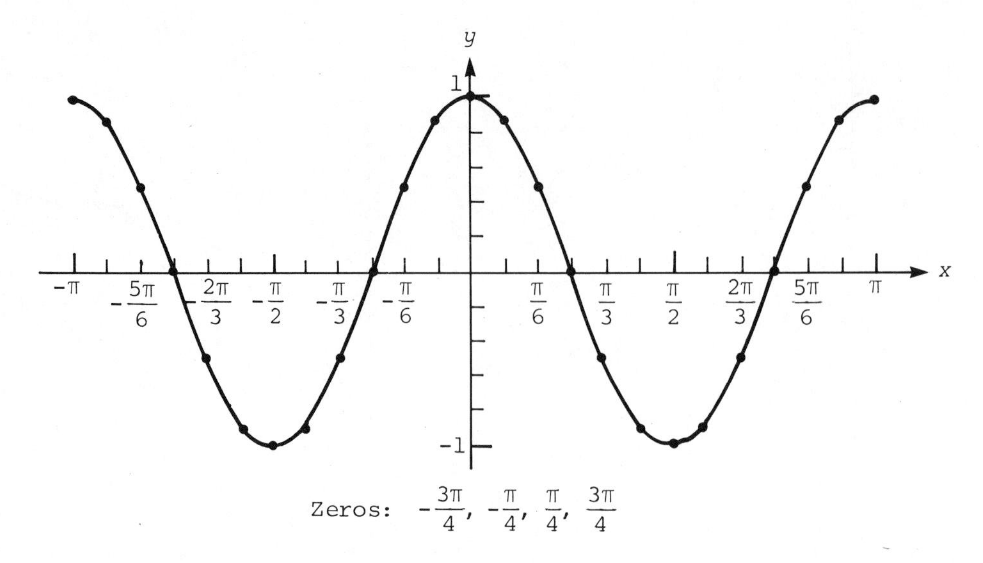

Zeros: $-\frac{3\pi}{4}, -\frac{\pi}{4}, \frac{\pi}{4}, \frac{3\pi}{4}$

29.

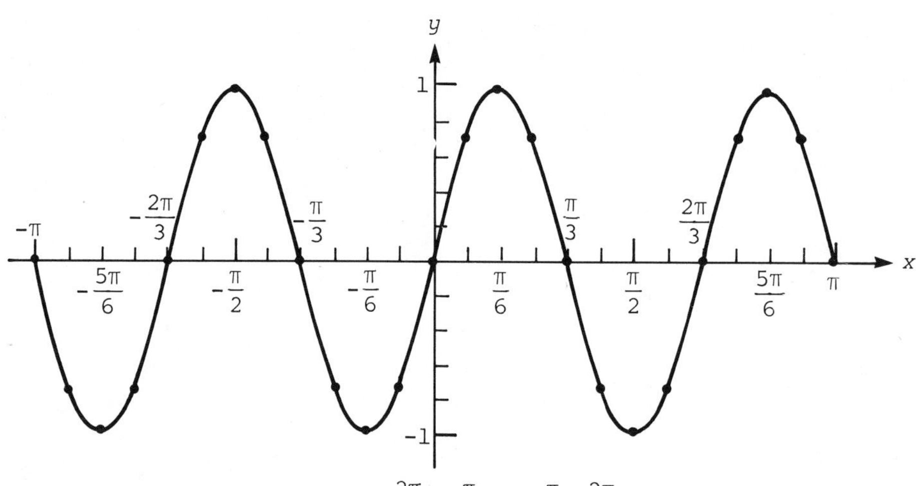

Zeros: $-\pi, -\frac{2\pi}{3}, -\frac{\pi}{3}, 0, \frac{\pi}{3}, \frac{2\pi}{3}, \pi$

EXERCISE SET B-12

1. 3.48 3. .0629 5. .288 7. 15.9 9. (a) $9^{1/2}$; (b) 3 11. (a) $49^{1/2}$; (b) 7 13. (a) $27^{1/3}$; (b) 3 15. (a) $125^{1/3}$; (b) 5 17. (a) $1^{1/4}$; (b) 1 19. (a) $625^{1/4}$; (b) 5 21. 2.339 23. 1.786 25. 2.446 27. 3.125 29. 2.154 31. .783 33. .250 35. .200 37. .426 39. .178 41. 1.498 43. .430 45. 6.082 47. 299.070 49. 7.990 51. 3.209 53. .164 55. .003 57. .125 59. .259

EXERCISE SET B-13

1. 199.52623 3. .00501187 5. 2.3442288 7. 49.402449 9. .02024191

11. 1.4190675

13.

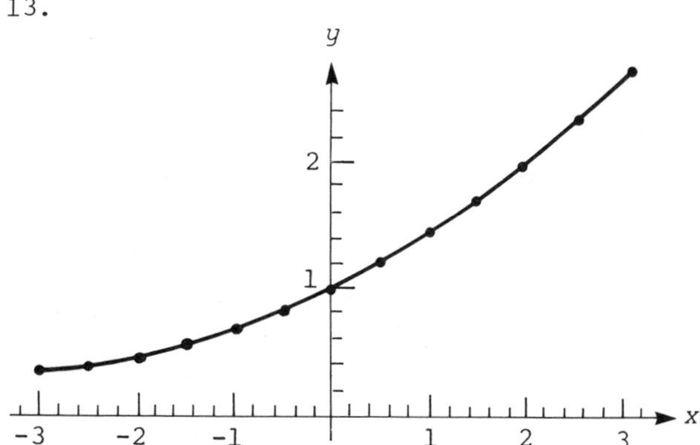

15.

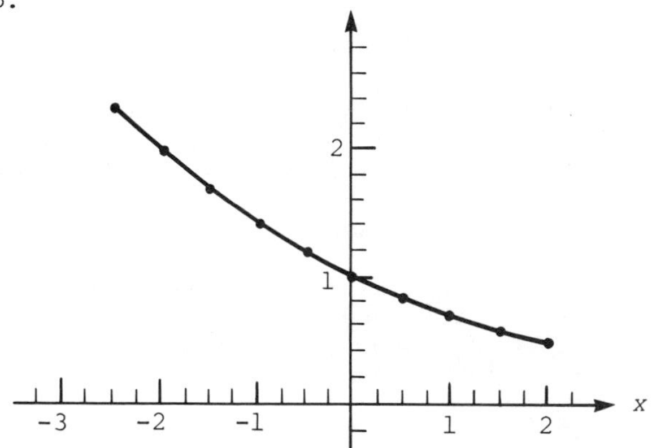

17.

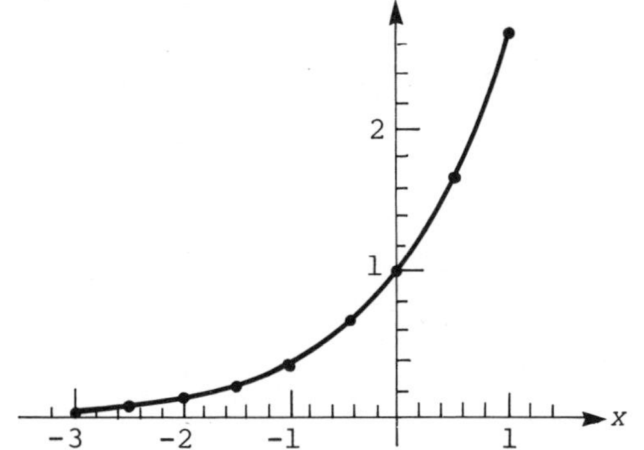

19. 375 21. 9375 23. $536.25

25. $953.00 27. 4.2 billion

29. 4.7 billion 31. 6.2 g 33. 3.8 g

35. $4606 37. $2404 39. $48,765

41. $100,505 43. .000063 45. .0013

47. 3.53, 2.31, 1.69, 1.50, 1.69, 2.31, 3.53

49. 2.62, 1.09, .11, -.40, -.51, -.32, .06

51. 14.21, 1.74, .85, .50, .28, -.20, -11.86

EXERCISE SET B-14

1. 2.48364 3. -1.24857 5. 4.55923 7. -4.84686 9. 2.6 11. -2.6
13. 2.6 15. -2.6 17. 915.02929 19. .01368623 21. 6.4476518
23. .15509522 25. (a) 702 yr; (b) 376 yr 27. (a) 4257 yr; (b) 8749 yr
29. (a) 13.86 yr; (b) 12.60 yr 31. (a) 13.87%; (b) 8.67% 33. -2.66, 1.08, .39, 1.74, 2.80 35. 13.39, 22.53, 37.97, 63.73, 106.42 37. 3.68, 2.50, 2.33, 2.57, 3.04
39. 10.69, 10.00, 27.22, 92.47, 306.28

41.

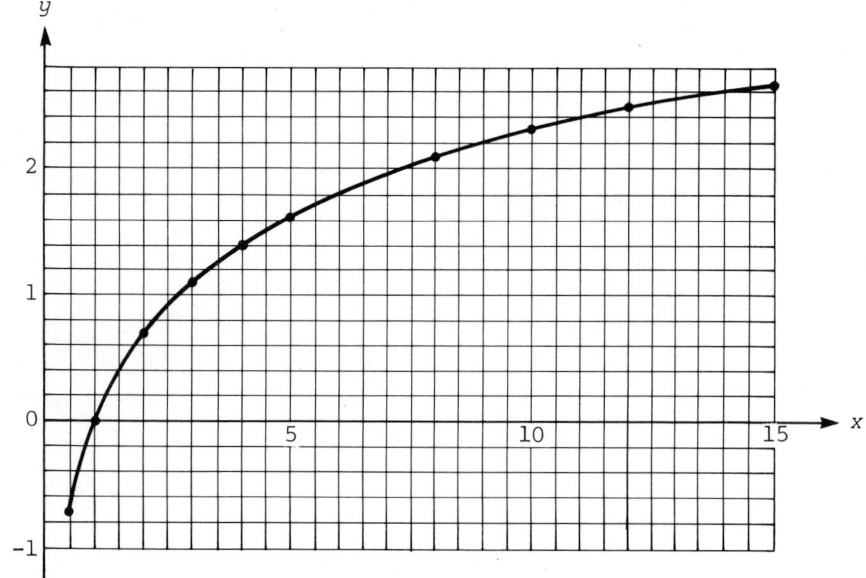

43.

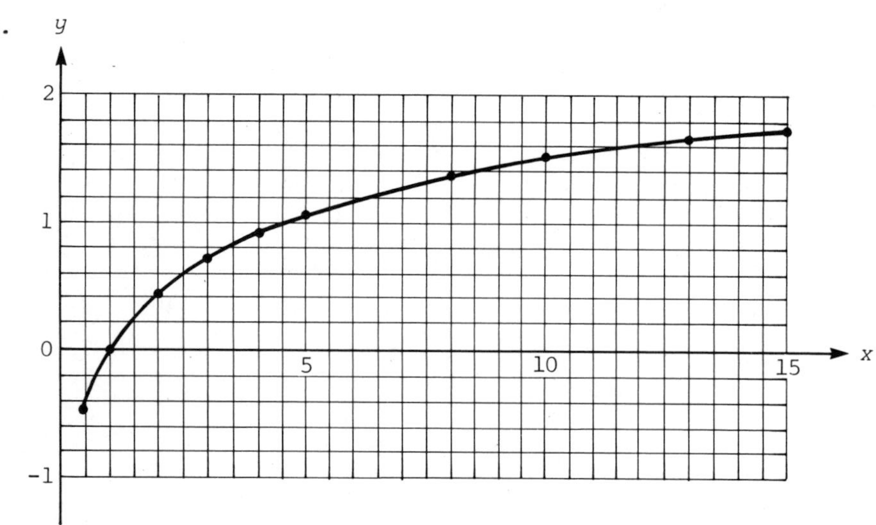

EXERCISE SET B-15

1. (a)

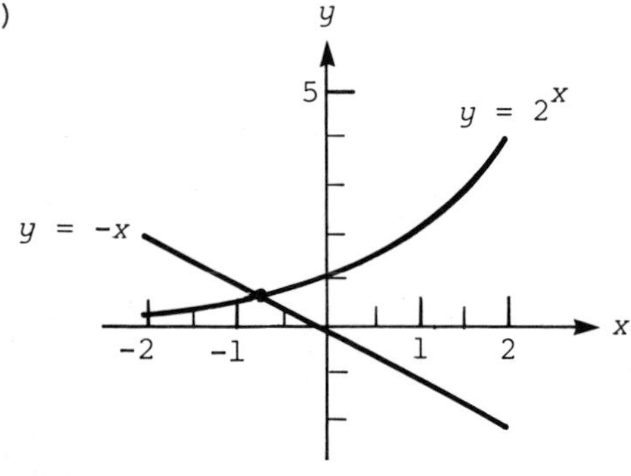

(b) -.64

3. (a)

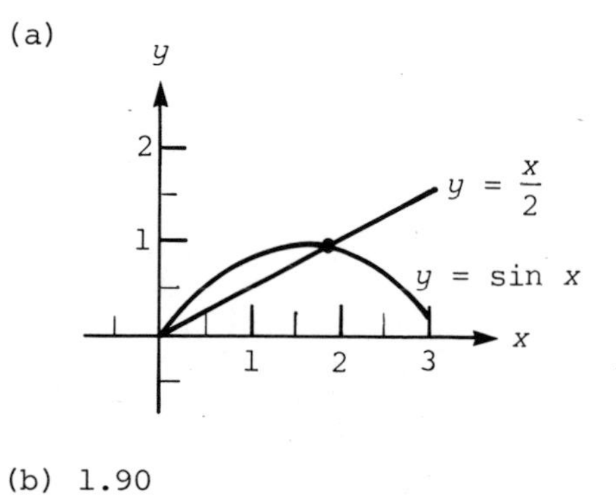

(b) 1.90

5. (a)

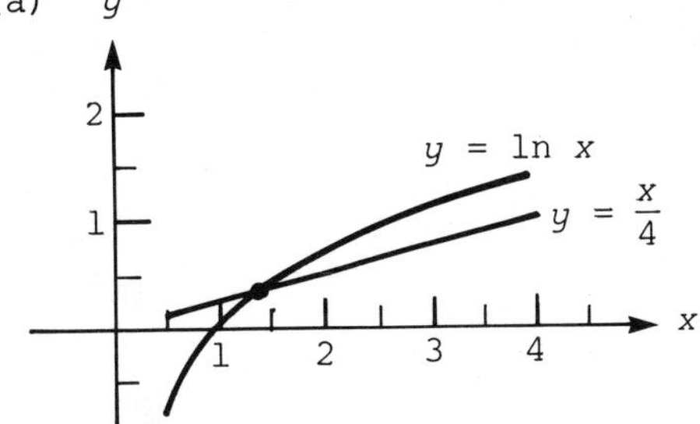

(b) 1.43

7. (a)

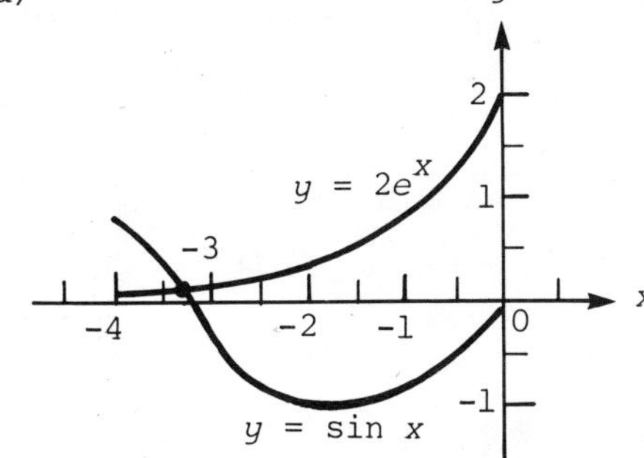

(b) -3.22

9. (a)

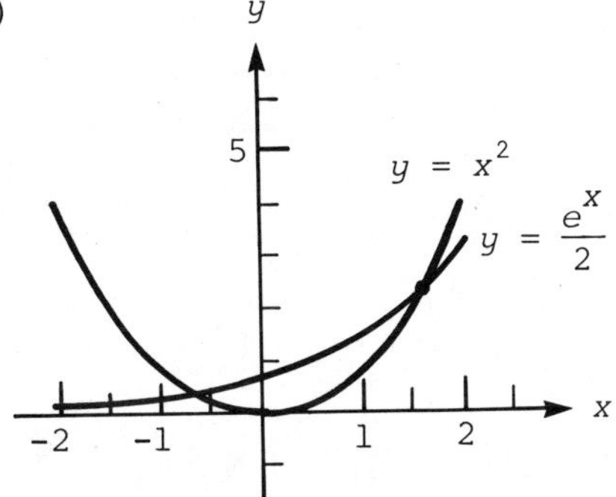

(b) -.54; 1.49

11. (a)

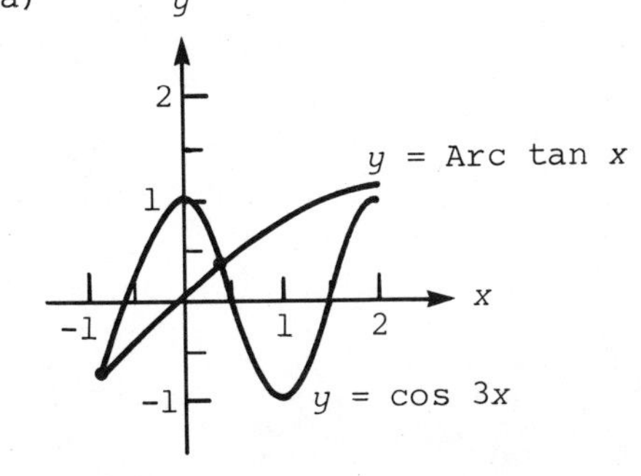

(b) -.76, .40

13. 2.04

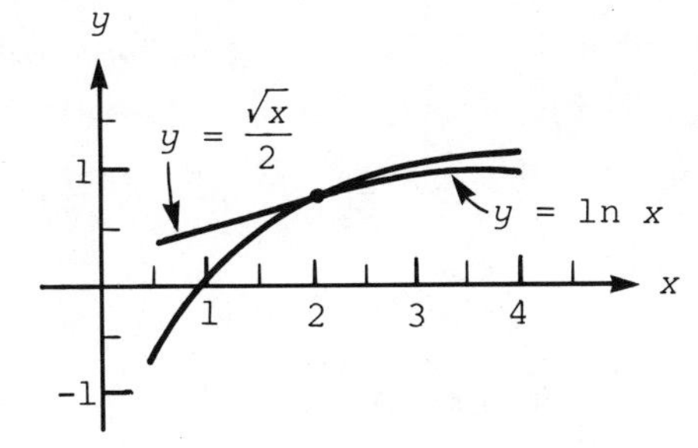

SECTION C

EXERCISE SET C-1

1. 57.0 sq ft 3. 10,875.8 sq cm 5. 286.0 sq in. 7. 5135.2 sq cm
9. 25,108.7 sq ft 11. 13,788.6 sq cm 13. 124.5 sq ft 15. 5890.9 sq mm
17. 273.9 sq cm 19. 7857.2 sq ft 21. 13.1 sq cm 23. .8 sq m
25. 1464.1 sq in. 27. 651.4 sq cm 29. 3379.9 sq ft 31. 1181.9 sq in.
33. 18,147.6 sq cm 35. 9 cu cm 37. 6636 cu m 39. 48,403 cu ft
41. 1722 cu cm 43. 7721 cu in. 45. 274,819 cu m 47. 6060 cu yd

EXERCISE SET C-2

1. 46% 3. 17.5% 5. 6.25% 7. 400% 9. .68 11. .006 13. 2.75
15. .0905 17. .18375 19. .00667 21. 37.5% 23. 127.5% 25. .6%
27. 77.78% 29. 457.52 31. 11.59 33. 3.84 35. 148.14 37. 22.47
39. 64% 41. 46.53% 43. 368.67% 45. 277.78% 47. 234.38 49. 4832.00
51. 249.57 53. 115.65 55. (a) $64.75; (b) $74.46; (c) $18.62 57. 57%

EXERCISE SET C-3

1. $24.38 3. $23.97 5. $113.55 7. $23.91 9. $160.02 11. $417.71
13. $59.85 15. 12.6% 17. 25.8% 19. 38.1% 21. 20.2% 23. 11.1%
25. $2277.68 27. $72.78 29. $12.59 31. $76.94 33. $59.60 35. $176.87
37. $39.91 39. $460.16 41. $229.84 43. $90.64 45. (a) $3613; (b) $4888
47. (a) $668; (b) $850 49. (a) $41,815; (b) $50,086 51. (a) $10,366; (b) $32,006
53. (a) $44,439; (b) $111,801 55. (a) $52; (b) $968

EXERCISE SET C-4

1. (a) $1341.00; (b) $8791.00 3. (a) $65.47; (b) $720.12 5. (a) $54.40;
(b) $534.40 7. (a) $338.25; (b) $1538.25 9. (a) $395.83; (b) $9895.83
11. (a) $26.36; (b) $661.81 13. 5.71% 15. 9.29% 17. 4.61% 19. 4.34%
21. 4.28% 23. 3.85% 25. 1.62889 27. 1.80094 29. 1.15439 31. 1.01612
33. 3.99546 35. 1.48595 37. (a) $12,535; (b) $35 39. (a) $65,289; (b) $289
41. (a) $19,808; (b) $108 43. (a) $15,794; (b) $119 45. (a) $9663; (b) $83
47. (a) $6620; (b) $120 49. $9890 51. $5922 53. $6129 55. $4946 57. $27

EXERCISE SET C-5

1. 87.22 3. 4.79 5. 2307.10 7. 1213.05 9. 6478.81 11. 162.9 gal
13. 419.8 mi 15. $18.91 17. $214.60 19. 8.0 cal 21. $1577.52
23. 43.942 cm 25. 42.099 m 27. 66.299 in. 29. 1093.613 yd 31. 15.190 ℓ
33. 2778.251 g 35. 24.132 kg 37. .359 lb 39. 3.329 gal 41. 1.022 ℓ
43. 45.710 pt 45. 90.192 a 47. 23.027 ha 49. 13.258 kwan 51. 614.238 lb
53. 18¢ 55. 39¢ 57. 79¢ 59. 63¢

EXERCISE SET C-6

1. 11.1 cm 3. 22.3 in. 5. 2.1 m 7. 7.6 yd 9. 27.1 cm 11. 173.8 ft
13. 259.1 cm 15. 80.3 ft 17. 420.3 m 19. 13.8 ft 21. 3.0 m 23. 456.0 ft
25. 42.8 mi 27. 75.0 km 29. 57.3 ft 31. 7.3 cm

EXERCISE SET C-7

1. 32.45 3. 77 5. 43.196 7. 67 9. Products: 284.4, 204.4, 214.2, 217.6, 147.6, 154.7; sum of products: 1222.9; $n = 87$; $m = 14.1$ 11. Products: 48.36, 57.46, 45.70, 83.16, 110.16, 61.50, 52.91; sum of products: 459.25; $n = 103$; $m = 4.46$

13.

Number	Frequency	Product
42.3	6	253.8
42.5	3	127.5
42.7	4	170.8
42.9	5	214.5
43.4	3	130.2
43.5	5	217.5
	$n = 26$	1114.3

$m = 42.9$

15.

Number	Frequency	Product
87.7	4	350.8
88.0	5	440.0
88.1	3	264.3
88.3	4	353.2
88.5	7	619.5
88.8	4	355.2
	$n = 27$	2383.0

$m = 88.3$

17. 54 19. $3.91 21. 49.3 mph 23. 1.9 25. 2.5 27. .033

29. $m = 406.9$, $s = 431.6$

List of Symbols

SYMBOL	NAME OF KEY	SECTION
[0] [1] [2] [3] [4] [5] [6] [7] [8] [9]	Number entry	A-0
[•]	Decimal point	A-0
[+] [-] [×] [÷]	Operation	A-0
[=]	Equals	A-0
[ENT]	Enter	A-0
[$\sqrt{\ }$]	Square root	A-5, App. A
[1/x]	Reciprocal	A-6
[y^x] or [x^y]	Power	A-7
[F]	Second function	A-7
[+/-] or [CHS]	Sign change	A-7
[EE] or [EEX]	Enter exponent	A-8
[STO]	Store in memory	A-10
[RCL] or [MR]	Recall from memory	A-10
[M+]	Add to memory	A-10
[M-]	Subtract from memory	A-10
[MC]	Clear memory	A-10
[SIN] [COS] [TAN]	Trigonometric	B-7
[ARC] [INV] [SIN^{-1}] [COS^{-1}] [TAN^{-1}]	Inverse trigonometric	B-7
[$\sqrt[x]{y}$]	Root	B-12
[10^x] [e^x]	Base 10, Base *e*	B-13
[LOG] [LN]	Logarithm	B-14
[%]	Percent	C-2
[x^2]	Squaring	App. B

Index